# MONETARY POLICY SINCE 1971

## Conduct and Performance

# Monetary Policy Since 1971

*Conduct and Performance*

**Maximilian Hall**

St. Martin's Press    New York

© Maximilian J. B. Hall 1983

All rights reserved. For information, write:
St. Martin's Press, Inc., 175 Fifth Avenue, New York, NY 10010
Printed in Hong Kong
First published in the United States of America in 1983

ISBN 0–312–54420–0

---

**Library of Congress Cataloging in Publication Data**

Hall, Maximilian.
    Monetary policy since 1971

    Bibliography: p.
    Includes index.
    1. Monetary policy—Great Britain.   2. Credit
control—Great Britain.   I. Title.
HG939.5.H24   1983     332.4'941      82–24043
ISBN 0–312–54420–0

To my Wife and Parents

# Contents

# Contents

# Preface

This book has resulted from a series of research papers written during my first three years as a lecturer in the field of monetary economics and reflects a personal bias towards the institutional framework within which monetary policy is conducted. Accordingly, the dependence of the efficacy of monetary instruments on the response of economic agents, notably the banks, to policy manoeuvres is stressed, reflecting the importance of the regulatory environment within which financial transactions are conducted. Apart from the establishment of the theoretical rationale for the adoption of individual instruments, emphasis is given to an assessment of the 'success' of policy action from the points of view of both the ability of the prevailing administration to meet its stated policy (especially financial) objectives and the overall effect on broader macroeconomic goals.

The starting-point of the text is a review of the recommendations of the National Board for Prices and Incomes (Report No. 34 on *Bank Charges*) and the Monopolies Commission (*Barclays Bank Ltd., Lloyds Bank Ltd. and Martins Bank Ltd., A Report on the Proposed Merger*) which, towards the end of the 1960s, inquired into various aspects of monetary policy, and reported critically on the harmful effects of 'direct' controls, such as lending ceilings and interest-rate agreements, for competition between 'like' institutions and within the financial sector more generally. In apparent acceptance of many of these criticisms a new monetary control regime was instituted in 1971 under the name of *competition and credit control* (CCC), which represented an attempt to improve the competitive environment in the financial field and to tighten control over credit and monetary aggregate growth through a respecification of balance-sheet ratio control and a revision of the Government Broker's dealing tactics in the gilt-edged market. By December 1973, however, with the appearance of the 'corset', all faith in the willingness of the monetary authorities to adhere to the principles of CCC had vanished. The reasons for this and the need for a new form of 'direct' control are closely documented, as are the *modus operandi* of the 'corset' and its extensive effects on the financial system.

Chapter 5 provides a review of the monetary reform debate (including a detailed analysis of the case for monetary base control, MBC) that arose as a result of dissatisfaction with the conduct of policy that persisted with the 'corset' scheme, and leads, in chrono-logical fashion, to the Tories' first year in office (1979). The pervasive, free-market philosophy embraced by the new administration first appears in the abolition of exchange control, and the monetary impli-cations of this move, both in theory and practice, are carefully elabor-ated. Chapters 7 and 8, respectively, cover the theoretical case for, and 'real-world' implications of, the Tories' full financial plans un-veiled in the guise of the *medium term financial strategy* (MTFS) in March 1980. The evidence presented to and views expressed by the Treasury and Civil Service Committee inquiring into the conduct of monetary policy are analysed within this context.

The final chapters cover the 'new' monetary arrangements intro-duced in August 1981 and early experience with the changed control techniques. The series of appendices is designed to clarify for the more discerning reader those, mainly theoretical, topics that are given only cursory treatment in the text.

The book is intended for second- and third-year undergraduate courses in monetary/financial economics and should also appeal to students undertaking the Institute of Bankers' Examinations in Ap-plied Economics and those generally involved or interested in the financial sector of the UK economy.

Finally, I would like to thank my colleagues at Loughborough and Nottingham Universities who provided helpful comments, suggestions and insights, especially Brian Tew, who enthusiastically undertook the daunting task of reading the whole script in draft form and provided much helpful advice and clarification. Last, but by no means least, I would like to express my sincere thanks to Su Spencer for all the patience shown and hard work involved in typing the entire script.

*Loughborough, England*                        MAXIMILIAN HALL
*November 1982*

# List of Tables

# Glossary

### Definitions of money

$M_0$ (monetary base): notes and coin in circulation with the non-bank public plus banks' balances at the Bank of England.

$M_1$: notes and coin in circulation with the non-bank public plus UK non-bank private-sector-owned sterling sight deposits (interest and non-interest-bearing) held with monetary sector institutions. (An adjustment is made for items in transit – *see* eligible liabilities.)

$M_2$: $M_1$ + clearing banks' 7-day time deposits.

$M_3$: notes and coin in circulation with the non-bank public, plus UK-owned (non-bank private and public sector) sterling deposits held with monetary sector institutions, plus all UK-resident-owned foreign currency deposits. (An adjustment is made for items in transit – *see* eligible liabilities.)

$£M_3$: the *sterling* component of $M_3$.

DCE: defined on p.50.

$PSL_1$: notes and coin in circulation with the non-bank public plus UK non-bank private-sector-owned sterling time (excl. deposits of an original maturity of over two years) and sight deposits (including certificates of deposit), certificates of tax deposit (*gross*), and Treasury bills, bank bills and local authority temporary debt (all *net*).

$PSL_2$: $PSL_1$ (*minus* certificates of tax deposit (*gross*)) plus UK non-bank private-sector-owned certificates of tax deposit (*net*) and savings deposits (with building societies and the National Savings Bank) and securities (premium bonds, British Savings Bonds, National Savings stamps and gift tokens) (all *net*).

### demand-for-money function

mathematical representation of the relationship between the demand for money (however defined) and its major determinants (e.g. income, wealth, yields).

**disintermediation**

financial transactions that bypass the banks, usually as a result of the imposition of *direct* controls on certain banking activities which are not extended to other types of financial institution or activity.

**eligible liabilities**

sterling deposits of the banking system as a whole, excluding deposits having an original maturity of over two years, *plus* any resources obtained by switching foreign currencies into sterling, *plus net* inter-bank deposit liabilities, *plus net* sterling certificate of deposit liabilities, *plus* the banks' *net* sterling deposit liabilities to their overseas offices. An adjustment was made for items in transit by subtracting 60 per cent of their net debit value.

**eligible reserve assets**

comprising: bankers' balances (excl. special deposits) at the Bank of England; money at call with the 'Discount Market'; British government and Northern Ireland Treasury bills; British government (and government-guaranteed nationalised industries') stock of less than one year to maturity; 'eligible' local authority bills; 'eligible' commercial bills (up to a maximum of 2 per cent of eligible liabilities); and company tax reserve certificates.

**Eurosterling market**

sterling liabilities and claims of banks located outside the United Kingdom.

**gradualist approach** (to curing inflation)

a 'medium-term' cure for inflation (in recognition of the significant short-run 'costs' of a sharp deflation) involving a progressive reduction in monetary aggregate growth as a means of favourably influencing inflation expectations.

**'hard' arbitrage** ('round-tripping')

the practice of borrowing from banks at 'base-related' rates of interest and redepositing (e.g. through the purchase of bank certificates of deposit) at 'market-related' rates whenever profitable opportunities arise.

**'natural' rate of unemployment**

defined on p.169.

**Phillips curve**

graphical presentation of the time-series relationship between inflation (originally wage inflation) and the level of unemployment.

**public sector borrowing requirement (PSBR)**

the difference between the expenditure and receipts arising from the various activities of the public sector as a whole (central government, local authorities and public corporations).

**reintermediation**

the reflux of business to the banks, usually as a result of the removal of distortive, *direct*, controls.

# Abbreviations

| | |
|---|---|
| *BEQB* | *Bank of England Quarterly Bulletin* |
| BIS | Bank for International Settlements |
| BL | British Leyland |
| BSC | British Steel Corporation |
| CB | Commercial Bill |
| CCC | Competition and Credit Control |
| CD | Certificate of Deposit |
| CEPG | Cambridge Economic Policy Group |
| CGBR | Central Government Borrowing Requirement |
| DCE | Domestic Credit Expansion |
| DM | Discount Market |
| ECF | External and Foreign Currency Finance |
| ECGD | Export Credit Guarantee Department |
| ECU | European Currency Unit |
| EEA | Exchange Equalisation Account |
| EFL | External Financing Limit |
| ELs | Eligible Liabilities |
| EMS | European Monetary System |
| ER | Exchange Rate |
| GDFCF | Gross Domestic Fixed Capital Formation |
| GDP | Gross Domestic Product |
| IBELs | Interest-Bearing Eligible Liabilities |
| (IB)ELs | Eligible Liabilities *and possibly* Interest-Bearing Eligible Liabilities |
| ICL | International Computers Ltd |
| IMF | International Monetary Fund |
| LA | Local Authority |
| LDMA | London Discount Market Association |
| LDT | Licensed Deposit-Taking Institution |
| LIBOR | London Inter-Bank Offered Rate |
| MBC | Monetary Base Control |
| MC | Monopolies Commission |
| MLR | Minimum Lending Rate |
| MTFS | Medium Term Financial Strategy |
| NBPS | Non-Bank Private Sector |
| NIBELs | Non-Interest-Bearing Eligible Liabilities |
| NIESR | National Institute of Economic and Social Research |

NIS    National Insurance Surcharge
OPEC   Organisation of Petroleum-Exporting Countries
PIB    National Board for Prices and Incomes
PRT    Petroleum Revenue Tax
PSD    Public-Sector Debt
PSFD   Public-Sector Financial Deficit
RAs    Reserve Assets
RPI    Retail Price Index
SDs    Special Deposits
SDR    Special Drawing Right
SSDs   Supplementary Special Deposits
TB     Treasury Bill
TCSC   Treasury and Civil Service Committee
TPI    Tax and Price Index
TSB    Trustee Savings Bank
TUC    Trades Union Congress
VAT    Value Added Tax

# 1 The Advent of Competition and Credit Control

In May 1971 the Bank of England published a consultative document entitled *Competition and Credit Control* which heralded the adoption of a new approach to monetary control. The aims of reform were threefold: to increase competition within the banking sector; to improve the bank regulatory system for demand-management purposes; and finally, to enhance the authorities' ability to control the money stock.

## COMPETITION

The measures introduced to deal with the non-competitive aspects of the banking system arose largely in response to criticism emanating from two quasi-official bodies, the National Board for Prices and Incomes (PIB) and the Monopolies Commission. The criticisms were contained in the PIB report on *Bank Charges*[1] and the Monopolies Commission's report on the proposed merger between Barclays Bank, Lloyds Bank and Martins Bank.[2]

A major point of concern was the clearing banks' interest rate cartel whereby, since 1955, the London clearing banks' seven-day deposit rate had been fixed at Bank Rate minus 2 per cent, with lending rates linked less formally to the Bank Rate. Since the rate agreements were oligopolistic in character they represented a legitimate area for scrutiny. However, although within a free market such arrangements may be open to criticism, the imposition by the authorities of restraints on the clearing banks alone effectively denied the existence of a competitive market whereby the public's preference for bank and non-bank liabilities would be fundamentally influenced by relative yields. Moreover, the clearing banks argued that 'without the agreements, they would end up paying more for the deposits they already receive and would therefore be unable to finance industry and commerce so cheaply'.[3]

Despite the apparent acceptance of these arguments by the Governor of the Bank of England and the Treasury,[4] both the PIB and the Monopolies Commission came out strongly against the cartel. It was argued that the cartel had a 'soporific effect' on the banking system,[5] led to excessive non-price competition, particularly in the form of an expanding branch network[6] and that its abolition would enable the clearers to recapture both lending and borrowing business lost to the 'secondary' banking sector.[7] Finally, the PIB argued that the cartel arrangement, together with the authorities' policy of imposing certain restrictions solely upon the clearers, led the clearing banks to conduct certain types of business through subsidiaries which, in the interests of efficiency, would best have been conducted in the clearers' own right.[8] This belief led the PIB to demand the abolition of the cartel and the extension of balance-sheet controls to all banks and near-banks.[9]

The whole question of the desirability or otherwise of the clearing banks' cartel was tied up with the controversy over whether or not banks could or should compete for deposits with other deposit-taking institutions. For analytical purposes it is useful to distinguish between competition with private-sector institutions (e.g. finance houses and building societies) and with public-sector institutions (e.g. the Trustee Savings Banks). As regards competition with the latter, there was general agreement[10] that the clearing banks could only gain from fighting off competition, as the loss of a depositor to a public-sector institution would result in a decline in both the clearing banks' reserves and deposits. However, there was less agreement on the alleged benefits of competing with private-sector institutions. Some took the view that competition was unnecessary since the clearing banks as a group could not 'lose' deposits to private-sector institutions. This belief was based on the argument that a transfer of deposits between a private-sector institution and a clearing bank simply involved a transfer of ownership of clearing bank deposits, since all such institutions banked with the clearing banks. This analysis, however, only describes the immediate effect of a transfer of deposits; the crucial question concerns the way in which the institution employs its newly gained funds. Firstly, the institution may have to, or indeed choose to, hold part of the increase in deposits as reserves, which might well be in the form of public-sector debt (as is the case for building societies); this in itself would constitute a leakage from the clearing banking system. Secondly, it is likely that the institution would seek to expand advances, if it were profitable to do so. If the on-lending of deposits eventually involves higher payments being made for imports or taxation, or the acquisition of public-sector debt, or the repayment of an overdraft at the clearing banks, then the clearing banks will again lose deposits. In the case where a borrowing customer is induced to switch to the competing institution, however, the decline in the clearing banks' deposits and advances would leave the clearing banks with an improved **liquid assets ratio** which would allow them to restore advances to the previous level, given the existence of profitable lending opportunities, unless the government undertook open-market sales or made further calls for **special deposits.**[11]

Before finally deciding to abolish the cartel the authorities gave further thought to the policy implications inherent in such a decision. For as well as threatening the revival of the industrial sector through the prospect of higher interest rates, the cartel's abolition raised fears of potential adverse (from the authorities' viewpoint) competition with the public sector savings media and of a serious loss of monetary control. The concern for monetary control was that the breaking of the link between the Bank Rate and the clearers' deposit and lending rates would seriously impair the authorities' ability to manipulate short-term rates to achieve balance-of-payments, funding or demand-management objectives. However, the development during the latter part of the 1950s and 1960s of London's 'parallel' money markets, in which no official transactions were conducted, had already 'opened the stable door'. On the savings front, the government feared that intensive bank competition would substantially reduce the inflow of funds to both building societies and the public sector, with important ramifications for the housing market and the reserve base of the banking system if the Exchequer's increased borrowing requirement could not be financed without recourse to the discount houses. These doubts remained to the end, so that even under the 'new approach' the Bank of England retained the discretion to impose ceilings on bank deposit rates as they thought fit.

Until 1967 the authorities relied heavily on hire-purchase terms control in conjunction with 'lending ceilings' to control bank and finance house lending to the private sector for demand-management purposes. This proved necessary because the preferred solution of limiting the availability of liquid assets provided insufficient restraint on bank lending. The authorities, however, were fully aware of the limitations of this approach. As far back as 1959, the Radcliffe Committee had noted that

> such arrangements are not satisfactory, notably in their long run effect on the efficiency of the services rendered by the banking system. They also tend to divert some business into institutions which lie outside the existing machinery of control. (Memoranda of Evidence: Vol. 1, p.39, para. 7, Cmnd 827)

Later evidence of an awareness of the distortions caused by ceilings control was contained in Mr Callaghan's budget speech of 1967 and in the writings of the Bank of England (*BEQB*, June 1969, pp 178-9). Indeed, Mr Callaghan went so far as to replace ceilings control over the clearing banks (but not the secondary banks) with the special deposit scheme (HC Debates, 11 April, 1967, col. 1001) but this change in policy was shortlived; the November devaluation saw the return of the tried and trusted ceilings. Nevertheless, on the introductions of the new monetary regime in 1971, ceilings control was banished, although the authorities retained the discretion to give guidelines on lending 'priorities'.


## CREDIT CONTROL

The need to use lending ceilings to control bank 'credit-creation' arose because (ignoring the growth of 'secondary' banks) the authorities failed to exercise proper control over the availability of liquid assets to the clearing banks. Two major factors[12] contributed to this failure: (a) the policy pursued by the Government Broker of 'leaning against the wind'; and (b) the rapid rise in popularity of **bill finance** for British industry. In order to broaden the long-run capacity of the gilt-edged market – 'to maintain market conditions that will maximise, both now and in the future, the desire of investors at home and abroad to hold British government debt' (*BEQB*, June 1966, p.142) – the Broker acted in such a way as to moderate fluctuations in bond prices and yields. In particular, the Broker was prepared to intervene to support a weak market. This, together with the Broker's unwillingness to drop bond prices in order to encourage sales (firstly because such a measure would prove ineffective as, in general, the gilt market was believed to respond perversely to price changes in the short run, and secondly because it would represent a serious 'breach of faith' with existing holders, which could only weaken the long-run capacity of the market),[13] effectively 'enabled the banks to transfer their holdings from one form of [i.e. non-liquid] government debt to another [i.e. liquid] in the short term without incurring too great a loss' (*BEQB*, June 1969, p.177). Thus the clearing banks' liquid assets plus investments (mainly gilts) ratio became the effective restraint on bank credit expansion and not the minimum liquid assets ratio.

The growth in popularity of bill finance for the industrial sector further augmented the availability of liquid assets, since eligible commercial bills counted as liquid assets, while the discount market's holdings added to bank holdings of liquid assets since the former's need for **call money**, itself a liquid asset, was increased.

Finally, the expansion of credit in the economy was fuelled by the rapid growth of the secondary banking sector, which remained largely unregulated – non-clearing banks were not subject to the 8 per cent **cash ratio**, nor the 28 per cent minimum liquid assets ratio, nor calls for special deposits. Although the authorities had recognised this problem some time earlier, they saw great difficulties in trying to apply similar balance-sheet ratios to all banks, with such diverse balance sheets and operations: a 'cash deposits scheme' was devised for non-clearing banks but was never applied (*BEQB*, June 1968).

Under the 'new approach' an attempt was made to deal with these problems by limiting the amount of commercial bills that were allowed to count towards the minimum reserve assets ratio, by limiting the creation of reserves in the form of call money through the imposition of portfolio constraints on the discount houses, by changing the dealing tactics of the Government Broker, and by extending imposed balance-sheet ratios to all banks and near-banks.


CONTROL OF THE MONEY STOCK

In 1959 the Radcliffe Committee took the view that bond trans-actions should be undertaken to influence interest rates rather than to control the money stock. The use of the quantity of money as a target variable was thought inappropriate as the level of spending in the economy was thought to be determined not solely by the amount of money in existence but rather by the public's total holding of liquid assets and the general availability of borrowing opportunities (Radcliffe Report, para. 390). The 'official' view attached more significance to the control of the money stock than interest rates[14] but nevertheless embodied the argument that the quantity of money alone did not determine spending – building society shares and deposits and short-term local authority debt were considered im-portant.[15]

No further official statements on the money supply were made until the publication of the *BEQB* in June 1966 wherein it was stated that control of the money stock was the 'dominant long-term consideration in debt management' (p.141). From 1967 onwards, however, official pronouncements became more regular. Following the devaluation of sterling in November 1967, the 'letter of intent' despatched to the International Monetary Fund (IMF) after nego-tiations of a stand-by credit facility accepted a money supply target, in the form of a limit on **bank credit expansion**, for 1968: 'bank credit expansion will be less in 1968 than the present estimate for 1967, both absolutely and as a proportion of GNP' (HC Debates,

30 November 1967, cols 648-52). A further target was accepted with the sending of a second 'letter of intent' to the IMF in May 1969. On this occasion a quantitative target for **domestic credit expansion (DCE)**[16] was set: 'The Government's objectives and policies imply a domestic credit expansion for the private and public sectors in the year ending 31st March, 1970 of not more than £400 million'.

Despite the acceptance of monetary targets, the authorities generally treated them as complementary indicators of monetary conditions in the economy. The ultimate objective, to influence the level and pattern of demand, remained sacrosanct, and neither the money supply nor the concept of DCE became the focal point of attention for the conduct of policy (*BEQB*, March 1971, pp. 43-4). However, following a theoretical reappraisal of the role of money ('The importance of money', *BEQB*, June 1970) the money supply became regarded as more than just one in a whole range of liquid assets, and its behaviour was considered an important indicator of the thrust of monetary policy. Accordingly, revised dealing tactics for the Government Broker and a respecification of balance-sheet ratio control were incorporated in the 'new approach' in order to tighten control over monetary aggregate growth.

# 2   Arrangements Under CCC

COMPETITION

In recognition of the views expressed by the Monopolies Commission
and the National Board for Prices and Incomes the following measures
were implemented: (a) the clearing banks' cartel on interest rates was
abolished, with each bank henceforth relating its lending rates to an
individually determined base rate in the light of commercial and
market considerations; (b) balance-sheet ratios were imposed on *all*
private sector banks and near-banks; (c) hire-purchase terms control
and lending ceilings were abolished[1] but the authorities retained the
discretion to use qualitative lending guidelines to determine the
distribution of credit; (d) clearing banks were asked to reveal their
inner reserves and true profits in their published accounts (true
profits had, in fact, been published for the first time in 1970 with
respect to the 1969 accounts); (e) the **collective tender** for Treasury
bills by the Discount House Syndicate was discontinued, although
the informal agreement to 'cover' the tender was retained.[2]

RESERVE REQUIREMENTS

To replace the 8 per cent cash ratio and the 28 per cent minimum
liquid assets ratio, hitherto imposed on the clearing banks alone, a
12½ per cent (minimum) ratio of **eligible reserve assets** to **eligible
liabilities** was imposed upon both clearing and secondary banks, and
both types of banks became liable to a uniform special deposit
ratio (special deposits to bear interest at approximately Treasury
bill rate). In addition, finance houses with deposits totalling more
than £5m. became subject to a 10 per cent minimum reserve assets
ratio and also became liable to calls for special deposits (in practice,
at the same rate as for the banks). Finally, the clearing banks alone
were asked to maintain 1½ per cent of their eligible liabilities in the
form of zero-interest demand deposits at the Bank of England in
order to allow for the settlement of inter-bank indebtedness and
the finance of the operations of the Bank at zero cost. This, together
with the exclusion of notes and coin (till money) and refinancable
export and shipbuilding credits from the list of eligible reserves,

effectively discriminated against the clearing banks and, as such, was against the spirit of CCC – although it must be said that the exclusion of local authority deposits likewise discriminated against the secondary banks, which did not benefit from interest-free current accounts because of the payments transmission mechanism.

The arrangements for the **discount market** involved members holding a minimum of 50 per cent (roughly the market average at that time) of their **borrowed funds** in certain categories of public sector debt.[3,4] In addition, each house was requested by the Bank to give a firm undertaking not to engage in short-term transactions with banks that were 'designed to substitute "window-dressing" arrangements for genuine observance of their minimum ratio obligation'. The Bank also reserved the right to call at any time for full information on the conduct of each house's book, with particular emphasis on the relationship between the house's total business and its capital and reserves.

Transitional arrangements under the new scheme allowed the finance houses twelve months in which to build up their reserves to the required level (although some sought full banking status after the announcement of the new rules), while the clearing banks were asked to subscribe to £750m. of government stocks of two, three and six years to maturity in order to reduce their reserve asset holdings towards the prescribed minimum. Other banks whose holdings of reserve assets had hitherto been well below the prescribed level were allowed to negotiate their own transitional period with the Bank within the time constraint of completion by the end of 1971.

## CONTROL OF THE MONEY STOCK

The essence of the new approach was a system under which 'the allocation of credit is primarily determined by its cost'.[5] It was envisaged that open market operations in gilts, backed up if necessary by calls for special deposits, would influence the level and structure of interest rates by squeezing the reserve position of the banks (see Appendix C). The subsequent changes in relative rates of return would induce shifts in the asset portfolios of both the public and the banks, hopefully in such a way as to restrain money stock growth. The mechanism might work as follows: (a) open market sales of gilts or calls for special deposits squeeze the reserve positions of banks (and finance houses) below the statutory/desired levels; (b) the banks respond to this pressure by disposing of non-reserve assets (such as gilts of greater than one year to maturity) which, presumably, are sold to the non-bank private sector, since the intervention of the

Broker, as a buyer, would only nullify the original policy stance, or by lending in the parallel money markets, e.g. to local authorities or in the inter-bank market, given that banks' cash is always held at or about the minimum level necessary to meet operational and possibly statutory requirements (i.e. the 1½ per cent minimum ratio of bankers' deposits to eligible liabilities imposed upon the clearing banks) and so leaves little room for manoeuvre;(c) the banks' disposal of non-reserve assets would exert upward pressure on a wide range of short-term yields, which would reinforce the upward pressure on interest rates on non-reserve-asset securities brought about by the original open market sales and by subsequent 'penal' lending to the discount market;[6] (d) the subsequent change in yields would cause portfolio adjustments by both the banks and the public; (e) some of these portfolio adjustments might slow down the rate of growth of the money stock, reinforcing the contractionary effect of earlier bank sales of non-reserve assets to the non-bank public. The major asset portfolio adjustment hoped for with respect to the operations of banks was a contraction in net bank lending to the non-bank private sector (see Appendix C) which might result from the increase in bank lending rates that would accompany the upward revision in bank base rates caused by the general increase in market interest rates. Thus, to a large extent, the intended 'transmission mechanism' of monetary policy under CCC was dependent upon the interest elasticity of demand for bank advances, a subject which is returned to later in Chapter 5. The authorities, however, had no doubts that the strategy would be successful:

> Of course the extent of the pressure we shall be able to bring to bear on interest rates. . . .will be affected by many factors: for example, the financial position of the central government or the current sensitivity of foreign exchange flows to short-term rates in London. However, *no limitation* is envisaged on the authorities' ability to neutralise excess liquidity or to bring about sufficiently strong upward pressure on bank lending rates. (*BEQB*, June 1971, p.197)

It is interesting to note that although the reserve system was tightened up somewhat as compared with the liquid assets ratio regime, for demand management reasons, it was 'not expected that the mechanism of the minimum asset ratio and special deposits can be used to achieve some precise multiple contraction or expansion of bank assets' (*BEQB*, June 1971). Indeed, given the 'loopholes' for reserve 'creation' (see appendix to this chapter) that still existed under the new control regime, operation of a classical reserves-deposits 'bank credit multiplier' scheme was never a realistic option. Nevertheless, there were officials at the time who paid more than lip-service to such possibilities.

To accommodate the move to a tighter control of the money stock, modified dealing tactics for the Government Broker were introduced to complement earlier reforms:[7]

(i)   the Bank will no longer be prepared to respond to requests to buy stock outright, except in the case of stocks with one year or less to run to maturity.

(ii)  they reserve the right to make outright purchases of stock with more than a year to run solely at their discretion and initiative.

(iii) they will be prepared to undertake, at prices of their own choosing, exchanges of stock with the market except those which unduly shorten the life of the debt.

(iv)  and will be prepared to respond to bids for the sale by them of tap stocks and of such other stocks held by them as they may wish to sell. (*BEQB*, June 1971, pp.191-2)

The changes helped to 'limit, further than can be achieved solely by alterations in the Bank's dealing prices, fluctuations in the resources of the banking system arising from official operations in the gilt-edged market' (*BEQB*, June 1971). They were designed to allow prices of gilts to reflect market conditions more fully and leave more room for other operators in the market. This latter result was thought particularly desirable since the Bank's close presence in the market had led to the emergence of only two views – that of the Bank and that of all other participants – which gave rise to large speculative transactions and made the speculative management of portfolios too simple. Finally, the adjustments left intact the system of continuous financing and refinancing of central government and also catered for the implementation of an easy monetary policy, through clause (ii), should that prove necessary.

Overall, the new tactics implied a reduction of official intervention in the gilt market, although it should be stressed that each year the Broker has to sell an enormous amount of stock to finance the **public sector borrowing requirement** and refinance maturing debt. Thus he continued to 'lean against the wind' on a rising market, as sales were made on a gradual basis without the price being dropped, but withdrew his automatic support of a weak market. Unfortunately, the experience of the early years of CCC failed to clarify the extent to which, in practice, the Broker's activities would be determined by the need to restrain the supply of reserve assets available to the banking system.

APPENDIX: RESERVE 'CREATION'[8]

The 'ideal' reserve ratio system for control of the money stock in the United Kingdom might be expected to incorporate the following elements: (a) the Bank of England would be the sole supplier of reserves and would maintain 'effective' control over this supply; (b) the banks (institutions), subject to the reserve requirements, would be the only bodies permitted to hold said reserves; and (c) the banks would maintain a constant or predictable reserve ratio. None of these elements featured under the minimum reserve asset ratio scheme[9] which had the following features: (a) although, over long-run periods of time, the public sector 'contribution' to reserve availability for the banks did not pose a serious problem for monetary control (see Appendix A), the Bank was not the sole supplier of reserves – the discount market (through call money), the non-bank private sector (through the commercial bill) and local authorities (through their bill issues) were able to generate reserve assets for the banks; (b) 'outside' holdings of reserves did exist which posed a potentially serious threat to monetary control; and (c) the banks' reserve ratio was not a constant nor did it always prove amenable to prediction.

The most serious potential 'loophole' in the reserve system instituted in 1971 concerned the ability of the discount market to generate substantial quantities of reserve assets for the banks (and finance houses). As distinct from the *generation* of reserves, which included mutually agreeable asset swaps by banks and discount market participants (e.g. the profferring by the banks of gilts of between one and five years to maturity – and hence eligible for rediscount at the Bank by the market operators – in return for gilts of up to one year to run till maturity or Treasury bills), the *creation* of reserves by the 'market' nearly always involved the extension of further call money to the 'market' (discount houses, 'discount brokers', 'money traders', 'money brokers' and the main 'gilt-edged jobbers'). Provided that the increase in call money was in excess of any extra payments made by the market to the authorities (and, of course, that the money was not used to purchase reserve assets from the banks) the commercial banks experienced an increase in reserve assets.

*Reserve creation* by the market might take one or both of the following forms: (a) the reclassification by banks of 'market loans' to the market as call money (only the latter counts as a reserve asset); and (b) the simple offering of more call money to the market by the banks. The first type of transaction allows the banks to offset any anticipated reserve squeeze (or alternatively to expand advances, usually the most profitable form of asset, presupposing an initial excess demand for bank credit) by generating for the banks an increase in reserves on an unchanged eligible liabilities base. In the second case, the increase in call money is initially matched by an increase in banks' liabilities in the form of deposits held by discount houses. The subsequent use to which the loan is put by the houses determines the ultimate impact on the balance-sheet position of the banks.[10] Assuming no 'leakages' in the form of discount house payments to the authorities (e.g. to purchase public sector assets or to reduce indebtedness at the Bank), the houses may choose to purchase assets from either the banks or the non-bank private sector. If the former course of action is taken a further distinction must be drawn, that is, between purchases of bank CDs and inter-bank lending (both of which increase bank eligible liabilities) on the one hand, and purchases of other non-reserve assets on the other. Call money returned to the commercial banks through inter-bank loans or purchases of CDs will not cause as great an increase in lending potential as would discount market purchases of other non-reserve assets from the banks, since the former transactions induce a higher level of bank liabilities and hence a lower consolidated reserve position for the banks (see Dennis, Hall, Llewellyn and Nellis, 1982, pp.188-9). Results similar to those likely to evolve from the use of call money to purchase bank CDs would be obtained if the call money were used instead to purchase assets from the non-bank private sector (see Zawadzki, 1981, pp.48-52) as once again the initial increase in deposit (eligible) liabilities would remain.

Despite the apparently serious design defects of the minimum reserve assets ratio control system, certain factors operated to limit the breaches in practice. With respect to the existence of 'outside holdings' of eligible reserves, the operations of the Government Broker in buying in gilts as they reached the one year to maturity threshold, the establishment of the '2 per cent of eligible liabilities maximum' for the commercial bill, the careful monitoring of acceptance business by the Bank (which rendered bills 'eligible' for rediscount at the Bank) and the restraint exercised on local authority bill issues through Local Government Acts, the 'Control of Borrowing Order' of 1958 and by executive action of the Bank and the Treasury (see Butler Till Ltd, 1978, pp. 48-50) operated to maintain reasonably effective, quantitative control over the availability of some categories of eligible reserve assets. As regards reserve creation by the discount market, a number of restraints came into play. First and foremost, discount houses were limited in the amount of call money they could take by the 'public sector debt ratio' (which later gave way to the 'undefined assets multiple') and by the requirement that their 'total business should bear an appropriate relationship to its capital and re-serves'.[11] Market restraints, notably expectations for future interest rates and relative rates of return on call money and other short-term assets, also had a role to play. In the absence of strong expectations for future rises in interest rates, a decline in call-money rates relative to yields on non-reserve assets would certainly encourage discount house participation in reserve creation for the banks, but the extent of the relative adjustment in yields would be dependent on banks' profitability considerations. If, however, perhaps because of the authorities' actions in the money markets, there was a general con-sensus that a rise in interest rates was imminent and likely to be sustained, the discount market operators would be reluctant to expose themselves to the risk of incurring capital losses on fixed interest securities and so would be less willing to participate in reserve-creating schemes. The strength of their reluctance to partici-pate would depend on their views regarding: (a) the expected future activities of the authorities and, in particular, the likelihood of their being forced to borrow from the Bank at 'penal' rates; and (b) the yields available on newly acquired assets relative to the present and expected future cost of borrowed funds. Finally, a prolonged rise in interest rates might dampen the enthusiasm of banks to initiate such transactions to the extent that any of the presumed excess demand for bank credit disappears. So although the design of the reserve asset system may have been unfortunate in a number of respects, a determination by the authorities to impose a monetary squeeze,[12] with its concomitant interest-rate effects, would effectively block many of the reserve-creating channels open to the banks.

# 3 CCC in Operation: Period 1 (October 1971 – December 1973)

This phase of CCC was associated with an intensification of competition within the banking sector, the floating of sterling, a rapid growth in money (on both the $M_1$ and $M_3$ definition) and credit and certain amendments and additions to the 'rules' and instruments adopted under CCC. The policy stance initially adopted was to stimulate demand in order to reduce the level of unemployment, but this gave way to a period of restraint, starting in July 1973, when a sharp upward movement in interest rates was sought for external reasons (*BEQB*, December 1973, p.476).

Of particular importance to the competitive environment was the entry of the clearing banks, in their own right and not through subsidiaries or associated companies as hitherto, into the 'wholesale' (e.g. inter-bank and CD) money markets, both as borrowers and lenders. As explained below, these developments led to a fundamental reshaping of CCC towards the end of 1973.

Before the major reappraisal of CCC took place, certain important amendments to the original 'rules' were made, notably in the money and gilt markets. Apart from the introduction of the undefined assets multiple (see Chapter 2) for the discount houses, the major policy change that occurred in official money market operations was the replacement of the Bank Rate, the Bank's traditional rediscount rate, by a market-determined **minimum lending rate** (MLR) in October 1972. Henceforth, MLR was to be determined by the formula: 'MLR equals average discount rate for Treasury bills at the tender plus ½ per cent, rounded up to the nearest ¼ per cent'. The change was introduced by the Bank because the Bank Rate had often moved out of line (and since 1971 to a greater degree) with the rates on non-reserve-asset securities and on loans not secured against reserve-asset securities since the latter part of the 1960s, the abolition of the clearing banks' interest-rate cartel accentuating this drift. Hence the new system provided the Bank with a 'penal' rate that responded more flexibly to changes in money market conditions. Although, in theory, the scheme allowed for the removal of the capricious political element from the setting of interest rates, it should be remembered that the Bank still retained the right to override the formula to signify a shift in monetary policy[1] and still sought to influence the Treasury bill rate through the signals that it gave to the discount market.

A second policy shift occurred in late 1973 (and again in early 1974) when, for the first time, the Bank broke tradition and acted to relieve pressure on interest rates in the local authority deposit and inter-bank markets by placing funds in the local authority market and by buying local authority bonds from the discount houses (Bank of England, *Report for the Year Ended 28 February 1974*, pp.12-13). This represented the first official attempt to influence such rates by transactions in the 'parallel' markets, the authorities' previous concern being exclusively with rates on eligible reserve assets and on loans secured against reserve securities and capable of being influenced through official transactions in such assets and loans.

Important developments also occurred in the gilt market. Although less systematic support was given to the market than in the 1960s, assistance was provided on various occasions in 1973. The support operations were described in the Bank's annual report for the year 1973-4 (p.14): 'During the period [early June to mid-September] there were moderate official net purchases, net sales of longer-dated stocks being exceeded by short-dated ones.' They were deemed necessary because of the weakness of the market, which was attributed to the general expectation that interest rates would have to be raised to offset the expansionary monetary effects likely to derive from the large public sector borrowing requirement.

This period of support was not the only occasion on which reserves were created for the banking system through official gilt operations. Following the floating of sterling in June 1972 the Bank made facilities available to the banking system for the temporary sale and repurchase of short gilts in order to alleviate the reserve asset squeeze caused by the outflow of funds abroad. In addition to these transactions the authorities were net purchasers of stocks in the June quarter to the tune of £442m., £432m. of which represented the purchase of next maturing stocks (Bank of England, *Report for the Year Ended 28 February 1973*, p.15).

Despite these operations it became obvious that the authorities were indeed willing to tolerate wider fluctuations in yields and prices than hitherto: the exit of two jobbing firms from the market in July 1972, together with the third biggest government bond dealer, Francis & Praed, was testament to this. These firms took the view that the fluctuations in the market carried too great a level of risk and that the Bank should have been willing to provide assistance on a greater scale. The Bank, however, was not unduly perturbed, maintaining that 'taken together these firms only accounted for a small part of the business in British Government stocks' (*BEQB*, September 1972, p.319). Not all onlookers, though, were so dismissive, and concern was raised about the possible effect of the firms' exit from the market on the marketability of gilts, since only two major jobbing firms were left dealing in gilts.

Finally, two innovations were undertaken in the gilt market to encourage sales: (a) a *convertible* stock – whereby the holder is given the option to convert from a medium to a long-dated stock at maturity at predetermined rates – was issued to stimulate demand at a time of uncertainty; and (b) £400m. of 3 per cent Treasury stock, 1979, was offered at £75 per £100 face value of bonds, the lowest initial issue price for a gilt since 1925, in order to seduce the private investor interested in capital gain rather than income (i.e. the high marginal-rate taxpayers, since capital gains were tax-free if the gilts were held for more than a year and taxed at only 30 per cent otherwise).

July 1973 witnessed the start of a more restrictive monetary policy. Offers of Treasury bills at the tender were sharply increased (to drive up MLR), signals were given to the discount market that the Bank desired a rise in MLR, and special deposits equal to 1 per cent of eligible liabilities (ELs) were called (to be made in August). Despite these measures and the subsequent reserve squeeze and rise in interest rates,[2] monetary growth continued at an undesirable rate, with the result that further calls (2 per cent of eligible liabilities) of special deposits were made on 13 November, of which ½ per cent of ELs was paid on 28 November and another ½ per cent on 12 December (the remaining two instalments of ½ per cent of ELs were subsequently rescinded on 17 December). In between these calls for special deposits, qualitative lending guidelines were issued[3] (on 11 September) according 'low priority' status to property and stock exchange speculation, and, for the first time in the United Kingdom, interest rate ceilings were introduced – 9½ per cent was to be the maximum banks could pay on deposits of less than £10,000. The latter measure was designed to reduce the competitive pressures faced by building societies in their attempts to attract investors in order to stall a rise in the mortgage rate and, like the reappearance of lending guidelines, was contrary to the spirit, though not the letter, of CCC. The restrictive stance of monetary policy culminated in the issue of further qualitative lending guidelines on 17 December, together with the reintroduction of terms control on hire-purchase transactions (hitherto rejected as too selective and hence inefficient) and the unveiling of a completely new device for restraining bank lending and the money supply - the **supplementary deposit scheme**, later to be termed the **corset**. The new scheme required each bank and finance house to place non-interest-bearing supplementary special deposits (SSDs) with the Bank whenever its interest-bearing sterling resources (**IBEL**s) grew at more than a specified rate ('Credit control: a supplementary scheme', *BEQB*, March 1974, p.37).

The reappearance of the new monetary instruments followed a reappraisal of the stated transmission mechanism of CCC - the allocation of credit by price. Despite significant increases in interest rates and calls for special deposits in the latter half of 1973, growth in the money stock continued unabated (possible reasons for this are considered below). This suggested that the interest-rate mechanism might have been: (a) ineffectual, (b) too slow in inducing the desired results, or (c) untested, by virtue of the fact that interest rates were not raised to the requisite levels. The authorities' response could be taken to imply an acceptance of each of these possibilities, for the corset was designed to bring about a speedy end to monetary growth by direct control of part of the banks' and finance houses' liabilities. In so far as an interest rate mechanism was involved, it worked by depressing banks' deposit rates and/or raising their lending rates relative to the levels that would have obtained in the absence of the corset, and so limited recourse to politically sensitive MLR adjustments. This refusal to allow free rein to market forces, the essential ingredient of CCC, characterises post-war efforts to control money stock growth in the United Kingdom, regardless of whether the underlying philosophical approach to control craves for market discipline or the application of official measures of restraint. The imposition of the corset, therefore, marked a return to reliance on quantitative controls on the banking sector, a heretical act for the original proponents of CCC.

Restraining **money supply growth** only became a feature of policy towards the end of 1972. Before that time, an acceleration in monetary growth was tolerated so as not to risk checking the rise in demand and hence the expansion of the economy. Morever, econometric research conducted at the Bank suggested that when real income is rising, a much more rapid rise in the money stock than in money national income is required if rates of interest are to be held within acceptable limits (i.e. the income elasticity of demand for money was calculated to be roughly equal to 2).[4] In the last quarter of 1972, however, emphasis switched to controlling inflation. At the same time the Bank's demand for money functions became discredited, and the Bank accepted that '$M_3$ is probably, at present, a less reliable indicator of the thrust of monetary policy, and assessments of monetary stringency must rest more than usually on a wider range of indicators' (*BEQB*, March 1973, p.12).

Three reasons were forwarded to account for the 'exceptional' rise in $M_3$ which continued throughout 1973: **reintermediation**; the 'precautionary' use of overdraft facilities; and **arbitrage**. Reintermediation involves the return of business to the banks which previously was conducted elsewhere in the financial system because of the nature of the distortive, direct monetary controls adopted by the authorities. Accordingly, a growth in bank liabilities, and hence the money stock, was only to be expected in the initial phase of CCC as banks sought to retrieve the ground lost to their competitors during the 1960s. Moreover, the (clearing) banks' willingness to enter into the 'parallel' money markets and undertake wholesale deposits business provided a new home for 'speculative' money (*BEQB*, June 1973, p.197) – that is, money seeking temporary abode (which previously might well have been placed on deposit with local authorities, outside the money stock definition) before the opportune moment to invest in gilts arises.

The economic effects of reintermediation and structural change[5] (i.e. the move to aggressive **liability management**) depend, respectively, upon the extent of maturity transformation (with concomitant 'liquidity' effects) involved and the degree to which the supply of liquid assets in the hands of the non-bank private sector is augmented rather than restructured. In the latter case, one must distinguish compositional changes in the existing supply of 'liquid' (money and near-money) assets involving a proportionate reduction in public-sector assets held in private portfolios from restructuring involving the substitution of bank assets for other private-sector assets. The economic effects of the latter depend on the liquidity implications of the switch, while, for the former, the monetary and credit ramifications of the resultant increase in government borrowing from the banks must also be considered.

Before moving on to consider the remaining causes of the rapid monetary growth during 1973, this is an opportune moment to consider in greater detail the issue of liability management, the advent of which greatly contributed to the demise of CCC in its original, 'pure' form. When CCC was first introduced the authorities presumed that a reserve-asset squeeze would cause banks to dispose (or at least to reduce net acquisitions) of non-reserve assets, including advances. The response of the banks, particularly the clearers, to the squeeze of mid-1972, however, did not follow the intended course; instead CD and inter-bank rates were 'bid up' (subject to marginal revenue/marginal cost considerations), as individual banks sought to obtain a higher share of the reserve assets available (in the form of bankers' deposits for clearing banks).[6] This resulted in a relative, and often absolute, decline in the yields available on reserve assets (e.g. Treasury bills) and other forms of public-sector debt, which naturally led to perverse, short-run rises in $M_3$ as the non-bank private sector switched into bank assets (after February 1973 the differentials narrowed again as CD and inter-bank rates dropped in absolute terms, only to widen once more in August 1973). Although liability management operations expanded $M_3$, it is important to appreciate that the figures exaggerated their significance, as it is difficult to argue that bank CDs and deposits are substantially more 'liquid' than Treasury bill holdings or deposits with local authorities. To this extent, even 'broad' definitions of the money stock should be treated with caution. Nevertheless, the growth in wider aggregates (e.g. DCE and '$M_3$ plus comparable liquid assets') gave the same impression of extremely rapid monetary growth in the fourth quarter of 1973.

Further monetary repercussions, in the form of (hard) arbitrage transactions, occurred in 1972–3 as a result of the practice of liability management. Arbitrage involved mainly large, corporate bank customers in taking advantage of the disparities in yield structures between the traditional and parallel money markets by borrowing on overdraft at 'base-related' rates (say base rate +1 per cent) and redepositing with the banks at 'market-related' (i.e. inter-bank or CD) rates whenever profitable opportunities presented themselves. Such opportunities arose, on occasions, in 1972 and 1973, but although adding to $M_3$,[7] the effects were temporary and cosmetic: unused overdraft facilities were exchanged for CDs, but only the latter potential source of spending power was included in $M_3$[8]. Measures designed to deal with the problem were eventually introduced in December 1973 when the London and Scottish clearing banks agreed to link lending rates for certain customers (local authorities, finance houses, other banks and certain corporate bodies) to money market rates rather than to base rate, and to ensure that movements in base rates more fully reflected market developments.

The final cause cited for the rapid monetary growth experienced towards the end of 1973 was the 'precautionary' drawing-down of unused overdraft facilities by the corporate sector, possibly due to the expectation of the reimposition of lending controls to contain the money stock 'explosion'. Cost factors were certainly conducive (Goodhart, 1981, p.128) to the simultaneous drawing on overdraft facilities and redepositing with the banks which was responsible for pushing up the recorded figures for the $M_3$ series.

# 4 CCC in Operation: Period 2 (January 1974 – April 1979)

## BACKGROUND

During the 1974-5 fiscal year industrial countries throughout the world faced the dilemma of whether to take measures to ward off an imminent recession that threatened to be as severe as that of the 1930s, or to combat inflation, which was being fuelled by large commodity price increases, particularly for oil (which also created acute balance-of-payments problems for many oil-importing nations). Initially, most countries pursued anti-inflation policies, but only to switch later to economic expansion once the depth of the impending recession had been fully appreciated. In contrast to the policies pursued in the majority of industrialised nations, the United Kingdom government was clearly more reluctant to halt accelerating inflation through deflationary policies that would lead to higher unemployment. The change to a Labour government in February 1974, following Mr Heath's confrontation with the miners and the introduction of the 'three-day working week', led to the first of Mr Healey's 1974 budgets. Although the first fiscal package was expected to cut the PSBR (by £700m.) below previous projections, the subsequent budgets of July and November - the latter to aid industry's financial position - were highly expansionary. A 'social contract' between the government and the Trades Union Congress (TUC) was devised as an instrument to fight inflation. In the event, output stagnated and inflation worsened, both absolutely and relative to most of the UK's trading competitors, although the current account balance did improve.

On the financial front, security prices fell sharply because of the industrial troubles, capital markets dried up, but the growth in the money supply decelerated. The slow-down resulted from a significant decline in bank lending in 1974, owing to the operation of the corset, the three-day working week, and the elimination (after February) of arbitrage opportunities that had done so much to swell

20

the 1973 figures. The end of the fiscal year witnessed a partial return to the spirit of CCC with the removal, in February, of the corset and the 9½ per cent limit on bank rates payable on deposits of up to £10,000.

For most countries the recession bottomed out during 1975, but for the United Kingdom both unemployment and business failures continued to run at high levels. The deflationary April budget provided no respite. Improvements were made on some fronts, however: the rate of inflation declined sharply during the 1975-6 fiscal year, while company finances and the current account payments balance (though still in deficit) improved. The major disappointment was the performance of sterling, which, despite measures taken to stem its fall on the exchanges, remained weak during the first quarter of 1976.

During the year, the rate of growth in $M_3$, which had declined in 1974 from the high levels of 1972 and 1973, continued to fall, so that its average growth in 1975 was of the order of 10 per cent per annum on the previous year. However, $M_1$ grew more rapidly (at a rate of approximately 20 per cent per annum), perhaps reflecting a higher transactions demand arising from upward revisions to anticipated inflation or the decline in the opportunity cost of holding non-interest-bearing money balances.

The weakness in sterling continued throughout the next financial year, causing sterling's depreciation against its Smithsonian parity to rise from 27 per cent at the beginning of 1976 to 41 per cent by October of the same year, although it recovered to 38 per cent by May 1977. This lack of confidence in sterling exacerbated, and in turn was influenced by, the pressures that had built up on the financial markets; interest rates were rising, money supply growth accelerated, owing to an increased level of bank lending to the private sector (arbitrage may again have been a problem) and difficulties experienced in trying to finance a growing PSBR in a non-monetary fashion, and inflationary expectations worsened.

Official concern about the growth in the money stock during this period was first expressed by the Chancellor in his budget speech of April 1976 when he stated that appropriate action would be taken should the growth in the money stock become excessive. In July he mentioned the figure of 12 per cent as being the appropriate rate of growth (assumed to apply to $M_3$) for the financial year 1976-7. By the end of October this figure had been described as a *target* of monetary policy. This aspect of policy assumed further significance when the 'letter of intent' was dispatched to the IMF on 15 December 1976: in return for assistance, a commitment was provided by the government to keep domestic credit expansion within specified limits (see p. 45). At the same time, cuts in public spending were announced, designed to hold the PSBR during 1977-8 to £8.7b. (Earlier concern about the *money* level as well as the *volume* of public expenditure culminated in the introduction of **cash limits** in February 1976 and a further £1b. of public expenditure cuts in July.) As a result of these measures, the hike in MLR in October and the resurrection of the corset in November, sterling staged a dramatic recovery which continued through the 1977-8 fiscal year.

Targets were again to the forefront in the March 1977 budget: the Chancellor stated that his 'best estimate' for 1977-8 was that the growth of sterling $M_3^1$ would be in the range of 9-13 per cent and reaffirmed that DCE was to be kept within the £7.7b. limit for 1977-8 (later extended until mid-July 1978). This commitment to monetary targets set the pattern for policy for the next five years.

During the first quarter of the 1977-8 fiscal year the PSBR fell more rapidly than expected, which, together with the continued presence of the corset, allowed the target for sterling $M_3$ (£$M_3$) to be met. Despite a resurgence in bank lending in the quarter to mid-July, the corset did not come into play and the scheme was indeed suspended in August. Large official sales of gilts in July and August ensured that £$M_3$ remained on target. By mid-October, however, £$M_3$ growth was above the target range, mainly due to the pressure from external capital inflows which was subsequently ameliorated by allowing sterling to float freely. A moderate increase in bank lending, a weak gilts market and an increased central government borrowing requirement (CGBR) in the final quarter helped to push £$M_3$ growth for the target period as a whole beyond 16 per cent, compared with the target range of 9-13 per cent. Accordingly, MLR was raised, by stages, from 6½ per cent to 9 per cent, with the Bank announcing on 25 May that henceforth MLR would be set by administrative action. This was followed in June 1978 by a package of fiscal and monetary measures, including a further increase in MLR (from 9 per cent to 10 per cent) and reactivation of the corset, designed to keep the trend growth in £$M_3$ within the target range for 1978-9 which had been set at 8-12 per cent. The ensuing gilt sales, together with the rapid growth in **disintermediation** (*BEQB*, December 1978, p. 499), helped to keep £$M_3$ on track.

On 9 November the Chancellor announced that the £$M_3$ target for the year to October 1979 would be 8-12 per cent. The accompanying rise in MLR to 12½ per cent stimulated substantial gilt sales but, despite this, monetary growth in the first three months of the new target period remained above the pre-set range. An expansion in bank lending in the first quarter of 1979 was responsible for keeping monetary growth above target, although, for the year to mid-April,

£M$_3$ rose by just 10½ per cent (unadjusted), comfortably within the previous target range.

## MONETARY INSTRUMENTS

The period in question was associated with a continued reliance on *lending guidelines* (and HP terms control), periodic calls for *special deposits*, frequent use of the *corset*, a return to an *administered MLR* and innovations in *official gilt market operations*.

### *Lending guidelines*

In its 'credit control' notice of 12 November 1974 the Bank asked banks and finance houses to retain the lending guidelines set out in the 'consumer credit' notice of 17 December 1973. This basically involved a request to the banks to restrain lending to persons and for purely financial transactions and to exercise restraint on lending to property companies (whilst avoiding aggravating their financial difficulties).

These guidelines were reaffirmed by the 'credit control' notice of 28 February 1975, which also asked banks and finance houses to ensure that any expansion in their lending was directed mainly to providing finance or facilities for the expansion of exports, the saving of imports and for domestic industrial investment.

Further qualitative guidance was contained in the credit notice of 17 December 1975, which requested that priority be given to the needs of manufacturing industry and to the provision of facilities for working capital, exports, import-saving and domestic industrial investment. 'Low priority' status was to be accorded to: loans to persons or check trading facilities for the purchase of goods covered by the Terms Control Order (finance was not to be given on easier terms than those permitted for hire-purchase contracts); loans to persons in general; lending to property companies; and lending for purely financial transactions.

Precisely the same guidance was contained in the next two credit notices, although that issued on 18 November 1976 carried one addition, namely that in providing acceptance credit facilities banks should observe the same degree of restraint as would apply to lending for the finance of the underlying transaction. Subsequent credit control notices issued on 12 May 1977, 11 August 1977, 11 April 1978, 8 June 1978 and 17 August 1978 carried the same requests.

Thus, throughout the 1974-9 period, qualitative guidelines on bank lending were observed by both banks and finance houses, at the behest of the Bank.

## Minimum Lending Rate

After 1975 the MLR instrument was assigned an increasingly important role in facilitating official gilt sales (see below, pp. 28-30). In addition, the frequent suspension of the market-related formula linking MLR to the Treasury bill discount rate led to its termination in May 1978.

## The special deposit scheme

The first use of the special deposit scheme during the 1974-9 period occurred on 4 February 1974, when SDs equivalent to ½ per cent of eligible liabilities were repaid by the Bank as the success of the corset in curtailing the growth of IBELs effectively removed the need for the special deposit instrument. Further releases of SDs equal to 1½ per cent of ELs were made in April (½ per cent on 8, 16 and 22 April) in order to counter rising market rates and provide the banks with resources to meet any industrial demands arising from recovery from the three-day week. (It is important at this stage to appreciate that Bank of England statements on the intended role to be played by the special deposit instrument were ambiguous, for it was never clarified whether influence was sought over banks' cash, i.e. bankers' deposits, or reserve assets as the means of influencing short-term interest rates, although the more frequent usage of the instrument after 1976 is usually associated with cash control. Certainly, in the absence of the corset, SD calls induce a rise in banks' wholesale borrowing rates, which, in a situation of reserve asset shortage, would widen the differential *vis-à-vis* eligible reserve asset yields.) The policy appears to have been successful in inducing the desired interest rate movements. During the 1974-5 fiscal year the Bank resumed payment of interest on SDs called against **non-interest-bearing eligible liabilities (NIBELS)**, which had been suspended late in 1973 because banks were deemed to be increasing their profits due to the 'endowment' element in their interest-rate structures.

No calls for SDs were made during the 1975-6 fiscal year as it became clear that there was insufficient demand for advances from the private sector to enable banks to expand the money stock in such a way as to create inflationary demand pressures within the economy. Only one release of SDs was made and this was only temporary - for three weeks from 19 January to 10 February 1976. Although such flexible use of the SD instrument had been envisaged when the CCC 'rules' were first drawn up, this was the first occasion on which it had manifested itself. The new strategy was implemented to counteract the anticipated interest-rate effects associated with the expected heavy concentration of tax payments which would otherwise have caused a severe but temporary shortage of funds in the money markets.

The next call for SDs was made on 16 September 1976, when banks and finance houses were asked to lodge 1 per cent of ELs with the Bank (½ per cent on 28 September and ½ per cent on 6 October) as part of the restrictive monetary policy pursued by the authorities at that time. Because the calls appeared to have a minimal effect in influencing either interest rates or the reserve asset position of the banks and finance houses, a further call, equivalent to 2 per cent of ELs, was made on 7 October. The first half of the call became effective on 2 November, but the other 1 per cent was subsequently deferred on 5 November and again on 10 December and was finally cancelled on 13 January 1977. At the same time (with effect from 17 January) SDs equivalent to 2 per cent of ELs were returned by the Bank to overcome the abnormally severe reserve asset pressure being experienced by the banks, mainly due to heavy official sales of gilts, and to try and hold down interest rates. The final SD manoeuvre of the 1976-7 fiscal year appeared in the shape of a temporary release (from 31 January to 10 March) equivalent to 1 per cent of ELs, again designed to ease market conditions until an expected improvement in the banks' reserve position materialised. As intended, short rates fell on release of the SDs.

The first operation of the 1978-9 fiscal year occurred on 15 June, when it was announced that the cumulative total of SDs lodged at the Bank was to be reduced from an amount equivalent to 3 per cent of ELs to 1½ per cent of ELs with effect from 19 June; the rate was to be restored to 2 per cent on 3 July and to 3 per cent on 24 July (later postponed until 11 September). When the desired fall in interest rates failed to materialise, a further temporary reduction of 1 per cent of ELs was announced, to take effect from 31 July and to be restored on 26 September. Again, the purpose of all these temporary adjustments was an attempt to use the SD instrument, rather than official transactions in the money market, as a smoothing device to moderate anticipated fluctuations in short-term interest rates arising from money-market pressures.

The penultimate SD venture of 1978-9 occurred on 17 August when £207m. of SDs were released to the clearing banks (out of their total of £288m.). This was in accordance with the Chancellor's undertaking of December 1976 to release SDs if the banks' position in relation to the corset was prejudiced by their commitment to find fixed-rate finance above 20 per cent of non-interest-bearing sterling sight deposits under the sterling export and home shipbuilding credit arrangements. Between 26 September and 19 February 1979 the banks' cumulative outstanding SDs remained at 3 per cent of ELs, but on 19 February the Bank released over £800m. of SDs (2 per cent of ELs) into the system to cushion the market from its ensuing gilt sales programme. The first tranche was due back at the Bank on 9 March (but was subsequently cancelled on 5 March because of the heavy strain imposed by massive gilt sales on banks' 'reserves') with a further 1 per cent due back at the end of March. The cancellation of the first recall meant that the cumulative level of SDs kept at the Bank remained temporarily at 1 per cent of ELs, and this was further reduced – to zero – when £252m. of SDs were temporarily returned to the banks on 15 March, to be recalled on 23 April. On this occasion, action was taken because the gilt sales had been responsible for opening up unacceptably high margins between short- and long-term rates of interest.

Although it is difficult to isolate the effects of SDs from more general developments in the economy, experience with the special deposit instrument during the years 1974 to 1979 suggests that it can be successfully used to induce *downward* adjustments to short-term interest rates but that it is less effective when used in a restraining capacity.


## *Official transactions in the gilt-edged market*

During the mid-1970s the Bank was known to be considering possible changes in government borrowing arrangements that might ensure a steadier flow of sales. Two basic ideas were canvassed, namely a system that allowed a more frequent adjustment of price, and issues by tender. Neither received official acceptance, although a partial move to a tender system was made in March 1979 (see below). However, in March 1977 a major innovation was introduced with the promise of a further one to come: two stocks were brought out for which only a part had to be subscribed at the time of issue. These became known as 'partly paid' stocks. The purpose of the innovation was to reduce the extent of short-run (i.e. month-to-month) variability in monetary growth by achieving a closer match between government payments and receipts.

The promise of a second revision to sales tactics was fulfilled in

May 1977 when £400m. of variable rate Treasury stock was offered to the market. In the words of the Bank, the introduction of variable rate stock was partly aimed at strengthening the total demand for government stock but was mainly designed for 'smoothing out the net flow of total sales, since such an instrument might, it was thought, prove particularly valuable on occasions when expectations as to the course of interest rates were uncertain'.

A variable rate stock would help to achieve this by compensating for a declining capital value when interest rates were rising or expected to rise, and so maintain the demand for gilts on occasions that had previously created acute funding problems for the authorities.

The first variable rate issue was quickly sold out, but a second issue, made on identical terms on 1 July 1977, sold much more slowly. The probable reason for this was the linking of the variable rate to the Treasury bill rate. The first issue had a rate of interest based on a daily average (over a six-month reference period) of the Treasury bill discount rate plus a fixed margin of ½ per cent. Although it proved popular (but, alas, mainly with banking sector institutions) it would probably have been more attractive if the rate had been linked to money-market rates (e.g. LIBOR, the six-month London Inter-Bank Offered Rate), thereby providing a *guaranteed* margin. This is because many institutions raise the bulk of their borrowed funds in the wholesale money markets, where rates, on occasions, have moved substantially out of line with 'traditional' money-market rates. For this reason most of the local authority variable rate security issues linked the interest payment to LIBOR, calculating the rate in advance but paying it six months in arrears.

On 23 March 1979 the first experiment at sales of gilts by tender was undertaken by the Bank: £800m. of Exchequer 12¼ per cent 1999 was offered at a *minimum price* of £97.50 for every £100 of stock. Subscribers were asked to tender either at the minimum price, which was closely in line with prevailing market rates, or in units of 25 pence above it. For investors the arrangements meant that an undersubscription of the issue would involve all applications being met at the minimum price (which proved to be the case), whereas for an oversubscription a cut-off price would be found that just cleared the issue and accommodated all applications at or above the cut-off price.

The general reaction of the market to the Bank's new initiative was lukewarm as it was seen as representing only a marginal change to existing procedures; for if the issue was undersubscribed (which was the normal outcome) then it would, to all intents and purposes, be exactly the same as a fixed price issue, whereas an oversubscription would enable the Bank to borrow on marginally better terms than would otherwise have been the case. The adaptation to policy did nothing to alleviate the difficulties faced in trying to sell gilts on a weak market.

The only other important feature of official dealing tactics during the 1974–9 period was the use of the MLR instrument to affect expectations in the gilt market. The phenomenon was christened the 'Duke of York' strategy by the market as it involved the authorities in blatantly engineering (or, indeed, officially pronouncing) a sudden jump in MLR whenever the funding season appeared on the horizon. The rationale behind the strategy was that the 'marching up' of MLR, along with long-term rates, to its peak would encourage the investor to expect a subsequent fall in rates, starting at the short end but transmitted to the long end by the familiar 'ripple effect', and hence to anticipate the accrual of a substantial capital gain. Once the funding operation was completed, MLR would fall back again, dragging down other short rates in the process and presenting the bulls (and 'stags') with their expected profits to go with the high, nominal fixed-interest payment (see Table 4.1 for instances of its application). Such activities, however, did not escape criticism. Apart from the general complaint of generating excessively high servicing costs (particularly if, as the authorities maintained, inflation moderated), vocal criticism came from the building societies which, because of their notoriously 'sticky' interest rates, were subjected to significant deposit withdrawals each time the strategy was attemped. Despite the concomitant implications for the housing market and, in

TABLE 4.1 Duke of York operations

| MLR change | Gilt sales generated |
|---|---|
| (1) *3 October 1975*<br><br>MRL raised from 11→12% (fell back to 11% on 2 January 1976 and to a trough of 9% on 5 March 1976) | Short tap stock, 9½% Treasury stock 1980, exhausted 10 October; 12¾% Treasury loan 1992 exhausted by November, along with official holdings of two other stocks. Official net sales of central government debt to non-bank private sector (NBPS) during fourth quarter of 1975 and first quarter 1976 totalled £1.9b. and £1.4b. respectively. |
| (2) *10 September 1976*<br><br>MLR raised from 11½%→13% | Substantial amounts of stock sold in second half of month: £600m. 14½% Treasury loan 1994 oversubscribed on day of issue (20 September); 9¾% Treasury stock 1981 exhausted. Official net sales of stock in third quarter of 1976 totalled £0.6b. |

TABLE 4.1 continued

| MLR change | Gilt sales generated |
|---|---|
| (3) *7 October 1976*<br><br>MRL raised from 13%→15%<br>(fell back to 14% on<br>7 January 1977) | Heavy official sales of stock made in October – 1979 and 1998 tap stocks exhausted on 4 November. Official sales of gilts to NBPS in three months to mid-January 1977 totalled £3b. |
| (4) *25 November 1977*<br><br>MLR raised from 5%→7%<br>(6½% by 6 January 1978) | Together with announcement of more favourable financial news, led to exhaustion of 1982 and 1992 stocks on 7 and 9 December respectively. Short-dated (1982) tap issued on 15 December exhausted on 4 January 1978. Long-dated (1999) stock issued on 22 December oversubscribed. Official net sales of stock during the December 1977 quarter totalled £2b. |
| (5) *11 April 1978*<br><br>MLR rased from 6½%→7½% | After announcement of increase in banks' base rates on 19 April substantial sales ensued: 1983 stock exhausted on 19 and 1995 stock on the 20 April. |
| (6) *8 June 1978*<br><br>MLR: 9→10% | Long-dated (1998) tap stock exhausted on 9 June; short (1982) tap stock exhausted on 12 June. Official net sales of gilts during June quarter totalled £1,9b. £1.9b. |
| (7) *9 November 1978*<br><br>MLR: 10→12½% | Official supplies of 12% Exchequer stock 1999/2002 and 10% Exchequer stock 1983 exhaused on 10 and 14 November respectively. Net sales during December quarter totalled £1.3b. |
| (8) *8 February 1979*<br><br>MLR: 12½→14% | Official supplies of three tap stocks exhausted shortly afterwards and two issues made on 22 February oversubscribed. First quarter (1979) sales totalled £2.3b. |
| (9) *12 June 1979*<br><br>MLR: 12–14% | With help of reports of sustained overseas buying, three stocks exhausted by 2 July. |
| (10) *15 November 1979*<br><br>MLR: 14→17% | Substantial sales made within a few days (incl. second tranche (£1,000m.) of 13¾% Treasury stock 2000/2003). Official third quarter net sales amounted to £2.7b. |

particular, the mortgage lending rate, the manoeuvre remained a significant feature of monetary control.

In contrast to the first phase of CCC, only once during the January 1974–March 1979 period was significant official support of the gilt market apparent to the observer. The occasion was during the second half of 1974 when persistent weakness, mainly at the long end of the market, led the authorities to support the market because 'The pressing need in the closing month of 1974 seemed to be the restoration of confidence in financial markets.'[2] The Bank described its intervention as follows:

> during this period the authorities, exercising the discretion provided for in the arrangements adopted in 1971, became net purchasers not only of stocks within one year of maturity, but to a modest extent of longer-dated stocks as well. (Bank of England, *Report for the year ended 28 February 1975*)

### The 'corset'

*Modus operandi and details of the scheme.* The 'corset' was designed to effect monetary restraint by providing a disincentive for banks (and finance houses) to manage their liabilities by bidding for funds in the wholesale money markets, in order to induce moderation in their rate of acquisition of assets (mainly in the form of loans). Each institution subject to the scheme[3] was allocated an 'allowable' or 'penalty-free' rate of expansion for its interest-bearing eligible liabilities (IBELS), expressed as a percentage rate of growth (on a three-month moving average basis) of IBELs on a specified 'base' level (see Table 4.2 for details). If an institutions's IBELs growth exceeded this threshold then that institution became liable to non-interest-bearing 'supplementary special deposits', on a steeply progressive basis (see Table 4.2). From the authorities' point of view, one of the scheme's great merits (apart from its moderating influence on interest rates) was its flexibility, for both the 'penalty structure' and 'penalty-free zone' could be readily changed to suit market developments and the base date could be set retrospectively to nullify any anticipatory action taken by the institutions concerned.[4]

The theoretical underpinning of the new scheme can perhaps best be illustrated by way of profit maximisation considerations. In a profit-maximising world, the level of bank liabilities (mainly deposits), and hence assets, would be determined where the marginal cost (interest and associated variable costs) of attracting an extra deposit unit was equal to the marginal revenue gained from the employment

31

**TABLE 4.2 Application of the corset**

| Dates operational | Base | Penalty-free zone | Penalty structure 'Excess' IBELs | Deposit rate required (%) |
|---|---|---|---|---|
| (1) 17 December 1973–28 February 1975 | | | (1) | |
| (a) 17 December 1973–11 November 1974 | (a) Average IBELs on make-up dates in October, November and December 1973 | (a) 8% growth in first six months followed by 1½% growth per month on a three-month moving average basis | (a) up to 1% / over 1% and up to 3% / 3%+ | 5 / 25 / 50 |
| (b) 12 November 1974–28 February 1975 | (b) " | (b) 1½% IBELs growth per month as above | (b) 3% or less / over 3% and up to 5% / 5%+. | 5 / 25 / 50 |
| (2) 18 November 1976–11 August 1977 | Average IBELs on make-up days in August, September and October 1976 | 3% for the first six months and ½% per month thereafter | (2) up to 3% / over 3% and up to 5% / over 5% | 5 / 25 / 50 |
| (3) 8 June 1978–mid-June 1980 | Average IBELs on make-up days for six months November 1977–April 1978 | 4% growth for average IBELs for three months August-October 1978 and thereafter 1% per month of the base average | (3) up to 3% / over 3% and up to 5% / over 5% | 5 / 25 / 50 |

Source: Dennis, G.E.J., Hall, M.J.B., Llewellyn, D.T. and Nellis, J.G., *The Framework of United Kingdom Monetary Policy 1971–81* (Heinemann, 1982) p. 183.

of that unit of deposit; expansion would take place as long as marginal revenue exceeded marginal cost. Now if bank operations were such that corset penalties were incurred, then, although the marginal cost of the liability management operations would be unaffected, the marginal revenue gained from employing the extra deposit unit would be lower than would otherwise have been the case, since a fraction of that extra deposit unit would have as its counterpart a non-interest-bearing deposit at the Bank of England. Obviously the higher the fraction, the less profitable bidding for deposits becomes. The corset thus acts as an additional constraint on bank liability management, i.e. it is additional to the market constraint on expansion of rising marginal costs (in fact the marginal cost curve will shift upwards owing to the rising cost of 'purchased funds', the industry's variable factor input) and falling marginal revenues,[5] the latter being experienced as loan charges are reduced to encourage the take-up of additional bank loans or as loans to less credit-worthy customers are made. Of course, in the real world profit maximisation may not always prevail; increasing the market share, maintaining goodwill or a concern with longer-term, rather than short-term, profitability (e.g. in attracting a student clientele) may all have an important role to play. Nevertheless, for the bulk of banking business, profit maximisation considerations apply, so that the corset is unlikely to fail on this count.

Apart from restraining bank expansion the corset was responsible for easing interest rate pressures in the money market by reducing the demand for funds emanating from the banks. As banks curtailed their wholesale bidding and took measures to increase inter-bank lending, either directly or through the purchase of other banks' CDs, in order to ease their 'corset' pressures, inter-bank and CD rates would fall absolutely and relative to other money market rates. This would serve to encourage depositors to switch to non-bank assets, thereby driving down interest rates in other markets (e.g. the local authority deposit, Treasury bill, commercial bill, inter-company and discount house deposit markets). To the extent that such disintermediation (discussed in more detail below) increased the flow of funds from the non-bank private sector to the public sector, the government's need for 'residual' finance from the banking system was reduced correspondingly, thereby providing a further monetary fillip in the shape of a reduction in the availability of reserves for the banking system and a fall in £M$_3$, although in 'liquidity' terms the latter would merely be cosmetic. The only problem with the interest rate effects of the corset was that the induced falls in money market rates might lead to falls in bank base rates and hence loan rates, which would undermine monetary restraint and create credit-rationing problems for the banks.

The first corset phase was terminated on 28 February 1975 because of slackness of demand for bank loans, which meant that most banks and finance houses were well within their permitted limits of IBELs expansion. The corset reappeared on 18 November 1976, following publication of the banking figures for October, which the Chancellor described as showing a 'continued growth of bank lending to the private sector which is inconsistent with my objectives for the future growth of the money supply'. The 'credit control' notice of 12 May 1977 extended the scheme for a further six months in an attempt to keep both DCE and £M₃ growth within previously announced limits. A ten-month corset-free period then ensued until the scheme was reactivated on 8 June 1978 to reinforce monetary restraint. With extensions, this third phase lasted until mid-June 1980, when the corset was finally abolished.

*'Penalty avoidance' and its effects.* In the knowledge that the corset might be reactivated at any time to contain monetary expansion (and especially when to raise interest rates would prove politically unattractive) the first measure the banks can take to avoid subsequently falling foul of the corset is to build up their IBELs. Despite the authorities' assumption of the power to set the base retrospectively, 'IBELs-building' operations (the opposite of those described immediately below) did feature in the run-up to the reappearance of the corset.

With the corset in operation, an *individual* bank might seek to reduce its own level of IBELs by reducing net inter-bank liabilities (by increasing inter-bank lending and/or reducing inter-bank borrowing), by increasing its holdings of other banks' CDs[6] or by lending more to the discount market on non-callable terms, for each operation is allowable as an offset against any recorded IBELs growth. Each of the first two forms of transactions simply redistributes IBELs pressure within the banking sector without achieving any relief for the banks as a whole, while all three (assuming, in the last case, that the net increase in market loans to the discount market is financed by an equal reduction in call-money loans) cause the bank in question to lose an equivalent amount of reserve assets. A shortage of reserve assets would therefore constrain the banks' ability to engage in such transactions, which, for the system as a whole, might simply result in a loss of competitiveness on the liability front with little IBELs relief being experienced.

Action taken by the banks as a group to reduce 'collective' IBELs is more important from a monetary standpoint because the success of such operations may thwart the ultimate objective of the scheme, which is to effect a deceleration in monetary growth, as measured by the $M_3$ (and later $£M_3$) statistic, with a lower level of interest rates than would otherwise be necessary. In view of this, transactions that succeed in reducing both IBELs and ELs[7] but not $£M_3$ require special consideration. The discount houses play an important part in this respect because each of the following transactions (some of which, namely (a) and (b), may be of minor practical significance but are included for the sake of completeness) result in a destruction of IBELs (and ELs) *relative to* $£M_3$: (a) a reduction in discount house bank deposits; (b) a reduction in discount house holdings of bank CDs; (c) a net increase in bank 'market' loans to the discount market; and (d) UK resident switches from bank deposits (with an initial maturity of up to two years) to deposits at discount houses.[8] In order that bank purchases of CDs from discount houses achieve the desired reduction in IBELs, they must be financed by means other than a reduction in market loans to the houses. The extent to which the finance is found by cutting net call money outstanding to the market is limited by the banks' consolidated reserve position relative to the prescribed minimum (12½ per cent of ELs). The same constraint may also operate to limit the banks' ability to generate a net increase in market loans to the houses by reclassifying callable loans as non-callable. More indirectly, reserve asset pressure would also serve to block the other two 'escape' channels, since competition for the available reserves would ensure that banks' wholesale (including CD) and retail deposit rates remained at levels competitive with alternative assets. Thus the yield incentives that are necessary for inducing (a) discount house switches out of bank deposits and CDs into, say, commercial bills, local authority loans or marketable central government debt, and (b) non-bank, private-sector switches to discount house deposits from bank deposits, are unlikely to be present when reserve pressure, as well as IBELs pressure, is brought to bear on the banks.

The preceding analysis covers mainly the direct and immediate effects of the corset, but to assess the ultimate impact on the economy the subsequent portfolio adjustments need to be traced. To continue the case of discount houses moving out of bank deposits and CDs, it is important to identify the subsequent balance-sheet adjustments made by both the banks and the discount houses. Assuming the banks have induced the reduction in their liabilities by allowing their deposit and CD rates to become uncompetitive, they have to decide which of their assets to dispose of. A corresponding reduction in call money to the discount market would be the most likely response, given a sufficiently healthy bank reserve position.[9] It is unlikely, however, that the discount houses would quietly accept a reduction in their 'book'. Indeed, perhaps without having to take positive steps to raise their borrowing levels from non-bank sources, the houses' problems might be solved, for the decline in bank deposit and CD rates is likely to cause non-bank (resident and non-resident) switches from these instruments to discount house deposits, thereby further destroying IBELs relative to £M$_3$.[10] This would allow the houses to build up their undefined assets in the form of loans (other than through the purchase of eligible bills and negotiable bonds) to local authorities or acceptances. If the former route is chosen, the local authorities are likely to use the funds to reduce their bank indebtedness, while the acquisition of acceptances from non-bank holders would provide the balancing entry in the banks' consolidated balance sheet in the form of increased non-bank-owned deposits.

With regard to the interest rate effects of the corset (and the related bank manoeuvres to avoid incurring penalties under the scheme) it is clear that, initially, bank deposit (including CD) rates decline absolutely and relative to the yields on other short-term instruments. As a result, funds both flow out of the banks and bypass the banks altogether as the ultimate users ('deficit' units) receive loans direct from the economic units in financial surplus. This phenomenon is termed disintermediation and is more likely to occur in markets where the maturity-transformation role of the banks is least important, i.e. at the short end of the loans market. In the UK context, disintermediation manifested itself in the local authority deposit market, the market for short-term public-sector debt, the acceptance market and, after the abolition of exchange controls, in the Eurosterling market (see pp. 81-3). The monetary effects of disintermediation are considered below, but in terms of 'allocative efficiency' the effects are likely to be minimal, as the major operators in the wholesale money markets are, on the whole, sophisticated corporate and financial bodies.

Disintermediation in the local authority deposit market results in a fall in £M$_3$ as the local authorities use the non-bank finance to reduce their indebtedness to UK banks. Hence both non-bank-owned deposits and bank loans are lower than they would otherwise have been. It is important to note, however, that this form of disintermediation leaves the banks with an improved reserve asset ratio, which, in the presence of an existing excess demand for bank credit at prevailing loan rates, could be used to rebuild deposits, and hence £M$_3$, to their previous levels. In the absence of such excess demand, though, £M$_3$ will fall, but the supply of credit and the non-bank private sector's holdings of liquid assets will remain the same. Hence little monetary significance can be attached to this brand of disintermediation. This is not so for non-bank switches into short-term public sector debt, e.g. Treasury bills or short gilts. In this case further repercussions arise as a result of the government's reduced need for 'residual' financing accommodation from the banks which will reduce both eligible liabilities (and £M$_3$) and bank reserve assets below the levels that would otherwise have obtained and so accentuate the initial reserve pressure and balance-sheet decline of the banks.

The third form of disintermediation resulted from the stimulation of the commercial bill market as a result of the relative decline in bank deposit rates and the eagerness with which banks sought commission by accepting commercial bills. Although the resurgence of activity in the commercial bill market meant less business for the banks, it did provide them with an opportunity for generating income in a manner that did not prejudice their position with respect to the corset. This is because fees could be charged for 'accepting', or lending one's 'name' to commercial bills (thereby enhancing marketability for the holder); IBELs would be unaffected as long as the accepted bills were discounted outside the banking system.

A complete analysis of the monetary effects of disintermediation in the acceptance market ideally requires a breakdown of discounts by type of purchaser (bank, discount house, Bank of England, non-bank financial intermediary, non-bank resident and overseas resident) and by source of funds (Dennis, Hall, Llewellyn and Nellis, 1982, pp. 193-6). However, if non-resident discounts are excluded (for which no reliable statistics are available), non-bank private sector discounts provide a good approximation as to the extent to which the acceptance market may be used to supply highly liquid assets to the non-bank public without either the ELs (and probably IBELs) or £M$_3$ figures being affected – non-bank private sector discounts simply cause a rearrangement in the ownership of existing bank deposits. The effect of disintermediation through the acceptance market is therefore to increase the supply of credit (to the issuers of the bills) for a given nominal money stock (£M$_3$), thereby evading the intended credit-restricting discipline of the corset. In this manner the statistics for both ELs and £M$_3$ are distorted as indicators of prevailing monetary conditions or the stance of monetary policy. Despite the constraints on acceptance market expansion – operating on both the demand front (risk/return considerations determine the proportion of acceptances held in portfolios) and supply front (individual banks are likely to limit the number of bills they accept to preserve marketability) – the magnitude of the growth induced by the corset was significant. However, due to the fact that, excluding non-resident discounts, market developments proved amenable to monitoring, the authorities took no direct action to limit the supply of acceptances, since to do so would only have redirected disintermediation into alternative and uncharted channels.

*Corset effects in practice.* To analyse the effects of the corset, it is convenient to split each corset period into three distinct phases: (1) the three-month period immediately preceding the announcement of the activation (or reactivation) of the scheme, during which time 'the banks' might have attempted to build up IBELs in anticipation of the reimposition of controls – this is termed the 'pre-announcement anticipatory action' phase; (2) the period running from the time of reactivation to the date the scheme becomes 'operative' i.e. when SSDs have to be made – this is termed the 'post-announcement, pre-operative action' phase; and (3) the period during which the corset remains operative – termed the 'corset experience' phase. Using this analytical framework, Table 4.3 highlights the corset's influence on the growth of $£M_3$, IBELs and bank lending to the private sector and on movements in private-sector liquidity resulting from the induced disintermediation.

*Summary.* Each 'post-announcement, pre-operative' phase was associated with a marked deceleration in the rate of $£M_3$ growth. If comparison is made with a monthly rate of $£M_3$ growth during the 'pre-announcement anticipatory action' phase, then for the three periods in question (i.e. mid-December 1973 to mid-June 1974, mid-November 1976 to mid-May 1977 and mid-June 1978 to mid-October 1978), the monthly growth rates fell from £670m., £390m. and £570m. to £200m., £30m. and £380m. respectively. This is consistent with the view that the corset was effective in restraining money stock growth, as measured by the $£M_3$ statistic, as intended (though also, unfortunately, with the view that $£M_3$ growth was stimulated in the pre-announcement phase) but one should be careful not to exaggerate its significance. It is undoubtedly the case that the imposition of the corset contributed to the deceleration in money supply growth, but to isolate and quantify its share of the total effect is an impossible task (this should be borne in mind when considering the remaining effects of the corset). It should also be noted that the restraint exercised wanes during each 'corset experience' phase so that, for example, the eventual money supply growth rate might prove higher than that experienced in the 'pre-announcement' phase, as was the case for the period mid-May to mid-August 1977.

A number of important observations can also be made with respect to monthly IBELs growth. First, 'anticipatory' action undertaken by the banks was responsible for a marked acceleration in IBELs growth

TABLE 4.3  Corset effects in practice[1] (£m.)

| Corset 'phase' | Δ£M₃ (seasonally adjusted) | ΔIBELs (unadjusted) | Destruction of IBELs relative to £M₃[2] | Δ£ bank lending to UK private sector[3] | ΔNBPS holdings of acceptances (i.e. 'bank bills,) | ΔNBPS holdings of local authority deposits | ΔNBPS holdings of Treasury bills |
|---|---|---|---|---|---|---|---|
| **1. 17 December 1973–28 February 1975** | | | | | | | |
| (a) Pre-announcement anticipatory action: mid-September 1973–mid-December 1973 | 2017 | 1098 | 919 | 1829 | NA | NA | NA |
| (b) Post-announcement, pre-operative action: mid-September 1973–mid-June 1974 | 1218 | 90 | 1128 | 2118 | NA | NA | NA |
| (c) Corset experience: mid-June 1974–mid-February 1975 | 2421 | 1054 | 1367 | 1523 | NA | NA | NA |
| **2. 18 November 1976–11 August 1977** | | | | | | | |
| (a) Pre-announcement anticipatory action: mid-August 1976–mid-November 1976 | 1164 | 2129 | −965 | 1484 | −35 | 249 | −697 |
| (b) Post-announcement, pre-operative action: mid-November 1976–mid-May 1977 | 186 | −2142 | 2328 | 797 | 78 | −220 | 65 |
| (c) Corset experience: mid-May 1977–mid-August 1977 | 1399 | 1376 | 23 | 901 | −56 | −269 | 102 |
| **3. 8 June 1978–mid-June 1980** | | | | | | | |
| (a) Pre-announcement anticipatory action: mid-March 1978–mid-June 1978 | 1709 | 1033 | 676 | 1407 | 70 | 38 | −143 |
| (b) Post-announcement, pre-operative action: mid-June 1978–mid-October 1978 | 1511 | −830 | 2341 | 1289 | 582 | 195 | −516 |
| (c) Corset experience: mid-October 1978–mid-June 1980 | 10,118 | 10,051 | 67 | 13,610 | 1865 | 1620 | 23 |

[1] Some of the figures are estimated from quarterly data.
[2] Δ£M₃ minus Δ IBELS.
[3] Banking sector lending plus Bank of England Issue Department's acquisition of commercial bills.

Sources: Data for £M₃, IBELs and bank lending to UK private sector taken from *Economic Trends*, Annual Supplement (1981), pp. 149–50, 190–1 and 149–50 respectively. Additional data for IBELs (October 1973–June 1974) taken from Table 37, *Financial Statistics*, October 1974. Private-sector liquidity details taken from Table 7.6, *Financial Statistics*, July 1980 and 1981 and *BEQB*, September 1979, p.281.

during the three months immediately preceding the reactivation of the corset: relative to the three-month period immediately preceding the 'anticipatory action' phase, the average monthly growth in IBELs rose from £280m. to £500m. and from £230m. to £320m. for the periods mid-August to mid-November 1976 and mid-March to mid-June 1978 respectively. Second, each 'post-announcement, pre-operative' phase was associated with an extremely rapid deceleration in IBELs growth (it became negative in two of the three cases), in both absolute terms and relative to $£M_3$ growth. The third column of Table 4.3 illustrates the latter point, indicating how loosely changes in IBELs and in $£M_3$ are related. The role played by the discount market in generating the destruction of IBELs relative to $£M_3$ is shown in Table 4.4, and demonstrates that the transactions identified account for between 34 and 39 per cent of the total.

As discussed earlier, the severity of the corset and hence its effectiveness in inducing demand restraint depends fundamentally on the supply of reserve assets available to the banks. The third row of Table 4.4 indicates that banks were sufficiently 'flush' with reserve assets to reclassify some call loans to the discount market as market loans in order to reduce IBELs pressure, but Table 4.5 provides a fuller picture. Those factors responsible for increasing the supply of reserve assets available to the banks (see pp. 133-6) and which are quantifiable are presented (together with qualitative evidence on official assistance given to the money market) to give a rough indication of the reserve pressure experienced by the banks while the corset was in operation. The overwhelming impression gained from casual observation of Table 4.5 is that the severity of the corset was substantially weakened by the ready availability of reserves to the banks. Taking the three 'corset experience' phases in chronological order, reserve asset creation totalling £137m., £793m. and £1535m. respectively is identified. While the creation of reserves through the discount market dominates the reserve availability scene in the period May-August 1977, the 'residual' supply of Treasury bills and the release of special deposits (apart from official money-market assistance given) dominate in the periods June 1974 to February 1975 and October 1978 to June 1980 respectively. Moreover, judging by the pressure put on the banks' consolidated reserve asset ratio, only in the latter period could 'official' action to increase reserve availability really be justified.

Finally, as was the case for the impact on $£M_3$ growth, the degree of restraint exercised on IBELs growth appears to wane during the 'corset experience' phase, for only four institutions in total (placing £2m. and £1m. at mid-January 1975 and mid-July 1977 respectively)

TABLE 4.4  Destruction of IBELs relative to £M$_3$ through the discount market (£m.)

| Transaction | (a) Mid-December 1973–mid-June 1974 | Corset phase (b) Mid-November 1976–mid-May 1977 | (c) Mid-June 1978–mid-October 1978 |
|---|---|---|---|
| Reduction in discount house holdings of bank CDs | 325 | 107 | 709 |
| Reduction in discount house holdings of UK bank deposits[1] | 54 | 59 | −57 |
| Increase in UK banks sterling 'market' loans to discount market[2] | NA | 731 (87) | 176 (58) |
| Identified destruction of IBELs relative to £M$_3$ through the discount market | 379 | 897 | 828 |
| % of total destruction of IBELs relative to £M$_3$ accounted for by discount market operations[3] | 34 (1128) | 39 (2328) | 35 (2341) |

[1] That is, reduction in 'funds lent to UK banking sector'.

[2] The figures in brackets give the corresponding fall in bank call money loans to the discount market, providing an indication of the extent to which call loans are switched to market loans.

[3] Total figure (in brackets) taken from Table 4.3.

Source:  *Financial Statistics*, December 1978, Tables 6.19 and 6.6; August 1977, Tables 6.21 and 6.9; October 1974, Tables 41 and 52.

**TABLE 4.5  Reserve asset 'pressure' during the operation of the corset (£m.)**

| Corset phase | Public sector 'contribution' to supply of reserve assets[1] | Net creation/destruction (negative) of reserve assets through DM[2] | Reduction in special deposits | Official money market transactions: qualitative evidence | Total effect[3] | Reserve ratio end-period |
|---|---|---|---|---|---|---|
| **1.** | | | | | | |
| (a) September 1973–December 1973 | -5 | 397 | -366 | — | 26 | 13.8 |
| (b) December 1973–June 1974 | -5 | -157 | 571 | (i) February–March 1974 – 'substantial' assistance in the form of purchases of TBs, CBs and LA deposits. (ii) End May–June 1974: assistance through purchase of TBs, CBs and LA bills. | 409 | 13.5 |
| (c) June 1974–February 1975 | 343 | -154 | -52 | End-November 1974 – 'large scale' assistance provided through purchases of TBs and LA bills. | 137 | 13.5 |
| **2.** | | | | | | |
| (a) August 1976–November 1976 | -339 | 799 | -762 | After end-September – 'exceptionally' large purchases of bills | -302 | 13.9 |
| (b) November 1976–May 1977 | 35 | -705 | 745 | 'Very large' assistance (including 'heavy' overnight lending) given during November–January period and at other times. | 75 | 14.0 |
| (c) May 1977–August 1977 | -180 | 1009 | -36 | Assistance given through purchases of TBs, CBs and LA deposits and overnight loans. | 793 | 14.5 |

*Continued overleaf*

**TABLE 4.5** continued

| Corset phase | Public sector 'contribution' to supply of reserve assets[1] | Net creation/destruction (negative) of reserve assets through DM[2] | Reduction in special deposits | Official money market transactions: qualitative evidence | Total effect[3] | Reserve ratio end-period |
|---|---|---|---|---|---|---|
| **3.** | | | | | | |
| (a) March 1978–June 1978 | -308 | 208 | 585 | 'Large' assistance given in June through purchase of TBs, CBs and LA deposits. | 485 | 13.8 |
| (b) June 1978–October 1978 | 300 | -226 | -400 | — | -326 | 13.4 |
| (c) October 1978–June 1980 | -48 | 532 | 1051 | 3 'sale repurchase' (gilts) arrangements: (i) 15 February– 13 March (extended to June) – £500m.; (ii) 11 April – June – £500m.; (iii) June – £700m. | 1535 | 13.0 |

[1] That is 'residual' supply of Treasury bills (see Table A.1, p.134).
[2] Approximated by net increase in UK banks' call-money loans to discount market (DM) minus increase in DM holdings of Treasury bills.
[3] A positive sign indicates relaxation in reserve asset pressure.

Sources: Column 1: Estimated from series for 'market bills' sold to UK banking sector to finance PSBR, Table 2.6, *Financial Statistics.*, August 1977, February 1979, May 1980, July 1981.

Column 2: *Financial Statistics.*: July 1974, Tables 37 and 52; July 1975, Tables 37 and 51; July 1977, Tables 6.9 and 6.21; December 1978, Tables 6.6 and 6.19; July 1981, Tables 6.6 and 6.7.

Column 3: *Bank of England Statistical Abstract* No. 2, 1975, Table 9; *Financial Statistics*, December 1978, Table 6.16; and July 1977, Table 6.3.
Column 4: *BEQB* (Financial Review).

were still incurring 'penalties' at the end of the first two corset periods.[11]

Growth in bank lending to the UK private sector also appears to have been successfully curtailed by the corset: monthly growth rates between 'pre-announcement' and 'post-announcement, pre-operative' phases fell from £610m., £490m. and £470m. to £350m. £130m. and £430m. respectively for the three corset periods taken in chronological order (see Table 4.3). Once again, however, other factors played a part in this, notably the pressure of demand for bank credit.

Disintermediation through the acceptance market (the 'bill leak') was most marked during the last corset period: private-sector holdings of acceptances rocketed from £217m. to £2664m. between June 1978 and June 1980. Likewise, the most marked increase in private-sector-held local authority deposits occurred during the same period, from £2322m. to £4137m. In contrast, disintermediation via the Treasury bill market was less significant, privately held bills actually falling by £493m. (to £244m.) between June 1978 and June 1980.

The influence of the corset on UK interest rates is particularly difficult to disentangle from other influences such as official money market operations, administered MLR changes and external developments. Nevertheless, as theory would predict, the banks' three-month sterling CD rate fell throughout the periods covered by the first two trials of the corset (see Table 4.6). This experience was not repeated under the final application of the scheme, primarily due to the interest rate effects of the reserve asset shortage caused by abnormally large official gilt sales to the non-bank private sector and to the strength of demand for bank credit, particularly from the corporate sector – 'involuntary' loan demand (see pp. 71-2). Following each application of the scheme the differential between the banks' three-month sterling CD rate and Treasury bill rate narrowed continually, as predicted (apart from the period October 1978 to June 1980 when reserve assets were frequently in short supply) while arbitrage opportunities (see column 5 of Table 4.6) were also eradicated as CD rates fell relative to bank base rates (apart from the period June to October 1978 when again reserve asset pressure was responsible – see *BEQB*, September 1978, p. 345).

## MONETARY TARGETS: JUNE 1976- JUNE 1979

Following the lead of West Germany (1974), Switzerland (1975) and the United States (1976), the UK government's intentions for monetary aggregate growth were publicly announced for the first time on 22 July 1976 when the Chancellor stated that, for the financial year

**TABLE 4.6   Interest-rate effects of the corset (% p.a)[1]**

| | | Three months' sterling CD rate | TB rate (average discount rate) | Base rate plus 1% | CD rate minus TB rate | CD rate minus 'base rate plus 1%' |
|---|---|---|---|---|---|---|
| 1. (a) September 1973–December 1973 | B | 13.375 | 10.94 | 12 | 2.435 | 1.375 |
| | E | 15.875 | 12.42 | 14 | 3.455 | 1.875 |
| (b) December 1973–June 1974 | B | 15.875 | 12.42 | 14 | 3.455 | 1.875 |
| | E | 13.5 | 11.24 | 13 | 2.26 | 0.5 |
| (c) June 1974–February 1975 | B | 13.5 | 11.24 | 13 | 2.26 | 0.5 |
| | E | 10.875 | 9.77 | 12.5 | 1.105 | -1.625 |
| 2. (a) August 1976–November 1976 | B | 11.25 | 10.94 | 11.5 | 0.31 | -0.25 |
| | E | 14.625 | 14.03 | 15 | 0.622 | -0.375 |
| (b) November 1976–May 1977 | B | 14.625 | 14.03 | 15 | 0.622 | -0.375 |
| | E | 7.75 | 7.43 | 9.5 | 0.32 | -1.75 |
| (c) May 1977–August 1977 | B | 7.75 | 7.43 | 9.5 | 0.32 | -1.75 |
| | E | 6.625 | 6.42 | 9 | 0.205 | -2.375 |
| 3. (a) March 1978–June 1978 | B | 6.75 | 5.99 | 7.5 | 0.76 | -0.75 |
| | E | 10 | 9.27 | 11 | 0.73 | -1 |
| (b) June 1978–October 1978 | B | 10 | 9.27 | 11 | 0.73 | -1 |
| | E | 10.875 | 10.28 | 11 | 0.60 | -0.125 |
| (c) October 1978–June 1980 | B | 10.875 | 10.28 | 11 | 0.60 | -0.125 |
| | E | 16.75 | 15.68 | 18 | 1.07 | -1.25 |

[1] Figures represent the average of spread (unweighted) rounded up to the nearest $\frac{1}{8}$% and are given for both beginning (B) and end (E) periods.

Source:   For CD and base rates, *Economic Trends*, Annual Supplements. For TB rate, *Financial Statistics*, April 1975, Table 112; July 1977, Table 13.10; July 1981, Table 13.9.

1976- 7 as a whole, $M_3$ growth should amount to about 12 per cent (*BEQB*, September 1976, p.296). By the end of October this figure had been described as a 'target' by the Governor of the Bank of England (*BEQB*, December 1976, p.454). Further quantitative commitments to monetary restraint were next provided by the government through the signing of the 'letter of intent' sent to the International Monetary Fund on 15 December 1976: domestic credit expansion (DCE) was to be kept within the boundaries of £9b. (first indicated to the IMF in a 'letter of application' in December 1975), £7.7b. and £6b. for the financial years 1976- 7, 1977- 8 and 1978- 9 respectively. At the same time the Chancellor announced that the sterling component of $M_3$ was to be held within a 9- 13 per cent range for the 1976- 7 financial year. The same 9- 13 per cent target range for $£M_3$ was announced in the March 1977 budget for the 1977- 8 financial year, and in July the Chancellor reaffirmed the government's commitment to the £7.7b. DCE limit for the fiscal year 1977- 8 (later extended to mid-July 1978). Finally, in the April budget of 1978, a target range of 8- 12 per cent for $£M_3$ was established for the 1978- 9 fiscal year.

The adoption of publicly announced targets by UK governments owed much to the spread of disillusionment with traditional demand-management policies (*BEQB*, March 1978, p.33) and to the growing acceptance (perhaps spurred through dealings with the IMF) of the view that control of monetary aggregates is at least necessary, if not sufficient, for the effective control of inflation. In addition, the move to explicit targets for monetary aggregates had been facilitated by a change in monetary strategy away from interest-rate stabilisation, which, arguably, becomes more important the shorter the time horizon the policy-maker is concerned with, and towards control of monetary aggregate growth. Three major factors were responsible for this: (a) the transition to a ('managed') floating exchange rate era which, in principle, allowed the authorities the opportunity to control monetary aggregates other than DCE; (b) higher and more volatile inflation rates, which had impaired the functioning of nominal interest rates as indicators and instruments of monetary policy; and (c) Bank of England studies which appeared to prove the existence of stable demand for money functions[12] and so could be construed as providing, first, evidence of the superiority of money stock control over interest-rate stabilisation as a policy for stabilising income;[13] second, evidence of the potential power of interest rates to control monetary growth; and third, an early, if only approximate, means of forecasting income movements.[14]

The rationale for the adoption of any intermediate target (i.e. lying between the tools or instruments of policy and the ultimate goals) is the provision of a diagnostic device for either forecasting ultimate goal variables, when data pertaining to the target variable are received more frequently than data concerning the goal variable and hence assist stabilisation policy by enabling the authorities to adjust their instrumental variables speedily in order to keep their goal variables 'on track', or for assessing the current stance of policy or state of economic activity. To use intermediate targets in the former capacity depends on the authorities' ability to identify close and systematic statistical links with goal variables (stable demand for money functions in the case where monetary aggregates are chosen as the intermediate targets), while their value as indicators derives from the information they provide to policy-makers, enabling continual revisions to be made to instrumental variables during the implementation of a particular policy, but in this case, to keep the target variable 'on track', consistent with the desired path for the goal variable.

The case for publishing targets is twofold: (a) expectations (e.g. concerning future nominal wages and prices) might be favourably influenced through the provision of a clear signal of government intentions to wage bargainers, foreign exchange, money and capital market operators and interested parties overseas (*BEQB*, March 1977, p.497); and (b) it might assist economic management in the long run by making it more difficult than hitherto for governments to retreat from the pursuit of their previously announced goals for reasons of political expediency. Proponents of the 'rational expectations' school in particular put great faith in the power of announced targets to condition rapidly, in a favourable fashion, expectations in the UK labour market, but their optimism was sadly misplaced, causing the Tories' post-1979 disinflationary policies to degenerate into a severe dose of 'old fashioned' deflation. The theory was that by announcing money stock targets for a certain period into the future and rigidly observing those targets, those involved in negotiating wages would eventually bargain on the basis of nominal wage and price expectations associated with the predetermined future rate of monetary growth.[15] Hence the only 'rational' approach from the employees' side in the face of government resolve to hold money stock growth below the current level of inflation is assumed to be to seek pay rises in line with productivity gains, since further rises, to the extent that they are reflected in higher prices for firms' output, can only result in higher unemployment.[16]

Further reduction in target ranges should, on this basis, gradually squeeze inflation (or at least that element not imported) out of the system. Unfortunately for the authorities, the theory overlooked, and policy-makers underestimated, the degree of entrenchment of labour-market practices. Moreover, it was fallacious to argue that under the previously stated circumstances there was only one rational response (assuming that the government was right in believing that trade unions would be more concerned with unemployment, and hence the size of their membership, than maximising the benefits for those remaining in employment). A number of responses were possible: (a) the unions might hope to force the government's hand - the more likely the nearer to a general election; (b) as a casual glance at the previous record of UK governments in adhering to targets would suggest, the unions might justifiably hope for a better out-turn than that promised because of the uncertain art of monetary targeting; and (c) even though pay rises in excess of productivity gains might be negotiated (perhaps conceded by firms as the more attractive alternative to industrial action) these would be unlikely to be fully reflected in higher prices, since profit margins, even though dangerously low in some cases, are temporarily pared in the expectation or hope of an imminent upturn in the economy. Even if all these hopes of the unions proved unfounded, one still has to consider the prime objective underlying their bargaining procedures. Any reduction in labour that may ultimately be required can be relatively painlessly achieved through a reduction in overtime working, early retirement or a slowdown in recruitment - the anguish caused by the last mentioned being ameliorated by government schemes to deal with youth unemployment.

The second strand of support for published targets can be criticised on the grounds that the government becomes a 'hostage to fortune' on the basis of policies founded on preconceptions about such issues as the stability of demand for money functions and the rationale of targets itself, which ultimately may prove misguided.

In the light of previous comments on the rationale for establishing intermediate targets and on the reasons for the change in monetary strategy away from interest-rate stabilisation, it is now opportune to discuss the alleged merits of selecting monetary aggregates to represent intermediate targets (see Artis and Currie, 1981, for the case for preferring the exchange rate). Least controversial was the Governor's assertion that published monetary targets were an essential foundation of monetary stability, a prerequisite of financial stability,[17] the provision of which he saw as 'the main role . . . for monetary targets'.[18] In the same vein, monetary stability was considered desirable as it contributed to stability on the foreign exchanges.[19] The second claim made by the Governor was that

the best way of giving a clear indication of the thrust of monetary policy is to state quantitative aims for the rate of expansion of one or more of the monetary aggregates. . . The growth of the monetary aggregates, properly related to the circumstances of the time, is perhaps the best indication of monetary conditions, and targets set in terms of monetary aggregates are useful in providing check points against which current developments can be compared and monitored. (*BEQB*, March 1977, p.48)

This was the indicator role to be played by monetary aggregates. Finally, control of monetary aggregate growth in the medium term was considered an indispensable part of anti-inflation policy in apparent acceptance of the view that 'a [longer term] relationship [between monetary growth and inflation] cannot . . . be doubted',[20] although others have questioned the statistical evidence for the UK.[21]

Having accepted the need for the establishment of intermediate targets in the form of growth ranges for monetary aggregates, policy-makers then have to decide upon the 'optimal' choice of aggregate (that there is a selection problem is evident from the low correlation between growth rates in different monetary aggregates – see Budd, 1981, p.15). To assist in the decision-making process two basic considerations are usually brought to bear on each variable (excluding the base)[22] (see Table 4.7). First, and most important, are changes in the potential control variable closely and systematically linked, preferably in a uni-directional, causal fashion to goal variables (e.g. nominal income) and is the target variable exogenous to (i.e. deter-mined independently of) the goal variable? Second, how precisely and at what cost can the target variable be controlled (and measured)? The 'official' line is that a money supply target is preferable to a DCE target when the balance of payments is in surplus,[23] while £$M_3$, despite its tendency to respond perversely to interest rate changes in the short run and the authorities' inability to identify a stable demand function for it, represents the 'best' money stock series because it allows identification of other 'key credit counter-parts, such as the PSBR, bank lending, government debt sales, DCE and external financial flows, in a way that helps our understanding of the course of monetary developments'.[24] It is also believed to be closely associated with price movements in the longer term, say five to ten years. Econometric evidence, however, if supporting any aggregate (which is debatable),[25] would tend to lean towards $M_1$,[26] whereas *a priori* reasoning would recommend moving further along the liquidity spectrum[27] than £$M_3$ to include assets such as Treasury bills, local authority deposits and building society deposits, which are close substitutes for assets included in narrower definitions of the money stock and hence could be legitimately regarded as a similar source of 'potential purchasing power', and even unused overdraft facilities and trade credit. Within the analytical framework

**TABLE 4.7** The relative advantages of different monetary aggregates as intermediate targets

| Aggregate | Arguments for | Arguments against |
|---|---|---|
| $M_1$ | (a) Readily controlled, even in short run, by interest rates. | (a) Stability of demand for $M_1$ function may be questioned on two grounds<br>  (i) since publication of Coghlan's work (1978) poor fore-casting performance;<br>  (ii) no presumption that $M_1$ would remain 'stable' if authorities sought to control it, i.e. UK banks might offer US-style interest-bearing current accounts (e.g. 'Now' accounts).<br>(b) On monetarist gounds, unsuitable as it is a 'demand-determined' variable.<br>(c) Too sensitive to changes in short-term rates of interest and intensifies difficulties in the interpretation of fluctuations.<br>(d) Ignores the potentially significant liquidity implications of wider (near-money) asset holdings. |
| $M_2$ | $M_2$ would provide (a) a broader aggregate than $M_1$, thereby overcoming some of the drawbacks associated with concentrating on too narrow an aggregate, yet (b) would exclude the highly volatile element of deposits – wholesale deposits – that plagues the prediction and control of $£M_3$. | (a) The additional of clearing bank 7-day time deposits to the $M_1$ series achieves only a marginal improvement in informational content – better to grade deposits by size but this would be arbitrary and impose a further, onerous, statistical collection burden on the clearers.<br>(b) Irrational to restrict a statistic purporting to measure private sector retail-type deposits to banks alone: why not include building society shares and deposits or deposits at savings banks? |
| $£M_3$ | (a) Can be linked to key credit counterparts in such a way as to aid interpretation of monetary developments, i.e. $\Delta M_3 \equiv$ PSBR plus sterling bank lending to the private sector and overseas minus sales of public sector debt to NBPS minus 'external and foreign currency finance' minus $\Delta$(banks' non-deposit liabilities).<br>(b) Proportionately less disturbed by transit items than $M_1$. | (a) Very difficult to forecast and control, partly due to volatile element of wholesale deposits.<br>(b) May be influenced, in unpredictable fashion, by 'structural change' within the financial system – see Artis and Lewis (1974) and Hacche (1974).<br>(c) No stable demand for $£M_3$ function yet identified, i.e. the very foundation of targeting policy is missing.<br>(d) As an indicator of monetary conditions, $£M_3$ is open to distortion by disintermediation in various forms.<br>(e) Ignores the potentially significant liquidity implications of non-resident-owned sterling bank deposits, resident and non-resident-owned foreign currency deposits held with UK banks and NBPS holdings of near-money assets (including acceptances). |

*Continued overleaf*

**TABLE 4.7** continued

| Aggregate | Arguments for | Arguments against |
|---|---|---|
| DCE | (a) Control of DCE the best way of ensuring adequate restraint over domestic financial situation, especially when priority is given to improving the UK's payments position.<br><br>(b) The domestic element of credit is most directly under the control of the authorities.<br><br>(c) Readily related to key credit counterparts: $DCE \equiv \Delta M_3$ + external financing of public sector + $\Delta$(overseas sterling deposits) + $\Delta$(banks' net foreign currency deposits) + $\Delta$(banks' non-deposit liabilities), i.e. DCE $\triangleq \Delta M_3$ + payments deficit/– payments surplus<br><br>(d) In so far as DCE includes the change in non-resident-owned sterling bank deposits, it improves $£M_3$ as a monetary indicator. | (a) Irrelevant when current account moves into surplus (e.g. because of North Sea oil), since DCE is simply an operational device for ensuring that the authorities make some cut in $£M_3$ growth when the payments deficit rises beyond a certain level (i.e. to ensure that the PSBR is not financed disproportionately by a payment deficit). |
| Broader aggregates than $£M_3$, such as $PSL_1$ or $PSL_2$ | (a) Any series measuring 'purchasing power overhanging the supply of goods and services' should rightly take into account assets beyond bank deposits, since it is difficult to substantiate the claim that bank deposits alone possess 'virulent liquidity' which would otherwise allow the authorities safely to ignore building society shares and deposits, savings bank deposits and local authority deposits, etc.<br><br>(b) The high degree of substitution between assets lying within and outside $£M_3$ (e.g. between CDs and Treasury bills or local authority deposits) supports the case for selecting a broader aggregate.<br><br>(c) The growth and evolution of the building society movement, which has blurred the distinction between deposits at banks and at building societies, has created a legitimate demand for extending the coverage of assets beyond those included in $£M_3$ to include, at the minimum, building society shares and deposits. | (a) Switching to a broader aggregate might impose a statistical collection burden on certain new contributors, e.g. local authorities.<br><br>(b) Such an aggregate might be beyond the immediate control of the Bank, e.g. holdings of local authority deposits are largely unaffected by official monetary measures.<br><br>(c) The cut-off point between those assets included and those excluded would be more arbitrary than before.<br><br>(d) The case for moving to broader aggregates lacks empirical foundation. |

developed earlier, therefore, both $M_1$ and $£M_3$ (the only two aggregates for which a substantial volume of evidence is available) would
score low on 'statistical association'[28] with nominal income which,
to many, would rule them out as target variables, although $M_1$ would
score higher on 'controllability' (given its higher sensitivity to interest-
rate changes) at 'minimum cost' to the real economy (see Chapter 8,
pp.114-18 for the 'real' costs of $£M_3$ targeting under the Tory
government). To take a positive view on the relative merits of sup-
planting $£M_3$ with a broader aggregate requires further evidence
on the practicalities of control and on the statistical links with goal
variables. Smith (1978) presented results for an $M_5$ series which was
very similar to $PSL_2$: this suggested that any instability was due to
the behaviour of its $£M_3$ component.

Once a decision has been taken on which aggregate to adopt as the
intermediate target, the authorities have to decide on the 'appropriate' target value or range. In the UK the general public is not privy
to such internal deliberations (the scientific rigour with which they
are constructed has attracted scepticism from the Governor himself),[29]
contrary to experience elsewhere in the targeting world. The West
German authorities in particular go to great lengths to explain how
the Bundesbank's target figures are arrived at, typically providing
estimates about the likely growth of productive potential, the
likely increase in capacity utilisation, the 'unavoidable' rise in the
price level and the expected change in income velocity.[30] Finally,
additional to the setting of target numbers, other technical difficulties have to be overcome. These comprise matching instruments
to targets, setting the base, dealing with variability in money demand,
and assessing the case for adopting 'rolling' targets.[31]

Whatever the arguments for the establishment of monetary aggregates as intermediate targets, a brief sketch of early targeting experience (see Table 4.8) suggests that the difficulties confronting
target practitioners are formidable. For the financial year 1976-7,
DCE was held to less than half the limit agreed with the IMF, $£M_3$
growth was well below the lower end of the target range, and total
$M_3$ growth was substantially less than targeted for. Such 'success',
if success is defined as not breaching the upper limit of targets and
serious under-shooting is not allowed to detract from this, was sharply
reversed in the following financial year when, although DCE was again
well within the agreed limit, $£M_3$ growth was well above the top end
of the target range. For the period April 1978 to April 1979, DCE was
allowed to exceed the agreed limit slightly, but for the first time the
rate of growth in $£M_3$ was held within the target range. Finally, $£M_3$
growth in the first half of the October 1978 to October 1979 target
period (the first occasion on which targets were 'rolled' forward)

**TABLE 4.8    Early UK targeting experience[1]**

| | DCE (£b.) | | £M₃ (%) | | M₃ (%) | |
|---|---|---|---|---|---|---|
| | Ceiling[2] | Out-turn | Target | Out-turn | Target | Out-turn |
| Financial year 1976–7 | 9 | 4.5 | 9–13 | 7.7 | 12 | 10 |
| Quarterly: April–July | | 2.5 | | 3.1 | | 3.6 |
| July–October | | 2.5 | | 4.2 | | 5.3 |
| October–January | | -0.4 | | -0.9 | | -1.2 |
| January–April | | -0.1 | | 1.5 | | 2.6 |
| Financial year 1977–8: | 7.7 | 4.4 | 9–13 | 16.4 | | |
| Quarterly: April–July | | 0.7 | | 2.5 | | |
| July–October | | -0.1 | | 3.2 | – | – |
| October–January | | 0.8 | | 4.1 | | |
| January–April | | 3.0 | | 5.7 | | |
| Financial year 1978–9: | 6.0 | 6.6 | 8–12 | 10.9 | | |
| Quarterly: April–July | | 1.9 | | 3.6 | | |
| July–October | | 1.0 | | 1.3 | – | – |
| October–January | | 2.2 | | 4.3 | | |
| January–April | | 1.7 | | 1.7 | | |
| October 1978–October 1979 | | | 8–12 | 13.3 | | |
| Quarterly: October–January | – | – | | 4.1 | | |
| January–April | | | | 1.6 | | |

[1] Mid-month, seasonally adjusted data.

[2] Agreed with the International Monetary Fund.

Source: *BEQB*, June issues, 1977, 1978 and 1979.

was only slightly above target, but subsequent experience caused the upper target level for the period as a whole to be breached. A more detailed analysis of monetary growth during the April 1976 to June 1979 period reveals some of the reasons responsible for the mixed 'success' achieved by the UK monetary authorities.

*Financial year 1976–7.* A rapid expansion in sterling bank lending to the private sector in June 1976 was responsible for the 'excessive' growth (relative to the quarterly growth rates implied by the targets) in DCE, £M₃ and total M₃ in the April to July quarter. Some of this was attributed to leads and lags in commercial payments and receipts from abroad as commercial enterprises sought to protect them-selves from any further depreciation in sterling by accelerating payments for imports and delaying foreign currency receipts from abroad, the banking sector being called upon to provide the necessary finance. Monetary growth inconsistent with all three targets per-sisted into the next quarter, mainly due to a pause in official gilt sales in the summer of 1976 and to a rapid rise in bank lending to the personal sector in the months to mid-September and mid-October (perhaps influenced by the general expectation that tighter credit controls were imminent). The authorities duly responded by raising MLR to a record 15 per cent in October, making special deposit calls and reintroducing the corset in November. As a result of these measures, falls for DCE, £M$_3$ and total M$_3$ were recorded for the October 1976 to January 1977 quarter, the growth in DCE being further moderated by heavy official gilt sales to the non-bank private sector (NBPS) and a lower than expected CGBR. DCE fell further in the final quarter, due to a lower than expected PSBR (£2½b. lower than the most recent forecast given only in December 1976) and heavier than expected net sales of gilts and national savings to the NBPS. Despite the re-acceleration in monetary growth partly caused by large capital inflows, neither target limit (for £M$_3$ or M$_3$) for the period as a whole was breached.

*Financial year 1977-8.* The first quarter of the new target period witnessed renewed growth in sterling bank lending to the NBPS, partly ascribed to lower interest rates and the completion of the unwinding of leads and lags in commercial payments, but this was insufficient to knock DCE and £M$_3$ growth off target. By mid-October 1977, however, £M$_3$ growth was just above target, the acceleration largely caused by the monetary effects of heavy capital inflows. Contrariwise, DCE slowed in the July to October period as net sales of central government debt to the NBPS (equal to £2430m.) more than offset the lower than expected CGBR (£560m.). In the third quarter of the target period, both DCE and £M$_3$ accelerated, the former due to a rise in the CGBR and the latter, still partially, to capital inflows, despite the decision taken in October 1977 to allow the exchange rate to float more freely. Unlike £M$_3$, however, DCE remained comfortably within the agreed limit. The final quarter developments confirmed the previous quarter's acceleration in monetary growth. £M$_3$ grew at an annualised rate of 23 per cent, causing the annual growth rate to exceed substantially (by over 3 per cent) the upper end of the target range. To be fair, however, this only became fully apparent after the revisions to the seasonal adjustments for the money stock series were carried out in May, leaving the authorities no time to undertake countervailing action (a determination to avoid a repetition of such events led to the introduction of 'rolling' targets in October 1978). At the same time, DCE expanded by an astonishing £3b. against a total for the year of £4.4b., as the expected level of gilt and other public-sector debt sales to the NBPS failed to materialise and the CGBR turned out to be higher than anticipated. The authorities responded by raising the MLR (by administrative action after May) and reviving the corset (in June).

*Financial year 1978- 9.* In the three months to mid-July 1978, £M₃ growth was more rapid than that implied by the target, despite the restraining measures imposed by the authorities and heavy demand for gilts. DCE was likewise slightly above the level implied by the agreement with the IMF. The subsequent three months witnessed a reversal of these expansionary forces as sterling bank lending to the NBPS grew more slowly (although the banks were facilitating the provision of credit by 'accepting' commercial bills). The third quarter was the first for the new target period October 1978 to October 1979, announced on 9 November; it bore the same target range, but because of the selection of the mid-October money supply figure, which lay below the lower limit of the previous target range, implied some tightening of policy. During the quarter, £M₃ growth was somewhat above target, as was the case for DCE. One of the reasons suggested for this was the lack of disintermediation that took place through the acceptance market, which had served to hold down £M₃ in the previous three months.

Finally, the January to April 1979 period was associated with a slow-down in monetary growth, due largely to exceptionally heavy net gilt sales to the NBPS, sufficient to leave the annual growth in £M₃ near the middle of the target range for the 1978- 9 financial year, but unable to prevent the DCE limit being breached.

To summarise the first three years' experience with monetary targets, it would appear that the authorities' ability to hold money stock growth within pre-set limits is seriously circumscribed by their inability to identify stable demand for money functions (*BEQB*, March 1977, p.49) or to forecast accurately and control certain financial flows, such as the PSBR, the CGBR, net gilt sales to the NBPS, foreign capital flows and sterling bank lending to the NBPS. Their problems are compounded by: the existence of long and variable lags in the process of collecting and analysing statistical data, undertaking remedial action and assessing the impact of such action; the interest-insensitivity (at least in the short run) of the corporate sector's demand for bank credit; and the *political* desire to exert some control on interest rates, be it as a move to restore confidence in financial markets (or sterling) through interest-rate stabilisation or to prevent undesirable developments in the housing market, such as an acceleration in house prices or a rise in the mortgage lending rate.

# 5 The Monetary Reform Debate

## WHY MONETARY REFORM WAS NECESSARY

To assess the deficiencies inherent within both the control system and the conduct of policy itself it is necessary to distinguish between short- and long-run control of the money supply. The major factor militating against effective *long-run* control was (and remains) the interest rate insensitivity of bank credit demand from the private sector (Moore and Threadgold, 1980) which proved greater than anticipated (Goodhart and Crockett, 1970; Artis and Lewis, 1981, pp.18-19). A rise in MLR would, by directly influencing base rates, eventually induce the banks to raise lending rates which, in theory, would reduce the private sector's willingness to incur bank debt. In practice, both halves of the 'transmission mechanism' occasionally proved faulty, for banks' lending rates sometimes proved 'sticky' when, for example, a squeeze in margins was tolerated in order to gain market share or to retain customer loyalty, and when the corporate sector's demand for bank loans proved unusually resilient to higher loan charges during cash flow crises. The latter flaw in the 'transmission mechanism' was evident during the 1979-80 recession, when, despite attempts to scale down both present and prospective activities, companies experienced an accumulation of stocks as a result of the depression in demand,[1] which, partly as a result of the authorities' funding techniques (i.e. the 'Duke of York' strategy to sell gilts) had to be financed from the banks by way of short- and medium-term loans (the new issue market did not revive until 1981).

Given that bank lending to the non-bank private sector is the major source of monetary growth in the longer term, it is not clear how restraint can be achieved without resorting to direct, quantitative lending controls. This, however, appears to have been overlooked in the reform debate, for the second factor cited as having impaired the long-run effectiveness of monetary policy was the use of direct controls such as the corset. It was argued that although the corset may have contributed to the control of £M$_3$ (and perhaps at a lower level of interest rates than would otherwise have been the case) by, for example, curbing liability management and 'hard arbitrage' transactions, such benefits were obtained at the expense of distorting the meaning of monetary aggregates, damaging the competitive environment in the financial sector, and reducing the allocative efficiency of financial operations. The harmful effects for competition, in particular, were emphasised:

(1) the more efficient and faster growing banks were penalised;
(2) 'subsidies', in effect paid by the banks and finance houses, were conferred on those whose debt instruments were classified as reserve assets (e.g. call money taken by the discount market);
(3) clearing and non-clearing banks were differentially treated which, arguably, favoured the latter. This was because under the minimum reserve asset ratio control system, the clearers alone had to observe a bankers' deposits ratio; the exclusion of till money from reserve asset status effectively discriminated against them as they alone ran the payments transmission service (which, however, supplied them with a higher proportion of non-interest-bearing balances); and their operation of the overdraft system and acceptance of responsibility for providing a lender of last resort facility to local authorities and nationalised industries made planning, particularly under the corset, more difficult;
(4) non-bank methods of finance were favoured, e.g. direct borrowing by local authorities from the non-bank public.

Despite these 'costs' and the tendency for 'direct' controls to induce a rise in the velocity of circulation of money, thereby partly offsetting any demand restraint obtained through money stock control, the authorities still had to face the fact that they themselves had set up monetary aggregates as the all-important statistics to control. If credibility in government policy is actively encouraged to rest so heavily on the authorities' ability to keep within prescribed target ranges for monetary growth, then surely logic demands that policy be adapted to ensure that targets are adhered to at all costs. In this context the ability of direct controls to affect the control of statistics such as monetary aggregates should have received greater weight; any criticism of the relevance of such control should have been redirected to the formulation of monetary strategy (for example, the merit of targeting any single aggregate can be questioned, as was formally accepted in the 1982 budget) and perhaps economic policy as well. perhaps economic policy as well.

The major discussions centred on the search for improvements to the techniques of short-run monetary control. One problem concerned the short-run efficacy of the interest-rate instrument: on the one hand, the 'Duke of York' strategy resulted in 'humped' or 'tidal' gilt sales, with monetary growth accelerating between funding periods (the strategy was also criticised as being disruptive, expensive and detrimental to the long-run broadening of the capacity of the government bond market); on the other hand, effective restraint demanded the control of interest-rate differentials between yields on public-sector debt instruments and bank deposit rates, which the advent of liability management had effectively denied to the authorities. Moreover, the tendency for changes in banks' 'wholesale' borrowing rates, tied to market rates such as local authority deposit rates, to *lead* changes in their lending rates, tied to base rates and hence linked to MLR, at times presented profitable arbitrage opportunities to astute 'wholesale' investors which swelled the money stock figures. More generally, the heavier the reliance placed on interest rates as the chosen instrument for effecting monetary restraint, the greater the 'costs' in terms of the deferment of investment programmes, the loss in corporate profitability (particularly for the export sector, which, under a floating exchange rate regime, is likely to face a loss of competitiveness as the exchange rate of sterling appreciates) and the political 'backlash' resulting from mortgage lending rate increases.

Partly to minimise the political opprobrium attached to often disruptive interest rate changes (and hence the likelihood of governments retreating from their commitments to curtailing monetary growth) but also to tighten short-run monetary control, demands were made to subordinate fiscal policy to monetary policy to a greater extent than previously attempted in the hope of reducing both the absolute size of the PSBR as a proportion of the gross domestic product (GDP) and the amount residually financed. Curtailment of the former would assist monetary policy by reducing the reliance placed on gilt sales which, *ceteris paribus*, might lower interest rates beyond the levels that otherwise would have obtained[2] and reduce the extent to which the private sector need borrow from the banks as a result of being 'crowded out' by government borrowing operations.

A third source of disquiet arose because of the nature of the minimum reserve asset ratio control system. Although it was claimed that the system had not been designed to be operated in a mechanical 'bank-reserves-to-deposits' multiplier fashion (hence the lack of restraint on banks' lending capacity and thus bank lending) but rather to enhance the authorities' control over the level and structure of interest rates, the latter role became redundant as soon as the clearing banks' 'bankers' deposits' ratio became the operative fulcrum for the authorities' official money market operations. In addition to this, the classification as reserve assets of short-term public-sector instruments (e.g. Treasury bills and gilts of up to one year to maturity) had added to the authorities' difficulties in trying to control interest-rate differentials, for reserve status ensured bank and finance-house demand for the said assets, thereby lowering their yields and hence reducing their attractiveness to the non-bank private sector. As a result, MLR hikes and reserve asset squeezes which led banks to manage their liabilities caused yield differentials to move against the authorities, causing perverse short-run increases in $£M_3$. The only redeeming feature of the reserve ratio system thus appeared to be its indirect function as a prudential control device, which, for a variety of reasons (see Green Paper on *Monetary Control,* 1980) was eventually also rejected.

Finally, an influencial group of economists (see Griffiths *et al.,* 1980, for example) were persuaded that attempts to control the money supply indirectly by controlling its demand (through control of the demand for bank credit) were inferior to direct control through the monetary base (see below). They argued that the uncertainty, with respect to both strength of association and the nature of time lags, surrounding the relationships between short-term interest rates and the demand for bank credit on the one hand and long-term interest rates and the non-bank demand for gilts on the other reduced the authorities to guessing the level and structure of interest rates that was compatible with the desired degree of monetary restraint, a process which arguably increased interest-rate and money-growth volatility.

Despite the weight of evidence suggesting that the authorities' reluctance to use interest rates to the full was at least as significant as the design faults of CCC in contributing to the lack of restraint exercised over monetary growth during the 1970s, the wide-ranging criticisms were sufficient to elicit a positive response from the authorities in the form of a Green Paper on *Monetary Control* in 1980. This consultative document considered the relative merits of certain alternative reform proposals as a means of improving the 'short-run' (which the authorities failed to define) control of money-stock growth. The 'medium-term' control effected through fiscal policy and interest rates was taken to be satisfactory.


## REFORM PROPOSALS

### Monetary base control

The first option analysed was **monetary base control** (MBC). The intuitive appeal of MBC results from the possibility that strict control over the supply of **base money** (this is normally defined to include banks' balances at the Central Bank, currency in circulation with the non-bank public and, sometimes, banks' till money) which, in theory, is susceptible to control by the Central Bank, will allow tight control over monetary growth. The theoretical foundations underlying a 'simple' base model involve a straightforward manipulation of identities for the money stock and base (or high-powered) money:

$$M \equiv C + D \tag{1}$$
$$B \equiv C + R \tag{2}$$

where $M$ = arbitrarily defined money stock, $C$ = notes and coin in circulation with the non-bank public, $D$ = some arbitrary measure of bank deposits, $R$ = banks' cash reserves.

$$\frac{(1)}{(2)} \Rightarrow \frac{M}{B} = \frac{C + D}{C + R}$$

$$\Rightarrow M = \frac{B(1 + C/D)}{(C/D + R/D)}$$

$$\Rightarrow M = \frac{B(1 + c)}{(c + r)}$$

where $c = C/D$, $r = R/D$

$$\Rightarrow M = mB \qquad \text{where } m = \frac{1 + c}{c + r} \tag{3}$$

According to equation (3) the (suitably defined) money stock depends upon only two variables: the **monetary multiplier** $m$, which itself is determined solely by the public's currency to deposits ratio and the banks' cash ratio, and the monetary base, $B$. Thus, if the supply of base money is wholly under the control of the authorities and the currency and reserve ratios can be shown to be stable and predictable under all prospective conditions, the money supply becomes exogenously determined, i.e. variations in the base can be used to control the money stock. Note, however, that should the authorities pursue a 'passive' money policy, simply adjusting supply to accommodate demand in order to stabilise interest rates, then despite their apparent ability to control money stock growth through manipulation of the supply of base money, the money stock is rendered endogenous.

Any examination of the relative merits of MBC obviously demands an analysis of the available empirical evidence on the stability and predictability of the aforementioned ratios. Together with a discussion of how the system was operated, such evidence fuelled the lengthy and vociferous 'orthodoxy *v.* new orthodoxy *v.* neo-orthodoxy' debate of the 1950s and 1960s (Pierce and Shaw, 1979, pp.142-64) concerning the necessity for and sufficiency of control of base money for the effective control of the money stock. While evidence was offered on the factors influencing the public's currency and the banks' reserve ratios, such as the yields on loans and securities for the latter and the level of income, interest offered on bank deposits, and social and institutional developments leading the public to economise on cash balances for the former, the general conclusion was that whether or not the authorities could have controlled bank deposit growth via bank cash, they deliberately chose *not* to do so. Empirical evidence on the stability of the ratios during the 1970s is sparse, but even if it had been plentiful and had demonstrated reasonable stability, this would still not have proved conclusive, for there could be no presumption that stability would be maintained in a changed institutional environment such as would accompany a switch to MBC. In particular, the greater uncertainty an individual bank is likely to experience in acquiring cash reserves at 'reasonable' cost to support previously agreed loans will almost certainly lead banks to maintain a margin over any prescribed minimum for prudential reasons. As banks become more active in bidding for the available cash reserves held by the non-bank public,[3] the latter's desired holdings are likely to become more interest-sensitive.

Whatever the transitional impact of MBC on the stability of the public's currency and the banks' cash reserve ratios, a second strand of analysis must concern itself with the ability of the authorities to set the base precisely at predetermined levels. A convenient starting point for an assessment of this subject is provided by Hansen's (1973) 'European-style' public-sector budget constraint:[4]

$$MAT + PSD_t \equiv MD + NMD + ECF + \Delta H$$
$$\Rightarrow \Delta H \equiv PSD_t + MAT - MD - NMD - ECF$$

where

   $MAT$ represents maturing public-sector debt
   $PSD_t$ represents the public-sector financial deficit (after allowing for financial transfers)
   $MD$ represents domestic sales of marketable public-sector debt
   $NMD$ represents domestic sales of non-marketable public-sector debt

*ECF* represents government finance raised from official intervention (sales of foreign currency) in the foreign exchange market (strictly *ECF* is that of the public sector: see p. 140)
and $\Delta H$ represents government finance raised in a form which directly increases the ('high-powered') monetary base.

The second presentation of the budget identity clearly identifies the financial flows that the authorities have to control in order to gain command over the monetary base.[5] Unfortunately for the proponents of MBC, both the financial flows $PSD_t$ and $MAT$ are largely beyond the control of the authorities – the size of the former being dependent more on political and social considerations than monetary requirements (and at any rate not susceptible to short-term manipulation for the purpose of influencing monetary growth) and the latter being determined by prior contractual arrangements, while both the flows *NMD* and *ECF* respond perversely to monetary-restraining interest-rate changes. This last point is significant, for it means that a general firming of interest rates required to effect monetary restraint will induce offsetting short-run expansionary forces in the form of outflows from *NMD*, owing to the traditional 'stickiness' of the associated interest-rate structures, and capital inflows which, even with a 'pure' floating exchange-rate regime, can cause an expansion in the money stock as measured by the £M$_3$ statistic (see Appendix D, pp. 144-50). While in principle offsetting transactions such as higher net sales of gilts can be used to overcome these problems in the medium term, assuming the relevant flows can be forecast accurately (which rarely appears to be the real-world situation), such measures themselves usually induce undesirable offsets elsewhere in the system (e.g. during 1980-1 when the corporate sector turned to the banks to provide extra working capital due to its reluctance to issue fixed-interest, long-term debt at interest rates anywhere near those offered by gilts of comparable term). Even accepting that an optimal funding strategy could be designed to cope with the variability in strength, direction and lagged pattern of response to official restraining measures introduced by the monetary authorities, the concomitant political requirements might prove as unpalatable as in previous control regimes. For example, the logic of 'tight' MBC demands that *all* interest rates[6] and the exchange rate are allowed to adjust to levels required to effect the desired degree of monetary restraint, requirements which at times might conflict with political desires to curb mortgage lending rate increases, avoid severe liquidity crises that threaten financial instability (technical insolvency might result from the interest-induced fall in capital values or from borrowing costs outstripping interest receipts) or preserve the country's exporting base. The second of these considerations calls into question the role of the Bank's 'lender of last resort' function (Congdon, 1981), and although most MBC supporters would not advocate its abrogation in the face of serious financial instability, they would argue for greater 'conditionality', perhaps in the form of the American system of progressive penal charges for persistent usage (although this implies the bypassing of the discount market) so that the loans are truly given on a 'last' rather than 'first' resort basis.

A Bank paper (*BEQB*, June 1979) had considered the remaining technical and operational problems inherent within any variant of MBC. Discussion was divided between an analysis of the likely implications of pursuing either a strict or a relaxed form of base control. The form of *strict* control set up for examination involved the Bank operating to predetermine the monetary base and the banks meeting their reserve ratio requirement exactly on a daily basis. Four problems of a technical or operational nature were envisaged with this proposed system:

(1) measures to mitigate the volatility of movements in central government balances suffered under the present institutional framework would have to be introduced, either by transferring the government's business accounts to the commercial banks – thereby isolating bankers' balances from unexpected movements in governmental balances – or by moving the banking system on to a next-day settlement basis for all transactions, a reform that would provide the authorities with one day's notice of unanticipated flows yet would constitute a retrograde step in administrative terms;

(2) even with the implementation of such reform the authorities would still have no advance warning of shifts in the public's demand for currency, which can be substantial even on a daily basis;

(3) given the complexities and uncertainties of the seasonal adjustment process for financial series and the necessity of working with a non-seasonally adjusted projection of the base to achieve smooth, seasonally adjusted growth in the base or alternative aggregates, only quarterly (or longer-term) base control would prove feasible;

(4) problems would arise over the banks' appropriate accounting basis – the previously used lagged accounting basis for calculating required reserves would prove unsuitable, while serious problems would be encountered in moving to either a current or lead accounting basis.[7]

A further problem arises over the manner in which banks would be able to adjust to a shortfall in reserves (i.e. when the base provided is insufficient to allow the banks to meet reserve requirements on their existing level of deposits), for many of the channels open to them could result in the exertion of upward pressure on short-term interest rates. For example, although banks as a whole could not avoid a multiple contraction in assets and liabilities (providing the authorities remained intransigent) except by attracting notes and coin from the public or, assuming lower reserve requirements on time than on sight deposits, by altering relative yields so as to induce switching from sight to time deposits, individual banks might try to improve their own position by disposing of certain marketable assets. In the process short-term rates would be forced to higher levels, thereby increasing foreign demand for sterling. Although the base could be protected from such developments by allowing the exchange rate to appreciate or by sterilising the capital inflow (e.g. through sales of Treasury bills) the former policy might prove unacceptable because of fears for industrial competitiveness, while the latter would simply intensify the pressure on short rates. Similarly, if the banks' response to the reserve shortage was to manage their liabilities and bid for funds, short rates would again be forced up, but the base would be left unaffected. Moreover, an acceleration in the interest-rate spiral might result as competitors responded to rising bank-deposit rates. Thus, the team at the Bank were led to duly conclude that

> strict control of the base (which would, of course, imply an end to all the present lender of last resort facilities) would continually threaten frequent and potentially massive movements in interest rates, if not complete instability . . . even for control over longer periods of time, strict control of the base would throw onto financial markets the whole burden of adjustment at present 'shared' by the Bank of England's lender of last resort facilities, its open market operations, its foreign exchange intervention, and the permitted short-run variability in the level of balances held by the clearing banks at the Bank of England. (*BEQB*, June 1979)

In addition to the above drawbacks, certain structural adjustments were seen as the natural outcome to the adoption of a strict form of base control. These included: the curtailment or disappearance of the overdraft system, since strict control of the base would entail considerable risk in the assumption of obligations to extend loans at some given date in the future; a general increase in the proportion of portfolios held in relatively liquid form by the banks and the private sector, since tighter control of the banking system raises the short-term risk of illiquidity; a rearrangement of banks' on-balance-sheet advances to off-balance-sheet acceptances; and a tendency for those not subject to reserve requirements to increase their holdings of liquid assets, although arbitraging between such assets and bank deposits would reduce the extent of interest-rate volatility. Taken together, these adjustments imply a growth in holdings of 'near-money' assets and an increased sensitivity of such holdings to changing interest differentials, both of which would reduce the significance of tight base and monetary control.

The 'relaxed' form of base control considered postulated that the authorities should be concerned with movements in the base over a six-month period, that the base need not average out at precisely the desired level, and that the lender of last resort and other facilities responsible for moderating short-rate instability should be in some degree retained.

On its potential as a leading indicator, even at the limit where no penalties are imposed for diverging from the prescribed ratio, the base was thought to be unsatisfactory, because movements in bank reserves would provide a poor indication of the stance of monetary policy. Even if a uniform reserve ratio were imposed (inequitable and possibly ineffective in practice – see Congdon, 1980) and the switch to a lead or current accounting basis were made, it would take several years before the data could be interpreted intelligently. Thus, although a relaxed form of base control would avoid many of the operational and adjustment problems associated with a stricter regime, its ability to provide an alternative and reliable leading indicator must be seriously doubted. Nevertheless, if such doubts proved ill-founded, the proposed system could be of benefit to the authorities in so far as it would allow an increase in the speed of adjustment to diverging monetary trends. Moreover, the change to such a system might entail or encourage structural change in financial markets conducive to a more effective regulation of governmental debt sales, as Wood (1979) argued. However, it should be appreciated that the logic of improving the functioning of certain markets does not demand the adoption of base control, which would prove a very indirect, and possibly highly costly, method – in terms of structural change and market upheaval – of achieving such reform. In summary, the Bank's economists concluded that:

the critics of the authorities' present approach to monetary management often contrast this with what might be obtained if the authorities were instead to adopt monetary base control. One purpose of this article is to show that there are several variants of monetary base control (an imprecise term) and to indicate reasons why rigid monetary base control would be unacceptable. More relaxed versions of such a control system might be accompanied by changes in the functioning of certain debt markets, though any such changes should perhaps be considered on their own merits quite separately, and might provide the authorities with additional information to allow prompter and firmer countervailing action. Any such putative benefits would, however, have to be weighed against the costs of making major structural changes in the system. (*BEQB*, June 1979)

Apart from underplaying the benefits to be derived from base control (although the Bank did recognise the possibility of making gains in the area of cutting delays in the collection and interpretation of data) the Bank's article may be criticised on the grounds that fears of greater rate volatility – a major element in the case against the adoption of base control – were exaggerated. Indeed, many would argue that monetary experience demonstrates that a substantial degree of volatility was present within both the pre- and post-corset regulatory and institutional frameworks and, moreover, likely to materialise under any form of tight monetary control.

Returning to the Green Paper on *Monetary Control*, the general need to minimise incentives to disintermediate was suggested as an important criterion against which reform proposals should be assessed. Thus while a non-mandatory base requirement system was rejected on the grounds that the uncertain benefits to be reaped (e.g. MBC might not yield the level and structure of interest rates required to keep $£M_3$ on target) would not outweigh the structural reform costs (e.g. the withdrawal of lender of last resort facilities) necessary to ensure continued stability between banks' holdings of base money and the money stock through time, proposals for MBC with a mandatory requirement had, ideally, to avoid inducing disintermediation[8] and bank liability management. As note (7) demonstrates, this implies trading off the provision of disintermediation incentives against the attainment of a close and stable relationship between banks' base money and the money stock, the 'optimal' trade-off appearing highly subjective.

A final criticism of MBC that is frequently raised is that it is merely a device for triggering interest-rate changes required to keep money stock growth on track. In the words of the Green Paper, 'The approach [MBC] therefore is intended to provide a means for the markets to generate the interest rates necessary to bring the rate of growth of the money supply back towards the desired path' (para. 4.2). In part this view reflects the blinkered approach of those nurtured on indirect control (from the demand side) of the money stock through interest-rate control of the demand for bank credit. The whole point of MBC is that demand-side control has proved unreliable, so that direct control of the banks' factor input, base money, and hence the money stock (since a given supply of base money sets an upper limit to monetary growth) should at least be given a chance. Admittedly, the device for equilibrating the demand for and supply of money (and also credit and the monetary base) will be interest rates, for example to ensure that the necessary volume of net sales of public-sector debt is made, but these will be used to adjust demand to an inelastic supply rather than vice versa. As Friedman explains,

> Trying to control the money supply through 'fiscal policy . . . and interest rates' is trying to control the output of one item (money) through altering the demand for it by manipulating the incomes of its users (that is the role of fiscal policy) or the prices of substitutes for it (that is the role of interest rates). A precise analogy is like trying to control the output of motor cars by altering the incomes of potential purchasers and manipulating rail and air fares. In principle, possible in both cases, but in practice highly inefficient. Far easier to control the output of motor cars by controlling the availability of a basic raw material, say steel, to the manufacturers – a precise analogy to controlling the money supply by controlling the availability of base money to banks and others. (Evidence submitted to the Treasury and Civil Service Committee, *Memoranda on Monetary Policy,* p.58, para. 14, Cmnd 720, HC, July 1980)

Wherever the balance of advantage lies in the weighting of the operational and structural costs of MBC against its potential advantages of providing banks (under a penalty system) with a greater financial incentive to keep net bank lending in line with the authorities' desires for monetary growth, 'de-politicising' interest-rate changes and broadening the range of funding instruments the authorities are able to offer, it must be stressed that MBC cannot offer a more effective form of monetary control unless the interest and exchange-rate implications are accepted unhesitatingly. Unfortunately, although the Bank of England in principle may be able to determine any prescribed level of the base through discretionary transactions in the money, bond and foreign exchange markets, all governments are likely to retain more than a passing concern in interest rates and the exchange rate, fluctuations in which are attended by their own vector of costs.[9]

*Indicator systems*

**Indicator systems** were considered as an alternative to MBC by the Green Paper as a means of circumventing the problems likely to be experienced in controlling the base and relating interest-rate changes to divergences of the base from its desired trend level (again reflecting the authorities' bias against perceiving interest rates as the equilibrating mechanism rather than as instruments of control). Two schemes were considered, one relating to the monetary base and the other to £M$_3$. Under the former, the base would be measured in arrears and divergences from the desired trend would be used to trigger changes in the Bank's lending rate according to a predetermined scale. It was envisaged that the requirement to hold base money would be mandatory, that last-resort lending facilities would be available, and that the desired path for the base would be such as to ensure a smooth, seasonally adjusted path for £M$_3$. The system related to £M$_3$ was considered more appropriate and operationally simpler, and involved the use of deviations of £M$_3$ growth from the desired trend to trigger changes in bank lending rates. In both cases a discretionary override power, at the disposal of the authorities, was deemed desirable.

The potential advantages of such schemes are, first, that they would involve little initial structural change to the financial system, and, second, that they would remove the perceived bias in·delay characterising the system of discretionary interest-rate adjustment and so might result in more effective control of the money stock. Against this, the authorities would still have to weigh the danger of premature action against delay, for it is always difficult to discern whether divergences in £M$_3$ growth from trend are likely to be temporary or sustained, a problem compounded by the necessarily arbitrary nature of the scale of response chosen. Further, the diminution of the authorities' discretion (frequent use of the override would eradicate any 'expectational' gains to be reaped from 'automaticity') might result in greater interest-rate volatility, and adoption of indicator schemes would preclude the use of interest rates for alternative purposes, such as to influence the exchange rate.

### Negotiable entitlements

The final proposal considered by the Green Paper was for the establishment by the authorities of a stock of **negotiable entitlements** (NEs) which would become the reserve requirement for the banks (as a minimum proportion of deposits). By making NEs saleable (and inviting bids for additions to the stock) the competitive and efficiency shortcomings of direct control would be mitigated. The scheme would work by raising the marginal cost of additional deposits to banks acquiring them in the situation where deposit levels threatened to rise above those implied by the existing stock of NEs and where the competitive bidding for NEs drove up their market rate. This would, in turn, cause the banks to raise their lending rates or restrict loans within a competitive banking system. As would be the case under MBC, however, the stronger the demand for bank credit, the greater the disintermediation incentive provided. Although a weak penalty system for inadequate NE holdings would reduce this incentive, the effectiveness of control would be impaired.

*Other*

Alternatives (or complements) to those schemes considered by the Green Paper[10] as a means of improving the efficiency of monetary policy are: (a) continued innovation in gilt marketing strategy, perhaps leading to full indexation or 'pure' auctions;[11] (b) a broadening of the range of public-sector debt instruments offered for sale either within[12] or outside[13] an MBC framework; and (c) more concerted efforts to adapt fiscal policy to the needs of monetary policy. The Thatcher administration's failure, despite lacking nothing in determination, to adhere to its PSBR 'projections' under the medium-term financial strategy (see Chapter 8, pp. 109-14) (through this is not to deny that fiscal policy was 'tight') led to a continuing campaign (e.g. Coghlan and Sykes, 1980) for cuts in the PSBR, if only to reduce the interest-rate pressures likely to cause governments to baulk at pursuing their stated monetary objectives.

The reforms eventually instituted in August 1981 (see Chapter 9, pp. 122-3) went some way towards MBC by instituting a cash ratio for all banks and 'licensed deposit-takers', but stopped well short of the full transition to controlling the money stock through rigid control of the supply of base money. Although MLR was abolished, the 'transmission mechanism' remained the 'indirect' control of $£M_3$ through interest rates, official changes in the latter being almost exclusively induced through open-market operations in bills. Despite the weaknesses of the $£M_3$ aggregate as an indicator, policy continued to be expressed within the framework of a progressive reduction in $£M_3$ growth, although movements in other aggregates (e.g. the base, $M_1$ and $PSL_1$ and $PSL_2$) were monitored (although in March 1982 $M_1$ and $PSL_2$ became complementary targets). This was especially puzzling since a growing volume of evidence pointed to glaring deficiencies in the interest-rate/$£M_3$ control mechanism. The problems were particularly acute in the short run, for the combination of a number of factors could actually induce a perverse response in £M$_3$. This was because a rise in interest rates would or could: (a) increase the PSBR, an important counterpart to £M$_3$ growth, by virtue of enlarged debt interest payments; (b) induce short-term capital inflows which, even within a 'pure' floating exchange-rate regime, can cause £M$_3$ to rise (see Appendix D, pp. 144–50); (c) cause £M$_3$ to rise because of outflows from ('sticky') non-marketable public-sector debt instruments; (d) cause non-bank residents' sterling bank deposits to grow because of the differential effects on banks' wholesale lending and borrowing rates, lending rates (tied to base rates) tending to react more sluggishly (perhaps as a result off 'cross-subsidisation' of wholesale business by retail profits, resulting largely from the endowment effect of high interest rates) and creating the opportunities for companies to engage in arbitrage operations; (e) cause banks to manage their liabilities and bid for deposits through the CD and inter-bank markets; (f) cause an increase in corporate bank borrowing as capital issues are shelved to await the return of lower interest rates, a problem compounded by the financing implications of 'involuntary' stock holdings resulting from the interest-rate-induced reduction in demand and the direct effect on debt servicing charges; and (g) cause an acceleration in £M$_3$ growth if the rise led to the expectation of further rises in the near future, thereby dampening non-bank demand for gilts. The long-run position was hardly more encouraging. Despite the long-run deflationary effects of policy (largely through exchange-rate changes) that contributed to a fall in the demand for money, the interest-rate sensitivity of bank credit demand remained ominously low.

# 6 The Tories' First Year in Office (May 1979 – March 1980)

The change in government in May 1979 introduced a new era in the history of economic policy-making in the United Kingdom. While it is true that publicly announced targets for the rate of growth of the money supply predated the Conservatives' return by some three years, the new administration elevated money stock targets (later to be complemented by 'projections' for the PSBR as a percentage of GDP) to the central plank of its economic programme. This was in apparent acceptance of the monetarist view that inflation and money stock growth are causally related, with a lag of anything up to two years, causation running from the money supply to prices and not vice versa. Fiscal policy (in the shape of the PSBR), exchange-rate policy and interest-rate policy were all supposed to support monetary policy, the prime aim of which was to achieve a 'progressive reduction in the rate of growth in the money supply' in order 'to squeeze inflation out of the system'. Incomes policy was eschewed as it was deemed distortive and ineffectual (other than temporarily), although cash limits announced for the public sector for the fiscal years 1981-2 and 1982-3 incorporated, in effect, pay norms of 6 per cent and 4 per cent respectively. Instead, the so-called 'supply-side' logic, involving the restoration of incentives through a switch from direct to indirect taxation, was adopted in an attempt to secure improvements in productivity, and hence economic growth, in the face of the demand restraint exercised through rigid adherence to monetary aggregates.

This philosophy permeated the budget measures introduced on 12 June 1979, which included: (a) a reduction in income tax at all levels of income (e.g. the standard rate fell from 33 per cent to 30 per cent); (b) a unification of the rate of VAT at 15 per cent; (c) an increase in MLR to 14 per cent; (d) a further extension of the corset (to mid-December 1979); (e) a revision of the target range for the growth in $£M_3$ - a range of 7-11 per cent (at an annual rate) was established for the period June 1979 to April 1980, based on June's inflated $£M_3$ figure, to be rolled forward in the autumn; and

(f) a pledge to cut the PSBR for the financial year 1979-80 from an estimated £10b. to £8.3b. As regards the monetary measures announced, it was recognised that the planned reduction in the PSBR would take time to effect any favourable change in £M₃ growth (which had jumped to 15½ per cent, at an annual rate, since the April 'caretaker' budget) so that MLR and the corset would have to be used to induce any immediate slow-down in the rate of monetary expansion. Finally, the *inflationary* dangers of the rapid rise in VAT were glossed over by statements emphasising the 'once-and-for-all' nature of the change which would drop from the retail price index (RPI) in July 1980, while employees were asked to assess the *deflationary* nature of the tax changes by referring to the new tax and price index (TPI), which provided a more realistic view of real take-home pay by taking account of income tax changes.[1]

In spite of the government's determination to fulfil its election promises, particularly on the monetary and inflation fronts, mixed results were achieved in the period to March 1980. Although the £M₃ target was met (despite the overshooting in the PSBR), inflation, which was the primary goal of policy, accelerated way beyond expectations. The reasons for this and for the out-turn figures for £M₃ and the PSBR are explored in more detail below.


TARGETING EXPERIENCE

In the first three months of the new target period, June 1979 to April 1980, the growth in £M₃ was somewhat above target, due mainly to an acceleration in sterling bank lending to the private sector in the month of August. This was in addition to the disintermediation that took place through the acceptance market (the **bill leak**), which expanded by £300m. in August alone, following a £400m. expansion in the three-month period to mid-July. Strong credit demand was ascribed to consumer buying in anticipation of the budget measures and, with respect to corporate demand, to growing cash-flow problems.

Rapid monetary growth continued throughout the late summer and early autumn, with a particularly sharp rise in October raising £M₃ growth for the first four months of the target period to over 14 per cent at an annual rate. The result was that the upper end of the target range (i.e. 12 per cent) for the year to October 1979 was breached, the out-turn figure being 13.3 per cent. The authorities' response came on 15 November when MLR was raised from 14 per cent to a record 17 per cent in order to encourage funding and discourage bank borrowing, the corset period was extended to

June 1980, and the 7-11 per cent target range for annualised £M$_3$ growth was extended to cover the sixteen-month period to mid-October 1980. Moreover, by not rolling forward the base, the Chancellor demonstrated his determination not to accommodate the recent surge in monetary growth. As in the previous quarter, the main cause of monetary expansion was sterling bank lending to companies (perhaps encouraged by a fall in *real* interest rates), which faced the pressures of accelerating wage and raw material costs[2] and financing unnecessarily high stock levels as a result of a fall in consumer demand and a determination to avoid clawback of stock relief. Given companies' reluctance to seek fixed-interest, long-term finance at what they regarded as excessively high nominal rates (partly due to the government's monetary stance) and the inactivity of the equity market since the autumn of 1979, the additional working capital had to be obtained through short-term bank borrowing. A second factor was the relaxation of exchange controls (see p. 81 below) which stimulated domestic credit demand as companies sought, partly as a result of the strength of sterling, to repay outstanding foreign currency loans and make new investments abroad, using sterling bank finance to purchase the necessary foreign currency. This, however, must be offset against the general contractionary effect of diversification out of sterling (e.g. through 'sales' of sterling bank deposits to non-residents) and repayment of foreign-currency borrowing using existing sterling balances, to the extent that such transactions are not reflected in a depreciation in sterling (which is the case when sterling is sold to the Bank of England for foreign currency).

Continued rapid monetary growth in the final quarter of 1979 (£M$_3$ rose by 12¼ per cent at an annual rate in the seven-month period to January 1980), despite the steep rise in nominal (though not real) interest rates, was followed by more moderate growth which allowed the June 1979-April 1980 £M$_3$ growth target to be met: the out-turn was 10 per cent, comfortably within the 7-11 per cent range. This was in spite of the persistently strong, interest-inelastic demand for bank credit from the company sector,[3] which had averaged £750m. per month throughout 1979 compared to £500m. per month the previous year, and the official assistance given to the money market throughout the period either to stabilise interest rates[4] or to relieve reserve asset pressure.[5] However, concern for credit rather than money might have tempered any jubilance among ministers and officials in the light of the continued expansion of the 'bill leak' (acceptances in the hands of the NBPS), which between mid-June 1979 and mid-April 1980 expanded from £1131m. to £2184m. (equivalent to 3½ per cent of £M$_3$), and the growth of DCE *relative* to £M$_3$, largely caused by a rapid build-up in overseas-owned sterling bank deposits, presumably attracted by sterling's petro-currency status and the relatively high interest rates on offer in the UK.


## THE PSBR

The government was thwarted in its attempts to hold down the PSBR during the 1979-80 fiscal year to £8.25b. (the out-turn being nearer £9.8b.) despite sales of public-sector assets (£1b.), including shares in British Petroleum (£290m.) and advance payments of petroleum revenue tax (£700m.), because of the following factors: (a) delays in the settlement of some telephone bills due to the Post Office strike; (b) local authority borrowing and interest payments on public-sector debt (which rose to approximately 4 per cent of GNP) turned out to be appreciably above forecast, reflecting the impact of higher than expected inflation on interest rates and general public-sector costs; and (c) an increase in the average lag between accruals and payments of VAT.


## INFLATION

Perhaps the biggest disappointment to the government in its first year of office was the unexpected acceleration in inflation as measured, for example, by the change in the year-on-year RPI, which stood at 10.3 per cent when the Conservatives came to power but had risen to 21.8 per cent by April 1980. Although some of the increase was predictable (though not necessarily desirable, e.g. the government-inspired rise in VAT which added approximately four percentage points to the RPI), the extent of the acceleration in oil prices (which added a further four percentage points to the RPI), other commodity prices and average earnings (firms having little option but to try to pass on the increases to consumers because of their perilously low profit margins) took the government, and outside forecasters, by surprise. In addition to these factors there was an increase in the cost of living (mainly to owner-occupiers in the shape of higher house prices and hence higher mortgage repayments, the interest element receiving less tax relief) and an increase in transport costs (reflecting higher oil prices, the budget increase in petrol duty and increases in some public transport fares). Allowing for an offset due to the appreciating exchange rate, these factors together yield the bulk of the final inflation figure.

In retrospect, the administration might have progressed more cautiously in improving incentives through the tax system to moderate its inflationary effects. Given the pre-eminence accorded to monetary control, even in the shorter term (i.e. quarter to quarter), Bank of England assistance to the money market might also have been curtailed on occasions to allow interest rates to perform their intended task of restraining monetary growth unhindered. Although the attempt to harmonise, in a more explicit fashion than hitherto, fiscal (as indicated by the PSBR) and monetary policy failed, the administration determined to persist with the strategy (formalised under the medium-term financial strategy embodied within the 1980 budget), marking the beginning of more concerted attempts to reform the system of monetary control in the United Kingdom.[6]

## THE ABOLITION OF EXCHANGE CONTROLS

One reform that was instituted in the government's first year in office was the abolition of exchange controls in October 1979 (although legislation allowing for the possible reintroduction of controls was retained). Up until this time exchange controls had been used for approximately forty years to: (a) strengthen the UK's external balance sheet by improving its liquidity, first by favouring an increase in official reserves rather than in private external assets, and second, in recognition of the importance of private holdings of sterling, by reducing the UK's vulnerability to volatile capital movements; and (b) hold the exchange rate at a level higher than would otherwise have been the case. For most of the period, policy was directed towards restraining capital *outflows* but, for a brief interval in 1971, temporary controls on short-term capital *inflows* were also imposed.[7] The strengthening of sterling due to North Sea oil (at September 1979 official reserves stood at $27.5b. compared with $4b. at the end of 1976) somewhat weakened the case for the continued existence of extensive controls which, at any rate, had been criticised as: (a) having distorted the flow of capital into overseas assets (international freedom of movement being a requirement of membership of the EEC), entailing some sacrifice in profitable longer-term investment opportunities; (b) being expensive, irksome and difficult to administer; and (c) proving ineffectual in practice.[8]

When the Tories came to power in May 1979 the exchange controls remaining[9] were performing, briefly, the following functions: (a) preventing the use of official exchange (i.e. preventing resident transactions from influencing the sterling exchange rate or the official reserves) for outward portfolio investment and for the purchase of overseas holiday homes; (b) restricting access to official exchange for direct investment abroad; and (c) blocking some of the channels that could be used for short-term speculation against sterling, e.g. access to the forward exchange market was limited to the covering of firm commercial contracts, advance payments for imports were restricted, as was sterling borrowing by non-residents, and a requirement for the repatriation of export proceeds was implemented. The first steps towards de-regulation were taken on 12 June, when it was announced that: (a) interest and other charges on foreign currency borrowing for portfolio investment abroad could be paid with official exchange; (b) the requirement to hold 115 per cent cover for such borrowing in the form of foreign currency securities and/or investment currency was abolished; and (c) the requirement to use investment currency to purchase private property abroad was abolished. Further measures were announced on 18 July which allowed for: (a) the repayment with official exchange of foreign currency borrowing for portfolio investment which had been outstanding for at least one year as at 19 July; and (b) the purchase with official exchange of most quoted foreign securities denominated and payable in the currencies of EEC member states and of foreign currency securities issued by EEC institutions and other international bodies to which the UK belonged. Other announcements, made on 12 June and 18 July, dealt with the dismantling of all remaining restrictions on the financing of outward direct investment and on the repayment of foreign currency borrowing taken to finance such investment. Thus, even before the removal of the final vestiges of exchange control (bar those necessary to allow continued sanctions to be taken against Rhodesia) on 23 October 1979, the Conservatives had virtually abolished controls on the financing of **direct investment** and had made significant inroads into dismantling controls on outward **portfolio investment**. The final move was made (partly in an attempt to hold down the exchange rate; other options, by expanding official reserves, were regarded as inflationary) at a time when sterling was viewed in a favourable light by the rest of the world, which served to minimise any panic that might be induced on the foreign exchanges, and in spite of political dissension over the issue of 'exporting' jobs.[10]

The monetary implications of the abolition of exchange control are potentially extremely serious, for the freedom given to UK residents (to arbitrage into foreign currency assets, lend to and borrow from abroad in sterling and foreign currencies and hold foreign currency deposits at home) and to UK banks (to switch, more or less at will, out of sterling and into foreign currencies and to finance third-party trade with sterling again) allows for the possibil-

ity that: (a) disintermediation through the Eurosterling market
(**offshore arbitraging**), by raising the volume of sterling credit for a
given money stock, will evade the corset control and reduce the
significance of $£M_3$ as an indicator; (b) $£M_3$ will be raised relative
to the volume of IBELs (e.g. as a result of 'switching-out' operations
of UK banks), thereby reducing the significance of the corset control
mechanism by weakening the leverage between IBELs and $£M_3$
growth; (c) sterling will resume its former reserve currency role; and
(d), perhaps a more distant threat, foreign currency will displace
domestic currency as the medium of exchange. In general, the net
monetary effects of a particular transaction will depend upon the
nature of the exchange-rate regime being pursued (fixed or 'pure'
float), the nature of the capital flow (source and destination) and
the implications of the transaction for the financing of the PSBR.
The effects are analysed below in terms of their impact on the flow
of sterling credit, $£M_3$ and the corset, and are summarised in
Appendix E.

### Portfolio diversification

The abolition of exchange controls, *ceteris paribus,* would be expected to precipitate net outflows of portfolio investment from the UK
as economic units rearranged their portfolios to embrace the new
investment opportunities open to them (particularly in the Far East,
North America, on Wall St, and on overseas futures and commodity
markets), which might be expected to yield an improved risk-adjusted
rate of return for the market portfolio.[11] In addition, interest
arbitrage opportunities (covered for exchange-rate fluctuations) will
always present themselves to the astute investor. Thus one would
expect the UK non-bank private sector to liquidate part of its holdings of bank deposits (IBELs), equities, government stock and other
sterling assets in order to finance the acquisition of foreign currencies, securities and claims. The examples presented below cover outflows from gilts, equities and IBELs, and the differential monetary
effects that arise under fixed and floating exchange-rate systems are
distinguished.

(1) NBPS 'liquidates' gilts to finance the acquisition of foreign
claims.

(a) *Fixed exchange-rate regime*: if 'liquidation' is taken to imply
sales (or the retention of maturity monies) to the Government
Broker, then the 'residual' monetary financing of the PSBR through

the banking system is necessarily raised. While this potentially raises the supply of reserve assets (RAs) available to the banking system, and (IB)ELs (for (IB)ELs read 'eligible liabilities (ELs) and *possibly* interest-bearing eligible liabilities (IBELs)')[12] and £M$_3$ as well, the government's commitment to maintaining a particular exchange-rate parity for sterling implies that the public sector, operating through the **Exchange Equalisation Account (EEA)**, stands prepared to meet the excess demand for foreign currency, the provision of which reduces the public sector's sterling borrowing needs as payment is made by the NBPS for the foreign currency. The net result is that expansionary pressures emanating from the initial debt-market transactions are cancelled by the monetary effects of EEA sales of foreign currency (see Appendix D, p. 141), leaving RAs, IBELs, ELs and £M$_3$ unchanged.

(b) *Floating exchange-rate regime*: under floating rates, the net monetary effects differ according to whether or not a UK resident supplies the foreign currency (the EEA is not involved). If a *non-resident* provides the foreign currency then the net impact on £M$_3$ will be neutral: the enlarged residual borrowing requirement resulting from the liquidation of gilts increases £M$_3$, but this is offset by the transfer of sterling bank deposits from residents to non-residents, whose holdings are excluded from £M$_3$ though represented in ELs. However, RAs and (IB)ELs will rise as a result of the larger 'residual' borrowing of the public sector. The net result is that (IB)ELs rise relative to £M$_3$, RA pressure on the banks is eased, and IBELs pressure is probably intensified, depending on the extent to which the extra sterling deposits created are held in interest-bearing form. Finally, although the easement in RA pressure may allow the banks to relieve IBELs pressure to some extent by reclassifying call-money loans to the discount market as 'market' loans, it is important to appreciate that this represents merely a *secondary* effect that may or may not follow the initial capital outflow according to how favourably disposed the discount market is to such manoeuvres. Should a *resident* supply the foreign currency, then £M$_3$ rises as a result of the enlarged 'residual' financing of the PSBR and the consequential growth in residents' sterling bank deposits, indicating that balance-of-payments transactions *can* influence the domestic money supply under a floating exchange-rate system. Similarly, (IB)ELs and the banks' RAs rise, any increase in £M$_3$ *relative* to IBELs being the result of the destruction of IBELs through subsequent bank transactions with the discount market.

(2) NBPS 'liquidates' domestic equities to finance the acquisition of foreign currency claims.

(a) *Fixed exchange-rate regime*: if 'liquidation' is taken to imply sales to *non-residents,* who are assumed to finance their purchases by running down their sterling bank deposits with UK banks, then the initial sale of equities will raise £$M_3$ but leave (IB)ELs unchanged. Allowing for the EEA's provision of foreign currency, £$M_3$ will fall back to its original level and (IB)ELs and bank-held RAs will decline. Although the banks might subsequently be able to generate RAs through discount-market transactions (at the expense of 'pulling in' the corset), dependent upon the severity of the prevailing corset constraint, their problems might be compounded by the ensuing reaction of the corporate sector to a possible slump in the equity market, which might force companies to satisfy a higher proportion of their borrowing needs from the banks, the latter lacking the reserves necessary for such an expansion of credit. In the face of a corset that 'bites', the banks' only option would appear to be to raise loan rates in an attempt to choke off credit demand, for it is clear from the table of results (p. 147) that, even with the abolition of exchange controls, there is no unambiguous route (either direct or indirect through residents' undertaking certain kinds of balance-of-payments transactions) through which RAs can be acquired in a way that ensures a quantitative rise in RAs relative to IBELs.

(b) *Floating exchange-rate regime*: under floating exchange rates the net monetary effects crucially depend upon the identity of the provider of foreign currency, i.e. whether the person is a resident or non-resident. If an *overseas resident* supplies the foreign currency, £$M_3$ will fall back to its initial level because non-resident holdings of sterling, although enlarged, are excluded from £$M_3$, while (IB)ELs remain the same. Allowance for any subsequent slump in the equity market and concomitant rise in corporate bank borrowing, however, would see £$M_3$ moving back up again and (IB)ELs increasing. In the case of a *resident* satisfying the demand for foreign currency £$M_3$ would remain at its higher level and (IB)ELs would remain unchanged. Again, if the effects associated with a sagging equity market are taken into account, both £$M_3$ and (IB)ELs are likely to rise (further in the case of £$M_3$), tending to intensify both corset and RA pressure simultaneously.

(3) NBPS diversifies from IBELs into foreign currency claims.

(a) *Fixed exchange-rate regime*: the EEA's provision of foreign currency causes a reduction in the sterling domestic borrowing requirement of the public sector and in the RAs held by the banking system, which may enlarge (as a result of the reduction in the banks' consolidated RA ratio) the *fall* in £$M_3$, ELs and IBELs resulting from the movement out of IBELs itself. In the process, RA pressure is increased, although the loosening of corset pressure may allow for the manufacture of reserve assets through the discount market.

(b) *Floating exchange-rate regime*: if a *non-resident* supplies the foreign currency then $£M_3$ falls, as a result of the movement out of residents' IBELs, but (IB)ELs and RAs held by the banks remain constant. However, should a *resident* supply the foreign currency required in the transaction, then RAs, $£M_3$ and (IB)ELs will all remain unchanged.

The extent of the surge in portfolio investment overseas that followed the abolition of exchange controls is indicated in Table 6.1.[13] From an outflow of £0.9b. in the whole of 1979, overseas portfolio investment accelerated to a rate of £1.2b. per quarter in 1981, despite the loss of dollar premium and the appreciation of sterling. This trend was confirmed in particular by the activities of pension funds, whose pre-abolition overseas portfolio investment levels of under £100m. per quarter rose to a quarterly average of between £300m. and £400m. This represented a jump in the share of pension funds' cash flow being invested in overseas securities (largely at the expense of investment in British government bonds) from 7 per cent in the first three quarters of 1979 to 25 per cent in the first two quarters of 1981.[14]

This, however, may overstate the underlying trend (as the figures for the third quarter 1981 suggest) as it includes a once-and-for-all stock adjustment effect as a reaction to the changed investment environment. Insurance companies also increased their overseas investment at a fast rate (see Table 6.1), so that by the first quarter of 1981 they were investing 17 per cent of their cash flow abroad, as against 4 per cent prior to abolition, representing a relative shift away from gilts and company securities and some reduction in liquidity. Finally, unit trusts acquired little except overseas assets, on a net basis, after the latter part of 1979, while the investment trusts' build-up of overseas assets involved disinvesting from the UK equity market. Although difficult to quantify, the overall impact of the acceleration in overseas portfolio investment is likely to have been to reduce the exchange rate (and hence add to inflation) below the level that otherwise would have obtained and, to the extent that the outflow was at the expense of investment in UK gilts or UK equities, to have caused some increase in $£M_3$ and interest rates (e.g. to stimulate funding or choke off the demand for bank credit, perhaps emanating from the corporate sector as a result of a lower level of new equity issues).

In contrast to the growth in overseas portfolio investment, little perceptible increase in *direct* investment abroad is apparent in the

**TABLE 6.1   Data illustrating the effects of the abolition of exchange controls[1]**

| Transaction | 1978 | | | | 1979 | | | | 1980 | | | | 1981 | | | |
|---|---|---|---|---|---|---|---|---|---|---|---|---|---|---|---|---|
| | I | II | III | IV | I | II | III | IV | I | II | III | IV | I | II | III | IV |
| Direct private investment abroad (incl. oil) (£b.) | ← | | -3.3 | ↑ | -0.3 | | -5.7 | -0.6 ↑ | -0.8 | -3.9 | -0.5 | -0.7 ↑ | -0.6 | -1.0 | -1.0 | -7.0 |
| Private portfolio investment abroad (£b.) | | | -1.2 | ↑ | | | -0.9 | ↑ | | -3.0 | | -1 | | | | |
| Unit trusts | -26.6 | -74.4 | -47 | +22.1 | -16.4 | +1 | -14.4 | -0.4 | -19.9 | -20.7 | -28.9 | -33.9 | -82.4 | -95.5 | -11.0 | -70.1 |
| Insurance cos | -19.8 | -22.1 | -39.0 | -64.0 | -32.4 | -48.3 | -55.4 | -86.5 | -122.6 | -153.4 | -222 | -192.1 | -263.3 | -271.4 | -163.5 | -239.8 |
| Pension funds | -55 | -76 | -116 | -125 | -50 | -40 | -107 | -187 | -264 | -209 | -303 | -408 | -353 | -433 | -338 | -332 |
| Investment trusts | +20.3 | -46 | +11 | +8.4 | -21.3 | +8.1 | -14.6 | -41.6 | -99.5 | -58.9 | -89 | -110 | -82.8 | -81.2 | -30.2 | -15.5 |
| UK private-sector o/s Investment* | -862 | -807 | -1169 | -1717 | -1520 | -1037 | -1834 | -1579 | -1856 | -1464 | -1392 | -1732 | -1769 | -2293 | -2002 | -2959 |
| Banking sector f.c. lending o/s | -1762 | -3337 | -7064 | -8036 | -1323 | -8516 | -12388 | -8138 | -10151 | -5676 | -3074 | -12299 | -9642 | -6589 | -11551 | -10219 |
| Banks' net position in f.c.s[2] | -103 | -545 | +16 | +9 | +337 | +123 | +513 | -506 | +104 | -470 | +180 | +479 | -140 | -401 | -576 | +474 |
| UK residents' f.c. deposits[3] | 43 | 442 | 157 | 253 | -191 | 368 | -35 | 660 | 299 | 119 | 408 | 554 | 1341 | 362 | 1247 | -468 |
| UK banks' £ lending o/s* | -646 | -294 | -47 | -75 | 82 | 22 | -92 | -1 | -423 | -606 | -807 | -958 | -1184 | -421 | -954 | -695 |
| Non-resident £ bank deposits[4] | 26 | -385 | 214 | 181 | 609 | 547 | 402 | 1441 | 439 | 1177 | 806 | 581 | 345 | 944 | 1055 | 193 |
| 'Official'[5] sterling balances* | 2995 | 2764 | 2773 | 2610 | 2748 | 2847 | 3259 | 3320 | 3777 | 4132 | 4475 | 4640 | 4730 | 4934 | 5073 | 4721 |
| 'Private'[6] sterling balances* | 4903 | 4751 | 4910 | 5258 | 5729 | 6088 | 6536 | 7839 | 8009 | 9020 | 9842 | 10321 | 10619 | 11512 | 12532 | 12943 |
| Size of Eurosterling market[7] (end-period £b.) | | | n.a. | | ↑ | 6.9 | 7.7 | 7.8 | 10.0 | 11.1 | 11.0 | 11.3 | 11.4 | 11.1 | 12.2 | 12.3 |
| Deposits by UK banks | | | | | | 0.6 | 0.6 | 0.7 | 1.0 | 1.7 | 2.1 | 2.6 | 3.0 | 3.2 | 3.3 | 3.3 |
| Deposits by UK non-banks | | | | | | 0.4 | 0.4 | 0.6 | 0.9 | 1.0 | 0.8 | 1.1 | 1.0 | 1.0 | 1.0 | 1.0 |
| Total claims | | | | | ↑ | 5.0 | 5.5 | 6.3 | 6.8 | 7.6 | 7.5 | 7.3 | 7.7 | 8.6 | 10.6 | 10.3 |
| Claims on UK banks | | | | | | 1.0 | 1.1 | 1.7 | 1.6 | 2.2 | 2.2 | 2.3 | 2.6 | 3.0 | 3.2 | 3.4 |
| Claims on UK non-banks | | | | | | 0.3 | 0.3 | 0.9 | 0.8 | 0.8 | 0.6 | 0.7 | 0.7 | 0.6 | 0.7 | 0.7 |

Unit trusts, Insurance cos, Pension funds: net acquisition-cash values' of overseas investments (mainly) company securities.

f.c. = foreign currency.
o/s = overseas.
* Seasonally adjusted.
† Amounts outstanding.
1 Outflows denoted by a negative sign unless stated otherwise.
2 '+ve': increase in net f.c. liabilities.
3 With UK banks and excluding valuation changes (increase '+ve').
4 With UK banking sector (the 'monetary sector' after August 1981).
5 Exchange reserves in sterling held by central monetary institutions.
6 Banking and money market liabilities (£) to other holders.
7 Sterling liabilities of banks in Group of Ten countries (excluding USA and – by definition – the UK) Austria, Denmark, the Republic of Ireland and Switzerland (true size of market understated due to lack of data from some countries).

Note: From 30 September 1981 the coverage improved, resulting in an increase of around £0.8b. in both liabilities and assets vis-à-vis 'other Western Europe' at that date.

Source: Financial Statistics, August 1981, Tables 6.2, 7.2, 7.3, 7.4, 8.11, 8.12, 8.14, and 13.4; BEQB, September 1981, pp. 369–73 and June 1981, p. 162; BIS data published in BEQBs.

post-abolition era. However, a noticeable change in the method of *financing* it can be traced, with a sharp swing towards sterling finance. Borrowing in foreign currency to finance UK overseas investment (reflected in the figures for the banks' net position in foreign currencies in Table 6.1) changed from a pre-abolition average in the six quarters preceding abolition of approximately £250m. per quarter to quarterly repayments in the second half of 1979 of nearly £400m. To the extent that this represented the repayment of foreign currency borrowing,[15] the main effect of such measures was to bring forward outflows that would have taken place anyway.

### Disintermediation through the Eurosterling market

Following the abolition of exchange controls, Eurosterling banks could bid for sterling deposits from some UK residents to on-lend to others when corset/RA pressure prevented domestic banks in the UK from satisfying domestic sterling credit demand.[16] Indeed, it is likely that some London banks at least, in spite of Bank requests to refrain from such tactics, directed customers to their own foreign offices/subsidiaries when profitability considerations precluded them from satisfying the credit demand themselves. The ramifications of such transactions are of supreme importance because of the *potential* size of the Eurosterling market. Four different examples are considered to illustrate the monetary effects that derive from Eurosterling market operations.

(1) Eurosterling bank induces a sterling outflow from UK residents' IBELs to on-lend to UK NBPS. When the Eurosterling bank on-lends its newly gained sterling resources to the NBPS, a slight net fall in £M$_3$ is recorded as a result of the Eurosterling bank keeping a small proportion, say 5 per cent, of the additional resources in the form of an interest-bearing sterling liquidity reserve (bank deposit) with a London bank. (IB)ELs, however, remain unchanged. The net result is therefore an increase in the volume of sterling credit granted to the UK NBPS on the basis of a lower stock of £M$_3$, achieved through an increase in the velocity of circulation of £M$_3$.

(2) Eurosterling bank induces a sterling outflow from UK NBPS-owned public-sector debt to on-lend to UK NBPS. As a result of the net reduction (achieved through sales to the Broker or the retention of maturity monies) in UK NBPS-held public-sector debt, the monetary effects associated with the enlarged 'residual' financing of the PSBR – higher (IB)ELs, £M$_3$ and RAs available to the banks – have

to be set against the impact of the sterling loan and the Eurosterling bank's addition to its sterling liquidity reserve in London. The net result is a rise in $\pounds M_3$, an even higher rise in (IB)ELs and a significant weakening in RA pressure imposed upon the banks which, depending on their position with respect to the penalty zone of the corset, may subsequently be used to destroy IBELs through discount-market transactions or to expand their balance sheets.

(3) Eurosterling bank induces a sterling outflow from UK NBPS-held equities to on-lend to UK NBPS. The initial sale of equities to non-residents (the most likely mechanism for achieving a reduction in NBPS holdings) will cause $\pounds M_3$ to rise (non-residents are assumed to finance their purchases by reducing their holdings of sterling bank deposits) but leave (IB)ELs unchanged. If allowance is then made for the operations of the Eurosterling bank (the net effect of the matching outflow and inflow causing $\pounds M_3$ to fall, in line with the growth in the Eurosterling bank's sterling reserves in London, but leaving (IB)ELs unchanged), the basic results will not be changed, although the growth in $\pounds M_3$ will be lowered slightly. Finally, if note is taken of the subsequent depression in the equity market and resultant expansion in bank lending to the corporate sector, (IB)ELs will rise and $\pounds M_3$ by even more.

(4) Eurosterling bank switches into sterling to on-lend to UK NBPS.

(a) *Fixed exchange-rate regime*: the operations of the EEA result in an expansion in the RAs held by the UK banking sector to match the rise in (IB)ELs and $\pounds M_3$ (to a lesser degree, as explained immediately above) caused by the Eurosterling loan. In this case, therefore, the expansion in the flow of sterling credit in the UK resulting from 'offshore arbitraging' is broadly matched by an expansion in $\pounds M_3$ (which ultimately may be greater as a result of the banks' improved RA position), posing less of a problem for the authorities in interpreting the signals given by the $\pounds M_3$ series.[1]

(b) *Floating exchange-rate regime*: under floating rates the net outcome depends on whether it is a UK resident or non-resident who provides the sterling to the Eurosterling bank. If a *resident* supplies the sterling (i.e. from IBELs) then the net result is a slight fall in $\pounds M_3$, corresponding to the increase in sterling deposits held by the Eurosterling bank in London, but (IB)ELs remain unchanged. If, however, a *non-resident* should supply the sterling (from IBELs) then a net rise in $\pounds M_3$ will result, as deposits are transferred from non-residents to residents, but again (IB)ELs will be unaffected. This provides another example of Eurosterling disintermediation raising $£M_3$ relative to IBELs, thereby weakening the correlation between the two variables.

An early indication of the level of activity in the Eurosterling market is provided by the relative movement of Eurosterling rates *vis-à-vis* sterling inter-bank rates, with competitive bidding by Eurosterling banks (perhaps with the intention of on-lending to UK residents) tending to increase the differential. This differential rose during February and March 1980 to reach a peak of 1.36 per cent in favour of Eurosterling, indicating a surge of activity which is borne out by the BIS data on Eurosterling claims and liabilities outstanding presented in Table 6.1. During the first quarter of 1980 the Eurosterling market expanded by £2.2b. or nearly 30 per cent, fuelled by almost 50 per cent expansion in Eurosterling deposits made by both banks and non-banks in the UK (£1.3b. to £1.9b.). The sterling outflow from the UK was not, however, matched by a significant expansion in Eurosterling market loans to the UK, as claims on both UK banks and non-banks contracted slightly during the first quarter of 1980. Although the Eurosterling market expanded by a further 10 per cent in the following quarter, subsequent growth was slow, despite the rising contribution from deposits of UK banks.[17] Claims on UK non-banks stabilised at about £0.7b. per quarter after mid-1980, but claims on UK banks continued to increase steadily in line with liabilities to UK banks.

The disparity between total Eurosterling liabilities and claims indicates that throughout the post-1978 period some of the sterling deposits were switched into other currencies, the proportion varying from 15 per cent at end-September 1981 to 35 per cent at end-December 1980, the latter high figure probably reflecting the low non-bank demand for Eurosterling loans and the increased direct access non-residents had to sterling borrowing in the UK. After that date, the Eurosterling banks' switched-out position (with respect to sterling) narrowed noticeably.

### *UK banks' 'switching-out'[18] operations*

Before the abolition of exchange control the banks' freedom to arbitrage out of sterling was closely regulated, so the new environment merits close inspection. Two examples are considered: a switch out of bankers' deposits – excess to requirements – and a switch out of non-reserve asset sterling securities (e.g. gilts of more than one year to maturity).

(1) Banks switch out of bankers' deposits. Under a fixed exchange-

rate regime (the only possibility if the banks' consolidated bankers' deposits position is to be reduced), bank RAs will fall simply as a result of the switch, as will (IB)ELs, because of the reduction in the banks' net 'switched-in' (i.e. net spot foreign currency liability) position. $£M_3$, however, is unaffected because residents' deposits are unaffected by the switch. As a result $£M_3$ rises relative to the level of bank IBELs.

(2) Banks switch out of (non-RA) sterling securities (e.g. gilts of more than one year to maturity.

(a) *Fixed exchange-rate regime*: should UK *residents* purchase the gilts then RAs fall as before, due to the intervention of the EEA, as do (IB)ELs – both because of the reduction in the 'switched-in' position and because of the resident purchases of gilts – and $£M_3$, due also to resident purchases of gilts. However, should *non-residents* purchase the gilts then, although the net result will be a fall in RAs and (IB)ELs for the reasons just given, $£M_3$ would not change because non-resident holdings of sterling bank deposits are formally excluded from this definition of the money stock. Finally, should the Government Broker acquire the bonds, the resultant increase in 'residual' public-sector borrowing would offset the monetary implications of EEA intervention, leaving $£M_3$ and bank RAs at the same level but inducing a fall in (IB)ELs because of the changed switched position.

(b) *Floating exchange-rate regime*: regardless of whether residents or non-residents purchase the gilts and supply the banks with foreign currency, the net impact on (IB)ELs is the same: the fall arising from the changed switched position and the purchase of gilts outweighs the rise resulting from the provision of foreign currency. Only in the case of the Government Broker absorbing the gilts would (IB)ELs rise (because of the implications for residual financing). As regards the net impact on $£M_3$, a number of permutations are possible according to the transactors involved: (a) if the gilts are sold to UK residents and residents provide the foreign currency, $£M_3$ stays unchanged; (b) if the gilts are sold to UK residents but non-residents provide the foreign currency, $£M_3$ will fall; (c) if the gilts are sold to non-residents and residents provide the foreign currency, $£M_3$ will rise; (d) if non-residents purchase the gilts and provide the foreign currency, $£M_3$ stays the same; (e) if the Government Broker purchases the gilts and residents supply the foreign currency, $£M_3$ will rise; and (f) if the Government Broker acquires the gilts but non-residents supply the foreign currency, $£M_3$ will again rise as a result of the monetary effects of the higher 'residual' public-sector borrowing from the banks. In cases (e) and (f) more RAs are also supplied to the banks in the form of bankers' deposits.

The examples indicate that switching-out (of sterling) operations of UK banks can, in theory, raise $£M_3$ relative to bank IBELs under both fixed and floating exchange rates. A brief glance at Table 6.1 ('banks' net position in foreign currencies') indicates, however, that during the last corset period, 'switching out' only occurred in two quarters – 1979 IV and 1981 I – reflecting to some extent the continuing confidence in the strength of sterling. The negative switched-in positions of the first three quarters of 1981 reflected in part the on-lending of the substantially increased foreign currency holdings of UK residents.

*UK banks foreign currency lending to domestic residents who switch the proceeds into sterling*

This type of transaction affords the banks a further opportunity for satisfying domestic sterling credit demand in the face of corset/RA pressure by encouraging clients to take foreign currency loans[19] and then to switch the proceeds into sterling.

(a) *Fixed exchange-rate regime*: assuming the UK banks borrow foreign currency in the Eurocurrency markets to on-lend to UK domestic residents, the banks' 'net external foreign currency liabilities' will increase, but their switched position will remain unaltered. Under fixed exchange rates, the absorption of foreign currency by the EEA and the concomitant provision of sterling finance to residents will cause banks' RAs, (IB)ELs and $£M_3$ to rise. To the extent that the discount market is subsequently used by the banks to destroy (IB)ELs, $£M_3$ will again be raised relative to the level of bank (IB)ELs, and domestic sterling credit demand will be satisfied despite any prevailing corset pressure.

(b) *Floating exchange-rate regime*: under a 'pure' floating system (IB)ELs remain the same whether it is a resident or non-resident who ultimately purchases the foreign currency. However, if a *non-resident* purchases the foreign currency $£M_3$ will rise, as sterling deposits pass from non-residents to residents, a resident purchase leaving $£M_3$ unaltered. Once again, $£M_3$ may rise relative to bank IBELs as a result of this form of transaction, while domestic sterling credit demand may be satisfied without registering any impact on $£M_3$.

*The build-up of resident-owned foreign currency deposits*

The figures in Table 6.1 showing movements in UK resident-owned foreign currency deposits held with UK banks demonstrate how rapidly foreign currency holdings have been built up since the abolition of exchange controls (which sanctioned only certain corporate holdings). Between the end of September 1979 and the end of June 1981 holdings rose by approximately £5b. (£1.1b. due to valuation changes).[20] Although the bulk of the increase is attributable to corporate enterprises (perhaps involving the matching of foreign currency liabilities or the retention of foreign currency export earnings in the hope of a fall in sterling – which materialised in September 1981 – or the building up of foreign currency balances to discharge previous foreign currency loans about to fall due), the balances of private individuals have been growing at the fastest rate. For the latter group the speculative motive, apart from a desire to benefit from relatively high foreign yields, is likely to have been stronger.


*The return of sterling to a reserve currency role*

Under the measures taken to deal with the 1976 sterling crisis, the Bank agreed with foreign monetary institutions that *official* sterling reserves would be held down to the level of 'working balances' required for day-to-day transactions. Although this still applies today, official balances rose continuously after the beginning of 1979, expanding by 81 per cent to £4640m. (see Table 6.1) in the period to end-December 1980. This is likely to understate the true position significantly. 'Private' sterling balances rose at virtually the same pace during the same period (i.e. by 80 per cent) so that by the end of 1980 they stood at £10,321m. (a further expansion of 25 per cent was recorded in 1981). Although sterling's share of world currency reserves is still of the order of a few per cent, compared to 50 per cent before the post-war balance-of-payments crises, there remains a danger that a North Sea oil-backed currency and a monetarist government determined to hold down inflation, together with a diversification of OPEC surpluses away from the traditionally strong European currencies, will combine to restore sterling at least someway towards its undesirable, former reserve currency status.

In conclusion, the abolition of exchange controls not only rendered the corset obsolete, but also complicated the task of monetary management, not least by reducing the significance of $£M_3$ as an indicator of prevailing monetary conditions and of the stance of monetary policy. A strong case can be made for including both resident-owned foreign currency deposits and non-resident-owned sterling deposits in the targeted aggregate (see Table 6.1 for an indication of the rapid build-up that has taken place in the last two and a half years, which may have been held up during the operation of the corset as such deposits expanded IBELs). Similarly, despite the apparent lack of supportive evidence provided by analysis of international experience, further consideration might be given to the reintroduction of capital inflow controls and the establishment of reserve requirements on domestic banks' foreign currency business. Finally, the authorities should be alert to the dangers associated with the growth in privately owned foreign currency deposits, not least the possibility of foreign currency deposits making a significant inroad into displacing sterling deposits as the means of payment.[21]

# 7 The Medium-Term Financial Strategy

The details of the Conservatives' 'medium-term financial strategy' (MTFS) were first outlined in Sir Geoffrey Howe's budget speech of 26 March 1980. It involved plans (including 'projections' for planned general government spending and receipts, nationalised industries' borrowing from the private sector and tax cuts) for the progressive reduction in both £M$_3$ target ranges and the PSBR as a proportion of GDP (at market prices). The precise plans were:

|  | *12 months to end-March* | | | |
|---|---|---|---|---|
|  | *1981* | *1982* | *1983* | *1984* |
| £M$_3$ growth | 7-11* | 6-10 | 5-9 | 4-8 |
| PSBR/GDP | 3.75 | 3.0 | 2.25 | 1.5 |

* For the period mid-Feburary 1980 to mid-April 1981.

The plans signified the final demise (at lease under the incumbent administration) of Keynesian demand-management policies, the planned cuts in the PSBR, in both absolute terms (forecast to fall from £9.8b. in 1979-80 to £8½b. by end-March 1981) and as a proportion of GDP (forecast to fall from 4¾ per cent at end-March 1980 to 3¾ per cent by end-March 1981 and to 1½ per cent by end-March 1984), coming at a time of severe depression. Even on Treasury calculations, the economy was expected to contract by 2½ per cent during 1980, which represented the largest ever post-war decline in GDP. The budget plans were expected to yield only 1 per cent growth per annum after that until 1984. Public expenditure, in volume terms, was projected to be 4 per cent lower in 1983-4 than in 1979-80. The shift (on incentive grounds) from direct to indirect taxation, first instituted in the 1979 budget, was maintained as the £1.2b. increase in tax allowances (in accordance with the 'Rooker-Wise amendment') was largely offset by increased duty on petrol, drink and tobacco. The short-run implication of the increase in duties (and prescription charges and council rents) for the RPI was, however, significantly less than that involved in the previous budget proposals; it was expected to add up to 1.3 per cent to the RPI as compared to the 4 per cent induced by the previous year's VAT increases.

In explaining the role to be played by the MTFS in the fight against inflation (reaffirmed as the priority of policy), the Chancellor made the following points:

> inflation cannot persist in the long run unless it is accommodated by an excessive expansion of money and credit . . . Restraint of the growth of money and credit is then essential. And it needs to be maintained over a considerable period of time in order to defeat inflation. That underlines the importance of the medium term financial strategy.
>
> it is not intended to achieve this reduction in monetary growth by excessive reliance on interest rates. The Government's financial strategy, therefore, plans a substantial reduction over the medium-term in government borrowing as a percentage of national income. The consequences of excessive borrowing have been high nominal interest rates and, in capital markets, the crowding out of business by the State. This has held back investment. From now on, however, given the shape of the Government's plans for public expenditure the Budget deficit should be reduced progressively to between 1 and 2 per cent of output.
>
> Some increase in the ratio of the PSBR to the national income may be consistent with the maintenance of a given monetary target and without itself requiring increases in interest rates. But, in practice, public sector borrowing has been too high during the past two years. That lesson, and the continuing high inflation rate, make a big cut in the underlying deficit imperative this year. (Budget speech, 26 March 1980)

The assertion that inflation cannot persist in the long run without monetary accommodation is undoubtedly true, but begs the question of how and why monetary accommodation takes place; the 'money/nominal income' causality debate has not yet been resolved.[1] Moreover, monetary control problems (discussed in detail in Chapters 3-5) are overlooked. On the link between the PSBR and interest rates, monetary growth and inflation, further exposition is necessary.

The relationship between the PSBR and changes in £M$_3$ may be derived from an analysis of the commercial banks' balance sheet and the financing options available to a government facing a positive PSBR. Taking the banks' consolidated balance sheet first, it is necessary to identify the asset counterparts to an increase in £M$_3$, defined to include notes and coin in circulation with the non-bank public plus all UK resident-owned (public- and private-sector) sterling bank deposits. Unfortunately, not all increases in sterling bank lending (to the UK public and private sectors and overseas) are reflected in changes in $£M_3$, so that measuring the change in $£M_3$ from the assets side requires the subtraction of certain liability items. These comprise, according to the definition of $£M_3$: (a) increases in non-deposit liabilities, such as capital reserves and internal funds; (b) any increase in non-resident-owned sterling bank deposits; and (c) any increase in foreign currency deposits, whether owned by residents or non-residents. Item (c), however, is normally subsumed within the net 'switched-in' item (i.e. change in banks' foreign currency deposits less foreign currency claims) which indicates the extent to which UK banks have acquired sterling lending resources (in the form of bankers' deposits in a fixed exchange rate environment) without directly increasing $£M_3{}^2$ and so also takes care of foreign currency assets acquired by the banks. Hence the increase in $£M_3$ may be written as:

> the increase in notes and coin in circulation with the non-bank public,
> *plus* the increase in UK sterling bank lending to UK public and private sectors and overseas,
> *less* the increase in non-deposit liabilities
> *less* the increase in non-resident-owned UK sterling bank deposits,
> *less* the increase in banks' net 'switched-in' position.

Turning to the financing of a given PSBR (representing the sum of the central government's borrowing requirement and 'contributions' to the PSBR from local authorities and nationalised industries), the following channels are open to the government: (a) subject to demand, the printing of more notes and the minting of more coin; (b) sales of marketable public-sector debt (e.g. gilts) to the non-bank private sector (NBPS); (c) sales of non-marketable public-sector debt to the NBPS; (d) sales of public-sector debt to the banks; (e) 'other' public-sector borrowing from banks, i.e. by local authorities and public corporations to finance their 'contributions'[3] to the PSBR; and (f) 'external finance', i.e. 'overseas financing' in the form of overseas purchases of public-sector debt, direct public-sector borrowing from overseas or a reduction in official foreign exchange reserves, plus foreign currency borrowing from banks. The differential, first-round monetary effects (in terms of the induced change in $£M_3$ and the implications for both the old minimum reserve assets ratio and the current cash ratio) of these alternative financing avenues are presented in Table 7.1, *ceteris paribus*. (Table A1 in Appendix A demonstrates the relative significance of the financing options as used during the 1970s.) A reduction in official foreign exchange reserves is chosen to illustrate the effects of channel (f).

If the public's demand for currency allows the PSBR to be financed by the increased issue of notes and coin to the NBPS, then, although $£M_3$ increases by virtue of the inclusion of currency in circulation in the statistic, no change in bank deposits, bankers' deposits or RAs will result. The addition to bankers' deposits resulting from the PSBR itself is cancelled when the banks exchange bankers' deposits for cash with the Bank of England in order to satisfy the public's enlarged currency demand.

As Table 7.1 indicates, the sale of public-sector debt (PSD) to non-banks represents the preferred financing option of governments because of the resultant neutral monetary effects. During the 1950s, 1960s and early 1970s transactions of this kind were predominantly in the form of open-market sales and new issues of gilts, but in more recent times national savings instruments have been asked to play

TABLE 7.1 The direct monetary effects of financing the PSBR

| Financing option* | Net monetary effects[1] | | | | |
|---|---|---|---|---|---|
| | $£M_3$ | Reserve assets (RA) | RA ratio | Bankers' deposits | Cash ratio |
| (1) Take up of notes and coin by the NBPS | ↑ | 0[2] | 0[2] | 0[2] | 0[2] |
| (2) Sales of public-sector debt (PSD) (market-able or non-market-able) to NBPS[3] | 0 | 0 | 0 | 0 | 0 |
| (3) Sales of PSD to banks:[4] | | | | | |
| (a) RAs | ↑ | ↑ | ↑ | 0 | ↓ |
| (b) non-RAs | ↑ | 0 | ↓ | 0 | ↓ |
| (4) 'Other' public-sector borrowing from banks | ↑ | 0 | ↓ | 0 | ↓ |
| (5) A reduction in official foreign exchange reserves | 0 | 0 | 0 | 0 | 0 |

* Strictly speaking item (1) is not an option. The possible take-up of notes and coin (or PSD) by the Banking Department of the Bank of England as a financing mechanism is ignored.

[1] '↑' indicates a rise, '↓' a fall and '0' no change.

[2] If some of the increase in legal tender is deposited with the banking system (and subsequently exchanged for bankers' deposits by the banks) then a rise will occur.

[3] And discount houses.

[4] Excluding discount houses and the Banking Department of the Bank of England.

a bigger role (the Chancellor's target for net sales - £3½ b. in 1981-2 - was comfortably met and the 1982-3 target is £3b.) in the hope of reducing long-term interest rates and so stimulating the revival of the corporate debenture market (with concomitant monetary gains as corporate bank borrowing declines). Whether the debt sold is market able or non-marketable, however, makes no difference to the resultant direct monetary effects; in each case the increase in deposits and bankers' deposits created by the positive PSBR itself (assumed to derive from a CGBR)[4] are extinguished as non-banks purchase the public-sector debt by drawing cheques on commercial banks which are then cleared at the Bank of England.

Sales of PSD to banks, however, fail to extinguish the rise in bank deposits resulting from the 'excess' central government expenditure[5] the financing transaction simply involves the banks in exchanging their newly gained bankers' deposits for the public-sector securities. The direct net effect will therefore be a rise in £$M_3$ (i.e. in non-bank, resident-owned sterling bank deposits) but no change in bankers' deposits. While this implies a fall in the cash ratio (bankers' deposits to eligible liabilities), the induced change in the reserve assets ratio will depend on whether the debt sold constitutes a reserve asset or not; if not, the reserve assets ratio will fall, but if so, the reserve assets ratio will rise, thereby raising the banks' lending potential. In spite of this, when the minimum reserve assets ratio was in existence, the main concern of the authorities was not to restrain the supply of reserve assets to the banks (the 'residual' financing of the PSBR) in order to avoid the potential secondary expansion in bank credit, but rather to minimise the *primary* increase in the money supply due to the banks' acquisition of *any* kind of central government debt. Nevertheless, as Table A1 in Appendix A demonstrates, on a long-term basis the authorities successfully limited their recourse to the banks.

Bank borrowing by either local authorities or public corporations to finance their 'contributions' to the PSBR will cause both bank loans and deposits (of the NBPS) to rise, thereby raising £$M_3$ but reducing both the reserve assets and cash ratios as bankers' deposits are unaffected. Subsequent bank action to improve these ratios to desired/prescribed levels, by either bidding for reserves and/or shedding deposits (eligible liabilities) would evoke secondary monetary repercussions.

Finally, by running down its official foreign exchange reserves the government has at its disposal a relatively simple means of financing a PSBR in a non-monetary fashion. As a result of the intervention of the Exchange Equalisation Account as a supplier of foreign currency against sterling, any reduction in official reserves relative to non-resident holdings of public-sector debt[6] of the same magnitude as the PSBR to be financed involves equal and opposite changes in both £M$_3$ and bankers' deposits to those resulting from the PSBR itself. In practice, however, the government is usually constrained by factors other than the need to contain money stock growth in determining its 'desired' level of foreign exchange reserves.

The **comparative static analysis** presented above implies that a government seeking to decelerate money stock growth should concern itself with maximising the proportion of a given PSBR financed through sales of PSD to non-banks or by running down official foreign exchange reserves. On a *ceteris paribus* assumption, both options have the desired effects, but in practice certain offsets inevitably arise. For example, open-market gilt sales might induce NBPS switches from non-marketable PSD as the relative attractiveness of the yield on the former improves, or they might induce higher corporate bank borrowing as the debenture market is effectively 'crowded out'. Even if the authorities consciously sought to expand a payments deficit (under a fixed exchange rate) they might find that the resultant reduction in national income was associated with a reduced non-bank demand, if only temporarily, for gilts or other forms of public-sector debt relative to the reduction in the demand for bank deposits (money).

By expressing the PSBR, as suggested by Table 7.1, as the sum of the available financing options (i.e. the increase in notes and coin in circulation with the NBPS, plus sales of PSD to NBPS, plus the increase in sterling bank lending to UK public sector, plus external financing of the public sector) the link between the PSBR and the increase in £M$_3$ can be obtained. This is done by substituting 'the increase in sterling bank lending to UK public sector' into the identity on p. 90. Substitution and rearrangement yield:

the increase in £M$_3$ ≡ PSBR
*minus* net sales of PSD to NBPS
*plus* increase in sterling bank lending to NBPS and overseas
*minus* external financing of the public sector
*minus* increase in non-deposit liabilities
*minus* increase in non-resident-owned UK sterling bank deposits
*minus* increase in UK banks' net 'switched-in' position.

The foregoing suggests that choosing a level for the PSBR compatible with a desired degree of monetary restraint is likely to prove an extremely hazardous task. This was confirmed by a paper by Middleton *et al.* (1979) based on simulations run on the Treasury model which suggested (paras 64 and 65) that the size and even *direction* of the change in the money stock associated with a given change in the PSBR are dependent upon the source of the change in the PSBR and the nature of the prevailing exchange-rate regime being pursued by the authorities.

That there is no simple one-for-one relationship between changes in $£M_3$ and the PSBR is evident from Table 7.2, which demonstrates the linkage for the years 1973 to 1980. Indeed, 'casual empiricism' of this type would suggest that, for this period, the 'increase in sterling lending to UK private sector' was more closely correlated (*ex post* data imply nothing about causality) with the increase in sterling $M_3$ than was the PSBR (i.e. while the accumulated increase in $£M_3$ was £44,263m., the accumulated increase in sterling lending to the UK private sector was £38,984m., compared to an accumulated PSBR of £69,434m.). This suggestion is supported by formal regression analysis conducted by Kaldor (1980, pp.117-19) (though note Hendry's qualification - 1981, p.15) and the National Institute of Economic and Social Research (1980, pp.152-5). Finally, even Friedman (1980, pp.56-7, para.9), the founder of 'monetarism', questioned the role assigned to the PSBR within the Tories' anti-inflation strategy.

The main strand of support for linking 'projections' of the PSBR with planned reductions in $£M_3$ growth within the MTFS comes from those who perceive a relatively immutable portfolio (stock) structure for the private sector in the medium to long term (e.g. Budd and Burns, 1979; Beenstock and Longbottom, 1980; Minford, 1980a, p.141; HM Treasury, 1981a, pp.82-5 and pp.91-3). Accordingly, given the private sector's subjective evaluation of the risks associated with different investment mediums and relative rates of return, a PSBR, by raising private-sector wealth, will induce proportionate changes in all assets held within the portfolio, including money. Further, a *permanent* rise in the relative yield obtainable on government bonds is necessary if the private sector is to be induced to increase the share of gilts within its portfolio on a continuous basis.[7] This approach, therefore, provides the intellectual foundation[8] to the MTFS and support for the Chancellor's view (see p.89 above) that 'excessive' PSBR levels have resulted in high nominal interest rates (to ensure their non-monetary financing). This has not yet become 'received wisdom',[9] at least not outside the City of London.[10]

The final area of controversy centres on the advisability (and practicalities) of cutting the PSBR for monetary purposes when the economy is in a recession (see Chancellor's quote on p.89 above). While Burns, the senior economic adviser to the Treasury, canvassed

**TABLE 7.2  The PSBR/£M$_3$ relationship 1973–80**

|  | Flows | 1973 | 1974 | 1975 | 1976 | 1977 | 1978 | 1979 | 1980 | 1973–80 |
|---|---|---|---|---|---|---|---|---|---|---|
|  | (1) Public sector borrowing requirement | 4195 | 6372 | 10521 | 9128 | 5995 | 8331 | 12587 | 12305 | 69434 |
| minus | (2) Net acquisition of public-sector debt by UK NBPS | 2283 | 3157 | 5606 | 5765 | 8456 | 6026 | 10906 | 9585 | 51784 |
| plus | (3) Increase in sterling lending to UK private sector | 5972 | 3435 | −385 | 3464 | 3188 | 4698 | 8585 | 10027 | 38984 |
| plus | (4) Increase in sterling lending to overseas sector | 189 | 289 | −65 | 647 | 405 | 1062 | −11 | 2794 | 5310 |
| plus | (5) 'External and foreign currency finance' | −868 | −2997 | −1338 | −2767 | 3432 | −378 | −2823 | −3335 | −11074 |
| minus | (6) Increase in banks' non-deposit liabilities | 485 | 682 | 802 | 1142 | 434 | 915 | 818 | 1308 | 6586 |
| equals | (7) Increase in sterling M$_3^1$ | 6702 | 3255 | 2326 | 3565 | 4130 | 6772 | 6615 | 10898 | 44263 |

Items (1)–(4) sum to 'domestic credit expansion'.
$^1$ Items (1)–(6) may not sum to item (7) because of seasonal adjustment processing.

Source: *Financial Statistics*, July, 1981, Table 7.3, p.80; February 1979, Table 7.3, p.84.

for the use of a cyclically adjusted PSBR[11] and Lawson (1980), the Financial Secretary to the Treasury, argued for a ' "stepped" public sector borrowing profile, with the PSBR not changing much as a proportion of GDP in recession years, but falling sharply in non-recession years', others (the Chancellor, Minford, 1980b) pressed for the override of automatic stabilisers. The extent of the (nominal) PSBR cuts formally demanded (although they failed to materialise – see pp.109-14 below) thus implied a rejection of the argument that the flow of bank lending to the private sector tends to fall relative to output during a recession, thereby making it possible to finance a higher PSBR with unchanged monetary growth.

Despite the public utterances of the government, one may conclude that the nature of the relationships between *discretionary* fiscal policy and the PSBR on the one hand[12] and between the PSBR, interest rates and changes in $£M_3$ on the other, are so complex as to deny to the authorities the ready availability of a simple rule of thumb that indicates how fiscal policy should be adjusted so as to ensure that the size and structure of the PSBR remain compatible with the stated monetary target. This poses an almost unbearable burden on practitioners who seek to use the PSBR, cyclically adjusted, inflation-adjusted[13] or otherwise, as a flexible instrument of monetary control, even in the medium to long term.

Looking beyond the statistical links between the PSBR and $£M_3$, the Treasury and Civil Service Committee (TCSC) also reviewed the conduct of policy and duly concluded that:

> The Medium-Term Financial Strategy was a bold experiment intended to change expectations about the future of the economy. As we conclude above, we believe that the view that declarations about monetary policy will quickly affect wage and price expectations is unsubstantiated. This clearly will not happen if the monetary targets themselves are not credible. Unforeseen external developments (such as a rise in the real price of oil) make achievements of immutable targets set for a period of several years difficult, if not impossible. We were warned by other Central Banks who have pursued monetary targets that the effective use of such devices is by no means a mechanical procedure. It evidently requires a degree of judgement and flexibility in the choice of the monetary aggregate, and in the setting and resetting of the targets for it, to ensure that the pursuit of such an intermediate target is consistent with and not inimical to progress in achieving the ultimate objectives of policy on which there is substantial agreement, namely growth, less inflation and higher levels of employment. (*Monetary Policy*, Vol. I, Report, para. 11.26, HC 163-I, 24 February 1981)

This conclusion brings together a number of criticisms that the Committee made about the conduct of monetary policy, and the separate strands require disentangling and elaboration.

The first point made was that the **announcement effect** of policy was weak:

> It is unrealistic to suppose that negotiated wages and administered prices respond rapidly and automatically to announcements about monetary policy, however credible they may be. The influence of monetary policy on wage and price inflation does not therefore appear primarily through the setting of targets or through expectations, but rather in the short term through the lowering of economic activity and the appreciation of the exchange rate. (*Monetary Policy,* Vol. I, para. 11.16)

This raises the question of whether or not some form of 'incomes policy'[14] should be introduced to alleviate the short-run costs of policy, in terms of the loss in industrial output, particularly in the manufacturing and construction sectors, the rise in unemployment and the reduction in investment (see Table 8.3, p. 116) by speeding up and strengthening the adjustment process from the setting of targets to nominal wages and prices. Closely aligned to this point is the criticism that the targets were not credible because of the authorities' failure to use 'either of its chosen policy instruments [interest rates and fiscal policy] to the fullest extent possible', which meant 'that there has been no true "monetarist experiment"'.[15] In addition to this, $£M_3$ was regarded as a poor target aggregate,[16] particularly as it was used as the sole monetary indicator (notwithstanding the authorities' willingness to monitor other aggregates). Finally, the MTFS itself was described as 'not soundly based',[17] not least because of its inflexibility and hence its inability to remain consistent with the achievement of ultimate goals other than inflation (though note that the Chancellor in November 1980[18] only committed himself to the 'thrust', and presumably not the figures, of the MTFS). The preoccupation of the authorities with the inflation goal was itself stigmatised as a 'single objective' policy.[19]

Disregarding the technical and operational problems inherent within the authorities' chosen policy path after June 1979, perhaps the major factor responsible for the Committee's anxieties was the apparent willingness of the authorities to countenance intolerably high short-run 'costs' in pursuit of marginal gains on the inflation front. To assess the validity of the latter claim it is necessary to consider both the actual and intended 'transmission mechanisms' of policy, bearing in mind that the control of inflation was regarded by the authorities as a prerequisite for sustainable growth of output and employment,[20] although others rejected this basic premise.[21]

HM Treasury argued that 'one of the first effects of a restrictive monetary policy will be to raise the exchange rate', which 'will have a direct impact on domestic prices - both by reducing the cost of imports and by putting pressure on producers of domestic substitutes to price competitively', and so 'help to moderate pay settlements'.[22] This fall in prices may stimulate consumption as the savings ratio falls in line,[23] but this is likely to be outweighed by the 'deterioration in competitiveness' - 'the more rapidly domestic wages and prices respond to monetary policy, the smaller this loss will be'.[24] Hence if 'price expectations are themselves dependent on announced monetary targets'[25] priority should be given to preserving credibility in the targets by consistently meeting them. (The Chancellor concurred on this point,[26] accepting the inevitability of short-run losses in output and rises in unemployment - due to the rise in the real exchange rate - as people took time to adjust to the changed monetary environment.) The short-run costs are also likely to be further augmented as a result of higher interest rates and a tightened fiscal policy designed to reduce the rate of monetary growth.[27] However, 'there is no reason why such transitory losses of output need have a permanently adverse effect on growth potential', for 'although spare capacity may hold down investment for a time, the prime determinants of capital formation are expectations of future output and profitability', which 'should be considerably enhanced by the reduction in inflation and the consequent reduction in uncertainty and risk'.[28]

The crucial issue at stake is thus the speed at which economic agents adjust, and can *reasonably be expected* to adjust, their expectations, and hence actions, in the light of the authorities' statements of intent and subsequent 'success' in adhering to such proclamations. Initial faith in the strength of the 'announcement effect' of policy, the foundation of which had always seemed shaky[29] and over-optimistic,[30] eventually evaporated and gave way to exhortations to the public to accept 'reasonable' wage awards. The explicit threat of unemployment for 'non-co-operation', though not necessarily for those who actually received higher remuneration, was backed up by the institution of cash limits on pay for public-sector employees. This in effect established public sector pay 'norms', although it was vigorously denied by the administration, which had always vehemently opposed any form of incomes policy. Rejection,[31] owing to doubts about the short-run predictions,[32] of the **rational expectations** school's approach)[33] led to the adoption of a **gradualist** approach for combatting inflation.[34] (Gradualists', like 'monetarists', believe in the concept of a vertical, long-run **Phillips curve**, but, unlike the latter, do accept the need for governmental intervention to mitigate the 'transitional' costs of policy[35] - higher unemployment, loss of real output, lower investment.[36] The Committee's concern that not enough was being done to mitigate and spread the considerable short-run costs of policy,[37] and that any success on the inflation front might only prove transient (i.e. until recovery occurred), [38] was undoubtedly a major factor behind their damning report.

Given the weakness of the 'announcement effect' of monetary policy, the conduct of policy bore all the hallmarks of 'old-fashioned', fiscal deflationary policies, except in this instance the depression in demand was induced, though possibly unintentionally,[39] through a rise in the (nominal) exchange rate. But what could be done to lessen the burden? Despite admissions by the Bank of England that the real exchange rate had been 'too high' and had led to a serious loss of competitiveness (accounting for between one-third and one-half of the loss)[40] and submissions by the Committee of London Clearing Banks (1981) and others on measures that might be used to influence the exchange rate, the authorities (at least until the intervention on the foreign exchanges in September 1981) remained sceptical about their ability to manipulate the exchange rate. The Governor of the Bank of England stressed the problems involved in trying to influence the nominal exchange rate and ruled out the interest-rate weapon as a possible candidate,[41] while the Chancellor questioned the effectiveness of capital inflow controls.[42] Reflation was also ruled out on the grounds that any temporary relief gained on the unemployment front would be at the expense of higher inflation in the future, while permanent relief could only be achieved through the removal of labour-market distortions. Outside observers were less dismissive, however. Despite the Prime Minister's repeated assertion that 'there is no alternative' credible strategy, a number of alternative reflationary packages, some involving the institution of some 'incomes policy' variant, were proposed as a means of improving economic performance and future prospects for recovery without jeopardising the inflation goal. One such package came from the 'CLARE Group' of economists (1981) who argued for a £5b. (at 1981-2 prices) reflationary package, including a reduction in the employers' National Insurance Surcharge, extra investment in the nationalised industries, a return to the (Rooker—Wise) principle of indexing income tax allowances, a cut in VAT, reductions in public-sector output prices, and increased government current expenditure. Another school, the Cambridge Economic Policy Group (CEPG), canvassed for the introduction of protectionist measures,[43] while the National Institute of Economic and Social Research argued for devaluation.[44]

To summarise, the MTFS may legitimately be criticised on the following grounds: (a) even if inflation is successfully cured by monetary policy, ensuing economic growth is not axiomatic; (b) monetary policy may not be sufficient to control inflation; (c) the technical problems associated with money stock control were underestimated; (d) the choice of £M₃ as the target aggregate, for which an identifiable stable demand function still proves elusive; (e) the apparent lack of coherent policy in the setting of target ranges; (f) overemphasis on the significance of the PSBR; (g) a failure to appreciate the difficulties likely to be experienced in cutting the PSBR at a time of depression and to avoid the 'soft' option of cutting public-sector investment disproportionately; (h) the imprudent adoption of an untried 'supply-side' doctrine; (i) too rapid a switch from direct to indirect taxation, with a concomitant failure to appreciate the likely inflationary consequences; and (j) too rapid an attempt, at an inappropriate time (i.e. of depression), to change long-standing attitudes, expectations and market actions of economic agents operating in the UK, with a 'benign neglect' of traditional policy goals.[45] Unfortunately, the failure of the government to achieve the £M₃ targets, the PSBR projections or its inflation goal (single figures by the end of 1981) leaves many of the controversial issues unanswered. Many will claim that the 'monetarist experiment' has not yet been tried and put to the test, much to the consternation of Galbraith (1980) and others who had hoped to damn monetarism forever as a result of its failure in the UK. While UK residents are certainly aware of the consequences of the recent *attempt* to implement a 'monetarist experiment', they can only speculate as to what might have been the outcome had the experiment been properly conducted. Nevertheless, the majority would probably condemn the broad conduct of economic policy since May 1979 as an abject failure, since, despite 'three years of unparalled austerity' (a phrase coined by John Biffen, Chief Secretary to the Treasury, in January 1980) the financial goals enshrined within the MFTS have, in the main, proved elusive. In this sense, naive monetarism, or the belief that rigid control of the money stock will impinge mainly on prices and not real output, is a poor substitute for naive Keynesianism, or the belief that an expansion in aggregate demand at less than full-capacity utilisation of resources will always call forth increases in real output and not raise prices. The fact remains that little is known about the precise distribution of a monetary impulse between prices and real output.

# 8 The Medium-Term Financial Strategy in Operation

## CONTROL OF THE MONEY SUPPLY[1]

Throughout the post-1979 period monetary policy was designed to enable the authorities to meet their prescribed £M$_3$ targets, but unfortunately only one of the targets (none since the introduction of the MTFS) was met – see Table 8.1.

In the four-week period to mid-April 1980, £M$_3$ growth was well within target, being only 0.3 per cent. This was the result of a large public-sector surplus and large sales of public-sector debt to the non-bank private sector outweighing a £1½b. increase in sterling bank lending to the private sector. Three major causes for concern remained, however: the continuing gap between domestic credit expansion (DCE) and £M$_3$ growth (which had been a prominent feature of monetary developments in the second half of 1979), the growth in sterling bank lending, and the continuing 'bill leak'. At mid-April, DCE was still running at over £7b. at an annual rate, or the equivalent of nearly 15 per cent of £M$_3$, while removal of the 'bill leak' would have expanded the reported figures by perhaps two percentage points.

The £M$_3$ figures for the period to mid-May demonstrated a marked acceleration in monetary growth. The 2.1 per cent recorded

TABLE 8.1  Targets' experience post-May 1979*

| Target period | £M$_3$ target | Out-turn |
|---|---|---|
| October 1978–October 1979 | 8–12 | 13.3 |
| June 1979–April 1980 | 7–11 | 10.0 |
| June 1979–October 1980 | 7–11 | 17.6 |
| February 1980–April 1981 | 7–11 | 18.5 |
| February 1981–April 1982 | 6–10 | 13.0 |

* % p.a. mid-month, seasonally adjusted data.

Source: *Financial Statistics* (various).

rise took the annualised growth rate in the first three months of the February 1980–April 1981 target period to one percentage point above the target range. The major contributory factors were a high CGBR and higher than expected private-sector borrowing from banks. Although monetary (£M$_3$) growth subsequently decelerated in the period to mid-June, the recorded monthly rise being only 0.8 per cent, this was immediately followed by explosive growth, largely as a result of reintermediation following the abolition of the corset in June. Despite the recorded 5 per cent jump in the month to mid-July, the Bank's judgement was that 'after making allowance for this readjustment of business and other special factors, it does not appear that there has been an acceleration in July'. Nevertheless, broader monetary aggregates, which were only partially affected by the corset, registered growth rates of between 18 and 22 per cent for the period since mid-February, not significantly different from the £M$_3$ growth rate of 23 per cent. The pressure for monetary expansion came from a high PSBR and strong private-sector bank credit demand.

Further details (using unadjusted figures) of the unwinding of corset distortions during the month to mid-July are presented in Table 8.2. The main effects were: (a) reintermediation from the acceptance market, which expanded sterling bank advances to the non-bank private sector by up to £997m.; (b) a switch from bank

**TABLE 8.2  The demise of the corset: expectations fulfilled**

|  |  | Changes between mid-June and mid-July 1980* | |
|---|---|---|---|
|  |  | £m. | % |
| (1) Reintermediation from the acceptance market (i.e. decline in NBPS-held acceptances) |  | 997 | 37.4 |
| (2) Switch by UK banks from 'market loans' (negative IBELs transactions) to the discount market to call-money loans to the market | MLs | −235 | −87.7 |
|  | CMLs | +874 | +25.6 |
|  | Turn-around | 1109 |  |
| (3) Increase in non-resident-owned UK sterling bank time deposits |  | 749 | 11.7 |
| (4) Expansion in sterling advances |  | 3272 | 6.8 |
| (5) Expansion in IBELs |  | 5353 |  |
| (6) Expansion in £M$_3$ |  | 3432 | 5.8 |
| (7) Expansion in IBELs relative to £M$_3$ |  | 1921 |  |

* Unadjusted data.

Source: *Financial Statistics*, August 1980.

'market loans' to the discount market to call-money loans, the incentive for 'negative IBELs' transactions having been removed (the turnaround was over £1.1b., which generated £874m. reserve assets for the banks); (c) a bank-induced increase in non-residents' sterling time deposits, since these deposits were not included in £$M_3$ and were no longer subject to corset discipline (the actual expansion amounted to £749m.); (d) an expansion in sterling advances (subject to the strength of credit demand and the availability of reserve assets which would be augmented by category (b) transactions) (the actual increase was £3272m., £3109m. of which represented lending to the private sector); and (e) an expansion in IBELs relative to £$M_3$, since banks no longer had any incentive to depress the level of IBELs relative to £$M_3$ artificially (see Chapter 4, pp.33–5).

Evidence of further corset distortions became apparent in the banking figures for the following month, which demonstrated that: (a) UK banks had added substantially to their holdings of gilts and other public-sector securities – to the tune of £0.6b. – which had been artificially depressed during the corset regime as banks sought to avoid corset penalties in the face of strong loan demand by selling public-sector debt to the non-bank private sector (perhaps encouraged by the authorities' apparent willingness to supply reserves on demand to banks, thereby diminishing the significance and need for secondary liquidity reserves);[2] (b) UK banks had significantly increased their sterling lending abroad (by £521m., compared to £393m. the previous month), a high proportion going to their overseas offices and banks abroad, probably reflecting Eurosterling business that they had previously been constrained from undertaking by the corset (the evidence suggests that the Governor's request not to circumvent the corset through Eurosterling-market operations went unheeded in some quarters); (c) UK residents had switched from foreign currency deposits and sterling deposits held abroad to UK bank deposits, presumably as a result of the restoration of bank competitiveness after the abolition of the corset. These factors, together with a recurrence of 'round-tripping' and a continued fall in the 'bill leak', contributed to the 3 per cent growth in £$M_3$ recorded for the month to mid-August. Even allowing for the distortions, monetary growth remained above target, although the substantially slower growth in $M_1$, the rise in *real* interest rates (as inflation fell more rapidly than expected), the strength of sterling and the perceived weakness in the real economy were accepted as evidence of the tightness of policy and hence the need to resist forces that might generate further increases in nominal interest rates.

After the débâcle over the banking figures for July and August, the authorities were relieved to find that £$M_3$ grew by only 0.6 per cent in the month to mid-September and by even less if a further reduction of £250m. in NBPS-held acceptances is allowed for (although an offset for the unwinding of round-tripping transactions should be made). The main reasons for the slow-down in growth were lower growth in bank lending to the private sector and in public-sector borrowing. The respite from monetary anguish was short-lived, however. Figures for banking October and banking November both confirmed 2 per cent jumps in £$M_3$, so that by mid-November (the out-turn figure for the June 1979 to October 1980 target period was 17.6 per cent compared to a target range of 7-11 per cent) recorded £$M_3$ growth since the start of the target period (mid-February 1980) was 17½-24 per cent at an annualised rate – compared with the target of 7-11 per cent. The main expansionary factors in October were sterling bank lending to the private sector, although the reported figure was probably inflated by the failure of the seasonal adjustments to keep pace with the changing pattern of VAT and interest payments, moves by private- and public-sector borrowers (i.e. local authorities) to draw on overdraft facilities to repay money-market debt as a result of 'high' money-market rates and, possibly, the growing current account surplus. Factors contributing to the expansion in November were a £0.5b. rise in sterling lending overseas (reflecting the continued unwinding of the corset-induced distortion to sterling bank lending generally), a £160m. reduction in the 'bill leak', and higher government borrowing (the government's deficit was £2.7b., much higher than anticipated). In recognition of the market confusion caused by the rapid monetary growth in the second half of 1980, the Governor of the Bank of England concluded that

> The lesson, perhaps, is the need to avoid attaching undue importance to short-term developments in any single monetary aggregate; it is sounder to take into account, as we in fact do, the underlying developments both in the aggregates as a whole and in the real economy. Taken overall, this evidence suggests that policy has been restrictive rather than otherwise. (*BEQB,* December 1980, p.458)

In apparent agreement with these sentiments, the Chancellor cut MLR from 16 per cent to 14 per cent on 24 November (see below), despite the monetary 'explosion', and decided against 'rolling forward' the target because of uncertainty over the factors influencing monetary developments in the economy. Targets continued to be framed in terms of the £$M_3$ statistic, however, although interest in the $M_2$ series was revived with an announcement that banking 'retail' deposit statistics were to be collected.

The December money supply figures, which showed a rise of just 0.5 per cent, were encouraging (although DCE was more than double the rise in $£M_3$) in that they marked the beginning of a slow-down in sterling bank lending to the private sector. After allowing for distortions caused by borrowers switching from foreign currency borrowing to sterling borrowing as a result of the relative decline in sterling interest rates, the 'underlying' rate of increase was estimated at £400-£500m., compared to £1.3b. per month in the four-month period to mid-October 1980. The slow-down in both $£M_3$ growth and sterling bank lending to the private sector was confirmed by the January banking figures, which demonstrated growth of 0.7 per cent and £388m. respectively. Although temporarily checked in February (when $£M_3$ rose by 0.9 per cent), the slow-down in monetary growth continued in mid-March, when reported $£M_3$ growth, despite a large jump in sterling bank lending (probably distorted by arbitrage transactions), returned to its January level. The significance of the $£M_3$ statistic as an indicator, however, was again questioned, this time in the light of the extremely rapid build-up of UK residents' foreign currency bank deposits, which expanded by over £700m. (after allowing for valuation changes) in banking January alone. Nevertheless, in the light of the recent monetary figures and other factors, a decision to cut MLR (from 14 per cent to 12 per cent) was taken on budget day, 10 March, and a new $£M_3$ target was announced – 6-10 per cent for the fourteen-month period from mid-February 1981 to mid-April 1982. Although the Financial Statement and Budget Report stated, 'it is the Government's intention to consider claiming back some of the past year's rapid growth of $£M_3$ by permitting an undershoot as and when the opportunity arises', the 'base drift' allowed for in the choice of February's money stock figure as the base for the new target period indicated a more pragmatic approach than the rhetoric implied.

Publication of the April banking figures, showing renewed acceleration in $£M_3$ growth (3 per cent), indicated that the target range for the February 1980 to April 1981 period (7-11 per cent) had been decisively breached. The 18½ per cent reported growth for the period, even after adjustment (perhaps by three percentage points) for corset distortions and the effects of the Civil Service pay dispute, which had inflated the figures at the end of the period as a result of delayed tax payments and correspondingly higher government borrowing, still represented a considerable overshoot. Nevertheless, monetary growth since mid-February 1981 was still held to be consistent with the new target. This remained the official view until July, despite the recorded 1½ per cent increase in May (three-quarters to one percentage point of which was attributed to the pay dispute) and the 2.2 per cent increase in July, which bracketed the freak 0.2 per cent rise reported for banking June.

The release of banking details in August 1981, which showed a 1.1 per cent jump in $£M_3$, was not accompanied by the Bank's familiar statement that the underlying increase was consistent with the prescribed target: the density of the 'fog' shrouding the statistics rendered calculations of the underlying trend unreliable.[3] For example, during banking August, at a time when seasonal factors normally give rise to a fall, sterling bank lending to the private sector rose by nearly £1.5b. (seasonally adjusted), distorted by the end of the Civil Service pay dispute, 'round-tripping' and borrowers switching from relatively expensive market sources to overdrafts. The August increase took $£M_3$ growth since the start of the latest target period (mid-February) to 17 per cent at an annual rate, compared with the target range of 6–10 per cent. The decision not to fund the displacement in the pattern of public-sector borrowing caused by the pay dispute was a major contributory (though unquantifiable) factor, as was the growth in bank lending to the private sector. Sterling bank lending to firms had risen in the spring of 1981 compared to the levels obtaining the previous winter, although the published figures did not fully reveal this because of the delays in the payment of taxes caused by the pay dispute. The subsequent improvement in the corporate sector's financial position (see below) and the reactivation of the new issue market (£0.9b. net was raised by UK companies in the six-month period to the end of calendar August) led to a fall-off in corporate loan demand, but this was more than compensated for by an increase in personal-sector lending (up 61 per cent on the previous quarter in the quarter to end-June 1980) both for house purchase (which increased by £440m., or 16 per cent, between mid-November 1980 and mid-May 1981) which, to the extent that it replaced lending by building societies, caused $£M_3$ to rise, and consumption (as the banks' share of consumer credit business was expanded). These factors, which created uncertainty in future monetary developments, led to a change of emphasis by the authorities towards the role of the exchange rate as an indicator of policy.

The rapid growth in bank lending to the personal sector continued during banking September (an increase of £1.2b. on the previous month was reported) and, together with large-scale 'unfunded' government borrowing (partly due to an increased rate of disbursement of VAT refunds compared with collections), helped $£M_3$ to grow by 2.1 per cent. This took recorded monetary growth during the first seven months of the target period to 19 per cent at an annual rate, or nearly double the top end of the target range. October's jump, of 1.7 per cent, confirmed this growth trend, but the remaining monthly banking figures for 1981 revealed a rapid deceleration: seasonally adjusted figures for $£M_3$ growth of 0.5 per cent and 0.25 per cent were recorded for the banking months to mid-November and to 9 December respectively. These results were all the more remarkable because of an explosion in bank lending to the private sector, which reached a record £2.58b. in November and amounted to just over £1b. in December. Despite continuing activity in the new issue market (the £3¼b. of new, excluding government, issues in 1981 was a record in nominal terms), part of the increase in bank loan demand came from the corporate sector, perhaps as a result of renewed cash pressures following the near completion of their rundown of stocks and the repayment of previously delayed tax dues or, in some cases, to finance restocking in anticipation of a gradual upturn in demand. To the extent that the increase in bank loan demand by the corporate sector was used to pay tax delayed by the Civil Service pay dispute, it did not contribute to monetary expansion. The remainder, perhaps a third or so of the total, came from the private sector, and was responsible for the growth in the banks' market share of both mortgage lending (up by £904m. in the three months to mid-November to a record 24 per cent, with their share of new advances at roughly 30 per cent) and consumer credit (the lowest quarterly figure for market share in 1981 was 86 per cent, compared with an average figure of 57 per cent in 1979). Apart from the obvious concern for monetary control, the authorities expressed anxiety that some mortgage lending was being used to finance consumption in the face of a sharp fall in real disposable income[4] and that the growth in personal-sector lending might 'crowd out' the corporate borrower. This led to widespread fear that controls on bank mortgage lending, similar to those applied earlier in 1981 to the Trustee Savings Bank, might be introduced, although, perhaps in an attempt to forestall this, the banks' activity in the market subsequently slackened. Despite this, a directive was eventually issued (20 January 1982) to all recognised banks and licensed deposit-taking institutions asking them to ensure that: (a) when a borrower sells his house and increases his mortgage, most of the increase is used in buying the new house or for its improvement; (b) when a mortgage is transferred from another lender without involving any property sale, its size is not normally raised unless required for home improvement. (Similar requests were made to building societies and insurance companies.) The directive thus ensured that all mortgages were henceforth applied to house purchase/improvement and stopped property vendors realising capital profits.

Although the 'improved' money supply figures were welcomed by the market, two points of concern arose. The first was a general reflection that even before excluding the increase in banks' mortgage lending (which, arguably, has the same credit effects as building society lending) on the grounds that it largely represented a diversion of loan demand away from building societies, the figures pointed to a particularly severe squeeze, which might have ruled out the modest recovery anticipated by the authorities. The second issue was more technical, however, and called into question the significance of the reported figures. The problem was that although the recorded increase in non-bank, resident-owned UK sterling bank deposits was substantially below the level of bank lending, this had been achieved, other than by collecting tax revenues and the proceeds of open-market gilt sales, by the Issue Department of the Bank of England acquiring substantial quantities of commercial bills (£1¾b. worth in November and £600m. worth in December, taking the year's purchases to nearly £4b.) and financing their purchase by running down its holdings of government stock. In this way the borrowing needs of companies were satisfied without the necessity for bank intermediation and hence an expansion in the money supply. While such activities contribute to the presentation of 'respectable' money supply figures in the short run, the danger arises, as was the case with the remarkable run-down during the 1970s by the banks of the share of government stocks within their asset portfolios (Greenwell & Co., 1981), if and when the trans- actions are subsequently reversed, which appeared likely if previous 'prudential' behaviour in backing the note issue with a higher propor- tion of government stock was anything to go on.

In spite of the above misgivings, the money supply figures at the end of 1981 held out the hope that the 6-10 per cent target for the fourteen-month period to April 1982 would not be breached by perhaps more than three or four percentage points (the actual annualised out-turn figure was 13 per cent), a considerable reduction on many previous 'informed' calculations (and hence the reason for 'merry-making', despite the further loss in credibility that would accompany yet another official failure to keep monetary growth on target!). This 'optimistic' outlook was taken in the knowledge that for the remainder of the 1981-82 financial year the PSBR would be significantly 'overfunded' (as indeed it was in the three months to mid-November to the tune of £1¾b.) as the £3½b. backlog of taxes outstanding at mid-December finally flowed to the Exchequer and the traditional tax-gathering came into play.[5] Taken in conjunc- tion with the effect of the addition to the money supply series (as from 18 November 1981) of a number of contributors whose depos- its were growing less rapidly than those of the clearers (notably the

Trustee Savings Bank), the tax factor was expected to ensure a substantial deceleration in $£M_3$ growth to take the annualised growth in the target period to mid-April 1982 to well below the 17.8 per cent (16.8 per cent on the new basis) and 15.3 per cent (new basis) figures recorded in banking November and December respectively.

## PSBR CONTROL

### *1980-81: 'blown off course'*

The first signs that the government's PSBR objective of £8½b. by the end of the 1980-81 financial year might prove elusive emerged early on in the year; by the end of the first quarter of the financial year the PSBR had already reached £4½b. Despite the above forecast level of current spending by local authorities and the higher than expected borrowing requirement of the public corporations (as anticipated by the Treasury and Civil Service Committee), this did not cause undue alarm, since the proceeds from the special asset sales, the EEC 'rebate' and payments of Petroleum Revenue Tax were not due until later in the year. Realisation that the steeper-than-expected recession and higher-than-expected debt interest payments would further augment the PSBR[6] finally forced the government's hand. Following a temporary moratorium on new defence contracts, the withdrawal of £200m. of Rate Support Grant from local government, and a moratorium on new capital spending on housing by English local authorities and, later, Scottish housing associations, more drastic measures were introduced in the November 'mini-budget'. Conceding that the 1980-81 PSBR out-turn figure was likely to be nearer £11½b. than £8½b. (it was £8b. at the end of the second quarter), with over half of the over-run ascribed to the deepening recession, the Chancellor sought to retrieve the situation[7] by: (a) cutting the defence budget by £200m.; (b) introducing a new tax on oil company revenues and raising employees' national insurance contributions (and, in the process, employers' contributions by nearly £1 b.), each of which was expected to raise £1b. during 1981-82; (c) cutting central government programmes, except health, by 2 per cent or £1b.; (d) cutting council spending by roughly 3 per cent compared with the planned level for 1980-81. All measures were to take effect from April 1981. In addition, the government suspended the Civil Service pay agreement (to avoid private-sector comparability) for 1981-82 and announced that only a 6 per cent increase in the wage bill would be allowed for in the Rate Support Grant for 1981-82. The measures were expected to yield a lower

PSBR figure for 1981-82 compared to 1980-81 and to depress the economy further during 1981-82: a GDP fall of 1½ per cent was forecast.

Between November and March 1981 a number of events conspired to raise the PSBR above the latest estimate of £11½b. to £13.2b. Of particular significance, given the Industry Secretary's known opposition to interfering in industry and particularly to supporting 'lame ducks', was the amount of government aid given to industry and the increased external financing limits (EFLs) granted to nationalised industries. During this period decisions were taken to: (a) fund Inmos, a microchip company; (b) provide British Leyland (BL) with an extra £990m., £620m. to be given in 1981 and £370m. in 1982; (c) extend the British Steel Corporation's EFL, initially by £500m. (to £6b.) and then by a further £150m. in 1980-81 and £730m. in 1981-82; (d) raise British Telecom's EFL first to £78m. and then to £223m. for 1981-82; (e) grant a £200m. loan guarantee to ICL (the computer specialists heavily involved in the supply of computer facilities to the government); (f) provide financial aid (although both offers were refused) to two other private companies, namely Talbot and Bowater. The effects of this industrial support (including the financial assistance granted to the National Coal Board) duly showed in the March 1981 White Paper expenditure review where, for example, the Department of Industry's budget for 1981-2 (excluding nationalised industries but including BL, Rolls-Royce and grants to steel and shipbuilding) was revised upwards from the March 1980 estimate by £644m. to £1554m., the continuing demands of BL and Rolls-Royce accounting for £580m. of the increase between them. The estimate for 1982-83 was similarly revised upwards, from £690m. to £1070m. (all prices expressed in terms of 1980 survey prices). Taken in conjunction with the continuing recession, these decisions not surprisingly caused a revision to the official estimates for planned public spending in 1981-82. The Chancellor's hopes (as expressed in the 'mini-budget' of November 1980) for a 1 per cent reduction in volume terms between 1980-81 and 1981-82 were dashed, and, in cash terms, the over-run was over £2b.

*1981–82: 'attempts to get back on course'*

Compared with the MTFS projection of 3.75 per cent, the actual out-turn figure of 6 per cent of GDP for the PSBR in the financial year 1980-81 represented a substantial overshoot. The estimate for 1981-82 - 5¾ per cent compared to the MTFS projection of 3 per cent - offered little consolation, although it should be stressed that 'flexibility' in the projections was admissable as long as the figures remained compatible with the £M₃ growth targets. In the March 1981 budget a PSBR of £10½b. for 1981-82 (4¼ per cent of GDP) was held to be consistent with a 6-10 per cent target (at an annualised rate) for $£M_3$ growth between February 1981 and April 1982. To this end a fiscal package was introduced, the direct effect of which was to reduce the PSBR by over £3¼b. below the level which would otherwise have obtained (assuming that non-indexation of duties, income tax allowances and thresholds would have featured under the 'old' plans). The budget measures included: (a) an increase in excise duties designed to yield £2.4b. during 1981-82; (b) a supplementary petroleum duty and changes in Petroleum Revenue Tax (both announced in the November 'mini-budget') expected to yield £1b. (net) in 1981-82; (c) a decision not to implement the 'Rooker-Wise amendment' on the indexing of income tax allowances and thresholds; (d) much to the consternation of the banks (which at the time were supporting ailing industry under the aegis of the Bank of England),[8] a once-and-for-all 'windfall' tax on banks' non-interest-bearing deposits, calculated to yield £0.4b.;[9] (e) a revised scheme for stock relief, designed to reduce the 'claw-back' of tax relief when stock levels fall,[10] which, together with capital taxation changes and new proposals to encourage enterprise, was calculated to reduce tax receipts during 1981-82 by £200m.; and (f) an increase in the contingency reserve and the EFLs of the electricity supply and gas industries which, together, were expected to boost public expenditure by £0.3b. in 1981-82.

In spite of vociferous argument to the contrary, the Financial Secretary to the Treasury claimed that the budget was not deflationary. Indeed, the deviation of the latest estimate for the PSBR as a proportion of GDP for 1981-82 (4¼ per cent) from the MTFS projection of 3 per cent was cited as an example of the government's flexibility in the face of a deeper-than-expected recession. Substantiation of the claim rested upon a belief that the demand withdrawn from the economy by the lower PSBR would be restored by virtue of stimulatory interest-rate and/or savings effects resulting from the budget. The interest-rate argument stemmed from a belief in a positive correlation between the PSBR and interest rates, higher yields being required to induce private investors to hold a higher proportion of gilts in their portfolios in order to minimise the monetary effects of financing the enlarged PSBR. A lower PSBR was therefore held to be associated with lower interest rates, which, it was hoped, would stimulate investment and perhaps the consumption component of aggregate demand. The available empirical did not provide much solace for those who expected a substantial regeneration of demand from this quarter, and at any rate it was not clear, even following the government's own line of reasoning, that the relevant rates, i.e. 'real' rates, would fall, since the budget was designed to assist movement to lower monetary growth[11] and hence lower inflation.[12] The savings argument reflected a belief in the reversibility of the phenomenon that has apparently existed in the UK since the late 1960s whereby savers, irrationally some might argue, seek to maintain the real value of their savings in the face of rising inflation. If the process is reversible, then a falling rate of inflation should induce a fall in the savings ratio, thereby boosting consumption.[13]

Within a month of the budget the Treasury had embarked on a new search for areas of public expenditure to cut in order to move the economy nearer to the 'projections' outlined in the MTFS and to enable the Conservatives to fulfil their election promise to reduce the tax burden by creating the scope for significant tax cuts at the next budget. (In practice, the March 1982 budget measures failed to achieve this, the tax burden on the average taxpayer having risen by 16¼ per cent since the Tories came to power. As the Chancellor admitted to the House of Commons on 11 March, after allowing for higher employee national insurance contributions, all but those on the highest and lowest income levels would pay more by Autumn 1982 if the Treasury's assumption of a 7½ per cent increase in income during 1982-3 proved correct.) To assist tight budgeting, the Public Expenditure Survey Committee changed its system of planning from one that revolved around 'volume' (physical quantity) plans to a new emphasis on projections based on expected cash outlay (see *Economic Progress Report,* November 1981). As a result, spending departments could not commit themselves to a particular level or volume of service because of the likelihood of changes in relative prices and costs compared to those projected in the spending plans.

In the first quarter of the 1981-82 financial year the PSBR amounted to £6.8b. (on a seasonally adjusted basis), £3.5b. of which was attributed to the Civil Service pay dispute. In view of the projections for North Sea oil receipts in the second half of the year, the figure was believed to be roughly in line with the projection for the whole year of £10.6b. The main expenditure decisions taken during the quarter (to raise the EFLs of British Telecom and the National Coal Board by a combined total of £430m. and to introduce special youth employment measures costing £150m. in 1981-82) were financed from the contingency reserve allowed for in the projection of the PSBR. By the end of the second quarter the PSBR had risen to £9.5b., approximately £4b. of which resulted from delayed receipts following the Civil Service pay dispute. Because most of this backlog was expected to be collected by March 1982, officials again asserted that the figure was in line with the March budget projection. Interpretation of the PSBR figure for October, however, was complicated by a £2b. boost to central government borrowing as a result of the decision taken to speed up VAT disbursements to companies in advance of collections.

The final attempts made during 1981 to limit future public expenditure and the PSBR were unveiled in November. The first consisted of a grand plan for the 'privatisation' or denationalisation of public corporations. In line with the Conservatives' 1979 election manifesto, British Aerospace had been 'privatised' some time earlier, but on 6 November the state-owned Cable and Wireless telecommunications group became the first body not on the manifesto list (which also included British Shipbuilders, National Freight, and subsidiaries of the National Enterprise Board) to be partially returned to the private sector, when just under half its shares were offered to the public. Other candidates known to be on the revised list included the British National Oil Corporation and the electricity, telecommunications and gas industries. Apart from an ideological appeal, the alleged benefit of 'privatisation' was that it would reduce the PSBR. This, however, is only true to the extent that the assets purchased are not financed by funds otherwise destined for the purchase of government securities, so that 'privatisation' might reasonably be regarded as just another diversified form of funding the national debt. Moreover, receipt of the sale proceeds would only bring about a once-and-for-all reduction and, in the long run, it is conceivable that the loss of revenue to the Exchequer might outweigh the short-run gains. Whatever the balance of argument, short-run political expediency won the day, and the decision of the following week to allow British Telecom to raise a £150m. bond issue in 1982, the transaction to be excluded from the PSBR, demonstrated the government's determination to press on with its 'privatisation' plans.

The second move arose out of fears that public spending in 1982-83 might rise by as much as £7b. above the £110b. planned for under the March 1980 White Paper. The overspending was expected to result from the deeper-than-expected recession, higher-than-forecast debt charges, the special employment measures outlined in July, and higher-than-anticipated inflation. Although the rise in spending would be accompanied by unexpectedly heavy tax receipts - perhaps £3b. more than anticipated - Treasury officials sought to limit the overshoot in spending in order to create more room for tax cuts in the 1982 budget. In the event, a £5b. overshoot in cash terms was sanctioned. The announcement of these revised plans on 2 December indicated where the extra finance would go: current expenditure by local authorities (£1.35b.); defence spending

(£480m.); employment and training measures (£800m.); increases in nationalised industries' EFLs (£1.3b.). The £6b. overshoot in spending was to be offset by £1b. of savings to accrue from higher prescription charges, a reduction in the real value of student grants and social security payments, and a squeeze on public administration costs. The increase in the social security budget arising from the uprating of pension payments (£1.5b.) and the expected further rise in the level of unemployment were to be financed from higher employee national insurance contribution rates.[14] In terms of their likely impact on the PSBR, the revised plans were expected to yield a figure for 1982-83 of roughly £9b. or just over 3 per cent of GDP.

This implied, however, an increase in public spending in volume terms compared to 1981-82, contrary to earlier government intentions. Nevertheless, the government remained hopeful that it could meet its borrowing 'targets' for two successive years (in the event, the 1981-82 PSBR 'target' was undershot by £1.9b.) although the merit of such a performance is none too clear, for the 'base drift' allowed for in the setting of £$M_3$ targets and the subsequent failure to meet them render the original PSBR projections outlined in the MTFS meaningless. After all, the PSBR projections were meant to be compatible with *lower* rates of £$M_3$ growth than those that actually transpired, and cuts in the PSBR as a proportion of GDP were supposed to contribute to controlling monetary growth and hence inflation. As such, they were a means to an end rather than a policy goal, and the marked difference in the extent to which the out-turn figures for £$M_3$ growth and the PSBR (as a proportion of GDP) deviated from their planned levels only serves to illustrate how tenuous the short-run PSBR/£$M_3$ relationship really is.

As part of the government's anti-inflation policy the MTFS now functions in a void and, despite the amendments made in March 1982 (see Postscript, pp. 154-5), credibility in the strategy can hardly be at a lower ebb. The retention of monetary targets (though revised for £$M_3$) and PSBR projections in the face of a political desire for interest-rate and exchange-rate 'objectives' and a willingness, on the part of the monetary authorities, to conduct policy in the light of movements in a series of both real and financial indicators, reflects a fundamental revision to the government's previous views on how the transmission mechanism of monetary policy is supposed to work, rendering policy unintelligible (Hall, 1982).

## THE 'COSTS' OF THE MTFS

It is, of course, extremely difficult to isolate the effects of domestic policy conduct from international influences bearing upon the development of the economy. Nevertheless, some of the more obvious contributions made by internal policy decision-taking (in the name of the MTFS) to the domestic economic climate may be analysed. The data relating to the major economic indicators presented in Table 8.3 overleaf facilitate this task.

The striking features of the output series (at constant factor cost) are the depth of recession experienced in 1980 – GDP fell by 5.2 per cent, total industrial production by 11.6 per cent and manufacturing production by 16 per cent (5.9 per cent in the fourth quarter), the largest annual fall recorded since the 1930s – and the slowness of recovery in 1981. Although the rate of decline decelerated in the first quarter of 1981, despite the direct and indirect effects of the steel strike, and manufacturing production actually rose by 0.7 per cent in the second quarter, GDP was still down by 1.1 per cent for the half-year period as a whole. Moreover, despite the slight rise (0.3 per cent) in GDP and the 1½ per cent jump in manufacturing production recorded in the third quarter, which suggested that the worst of the recession was over, industrial output during 1981 was 5 per cent less than in 1980, and manufacturing production remained about 14 per cent below the average for 1979. A sustained recovery was dependent upon a continued slowdown in industrial destocking and further improvements in competitiveness.

A major factor influencing the development of the 'real' UK economy in 1980 was undoubtedly the serious loss of competitiveness that domestic producers experienced as a result of a relatively high domestic inflation rate and the appreciation in sterling in 1979 and 1980. Although the **petro-currency** status of sterling was certainly a determining factor, so also were the government's monetarist policies, which were at least partially responsible for the relatively high level of interest rates in the UK – real and nominal – and indirectly boosted the demand for sterling by providing foreign investors with an assurance that the administration's anti-inflation policy would not lack resolve. Beyond this, the government contributed directly to depressing demand through discretionary cuts in the PSBR and by inducing a slow-down in the rate of flow of interest-sensitive expenditures.

The exchange rate series presented in Table 8.3 indicates the extent of sterling's appreciation in 1979 and 1980. In terms of the effective exchange rate, sterling appreciated during 1979 by some 10 per cent (4½ per cent in terms of the ECU basket) which, together with a relatively high domestic inflation rate, resulted in a 20 per cent loss of competitiveness in terms of relative normalised unit labour costs.[15] This was followed in 1980 by a further 13 per cent appreciation in effective terms (10.7 per cent against the US

116

TABLE 8.3 Indicators of economic 'performance' (April 1979–December 1981)

| Indicator variable | 1979 II | 1979 III | 1979 IV | 1980 I | 1980 II | 1980 III | 1980 IV | 1981 I | 1981 II | 1981 III | 1981 IV |
|---|---|---|---|---|---|---|---|---|---|---|---|
| **Output at constant factor cost†¹** | | | | | | | | | | | |
| GDP | 112.1 | 110.0 | 110.6 | 109.8 | 108.1 | 106.3 | 104.7 | 104.3 | 103.7 | 104.0 | 104.8 |
| Total industrial production | 115.2 | 112.8 | 112.6 | 110 | 106.8 | 103.3 | 99.5 | 98.8 | 98.5 | 100.3 | 99.0 |
| Manufacturing production | 107.5 | 103.6 | 104.4 | 100.4 | 97.4 | 93.4 | 87.9 | 87.6 | 88.2 | 90.3 | 88.1 |
| **GDFCF at 1975 prices (£m.)†** | | | | | | | | | | | |
| Total | 5196 | 5281 | 5363 | 5356 | 5205 | 5141 | 5059 | 4818 | 4921 | 4798 | 4839 |
| Private sector | 3528 | 3531 | 3700 | 3708 | 3533 | 3546 | 3540 | 3366 | 3480 | 3583 | 3594 |
| General government | 809 | 876 | 814 | 768 | 750 | 726 | 688 | 629 | 566 | 441 | 457 |
| Gross fixed investment in manufacturing at 1975 prices (£m.)† | 987.9 | 987.0 | 1004.1 | 958.6 | 917.9 | 892.7 | 808.1 | 781.2 | 760.4 | 726.1 | 700.6 |
| UK unemployed (excl. school leavers) (000s)† | 1305.2 | 1266.8 | 1287.1 | 1373.9 | 1497.7 | 1699.0 | 2019.8 | 2304.4 | 2506.4 | 2627.1 | 2781.6 |
| UK unemployment rate†² | 5.4 | 5.2 | 5.3 | 5.7 | 6.2 | 7.0 | 8.4 | 9.5 | 10.4 | 10.9 | 11.4 |
| Retail Price Index | 11.4 | 16.5 | 17.2 | 19.8 | 21.0 | 15.9 | 15.1 | 12.6 | 11.3 | 11.4 | 12.0 |
| Tax and Price Index (year on year % change) | 13.8 | 14.1 | 14.9 | 17.6 | 17.4 | 17.3 | 16.4 | 13.4 | 14.9 | 14.9 | 15.6 |
| **Average earnings (GB)†³** | | | | | | | | | | | |
| Economy (% increase on previous year in brackets) | 146.6 (13.4) | 153.9 (15.7) | 161.8 (18.5) | 168.8 (19.7) | 178.0 (21.4) | 188.1 (22.2) | 193.3 (19.5) | 196.5 (16.5) | 201.2 (13.0) | 209.6 (11.4) | 216.5 (10.1) |
| Manufacturing | 152.7 (15.4) | 155.0 (13.8) | 166.2 (18.1) | 170.6 (17.3) | 179.9 (17.8) | 188.3 (21.4) | 191.3 (15.1) | 196.9 (15.4) | 200.5 (11.5) | 212 (12.6) | 216.6 (12.5) |
| Exchange rate: effective¹ | 87.0 | 91.3 | 88.5 | 93.0 | 94.5 | 96.7 | 100.2 | 101.4 | 97.8 | 90.6 | 89.7 |
| $ | 2.081 | 2.234 | 2.157 | 2.254 | 2.286 | 2.382 | 2.387 | 2.309 | 2.079 | 1.839 | 1.905 |
| Gross trading profits of industrial and commercial companies (£m.)†⁴ | 7518 | 7826 | 8147 | 8091 | 7136 | 6353 | 6549 | 6886 | 7266 | 7880 | 8713 |
| Financial surplus/deficit of industrial and commercial companies (£m.)⁵ | −77 | −747 | −1357 | −988 | −679 | −1698 | 423 | 574 | 1450 | 112 | −479 |

† Seasonally adjusted.
¹ 1975 = 100.
² Numbers unemployed (excluding school leavers) expressed as a percentage of estimate of 'unemployed plus employed'.
³ January 1976 = 100.
⁴ Before providing for depreciation and stock appreciation.
⁵ Saving plus capital transfers less gross domestic fixed capital formation (GDFCF) less increase in value of stocks and work in progress.
Source: *Economic Trends*, Annual Supplement, 1982, pp. 55, 58, 86, 105, 109, 113, 118, 145 and 176; December 1981 issue.

dollar). Despite the 9 per cent fall between December 1980 and August 1981 (as a result of the availability of higher real interest rates in the USA and West Germany, lower dollar oil prices and the erosion of the previous year's massive surplus on current account) cost competitiveness improved by only 10 per cent, representing perhaps one-fifth of the loss experienced during the previous two years.

The induced fall in investment is evident from the data series for real gross domestic fixed capital formation (GDFCF). Total quarterly GDFCF fell (by 10 per cent) continuously in the five quarters to March 1981, the steepest fall occurring in the first quarter of 1981 – 19 per cent at an annual rate. The rate of decline of the private sector's component was less marked (9 per cent over the same period) but gross fixed investment in manufacturing was severely curtailed: in the same five-quarter period it fell by 22 per cent, and, in contrast to the other two indicators, it continued to fall (by a further 2.5 per cent) during the second quarter of 1981. The worst effects, however, were felt in the investment areas of housebuilding (Fleming and Nellis, 1982) and public services. At 220,000, housing starts in 1979 were at their lowest level for thirty years, and the October 1980 moratorium on public-sector housing expenditure contributed during the first quarter of 1981 to a halving of the rate of housebuilding experienced in the mid-1970s. Despite the strong revival (from a very low base) in private-sector housing in the first quarter of 1981, both total housing starts and the number of houses under construction declined in the second quarter of 1981, causing the figure for total UK investment in housebuilding to fall to its lowest level since 1960. For 1981 as a whole, total housing starts fell to their lowest level (153,000) since the 1920s, the 33 per cent drop in public-sector housing starts (following 31 per cent and 25 per cent falls in the previous two years) outweighing the 18,500 increase in private-sector starts. House completions in 1981 were also down in both the public and private sectors, as was the number of improvement grants made by the government.

Real GDFCF by general government fell continuously throughout the two-year period to end-June 1981. The registered fall was 35.4 per cent or 17.7 per cent at an annual rate, with the steepest rate of decline occurring in the second quarter of 1981 (40 per cent at an annual rate).

Appalling as they were, the output and fixed investment figures were overshadowed by the unemployment statistics. From a seasonally adjusted level of 1,266,800 (excluding school leavers) at the end of September 1979, which represented 5.2 per cent of the working population, unemployment rose continuously (on a quarterly basis) to 2,781,600 by the end of 1981, which in unadjusted terms was 2,940,700 or 12.2 per cent of the working population. If allowance is made for special employment measures, the unregistered and those who left the labour force despairing of ever finding a job and so gave up searching, the figure rises to nearer four million than three.[16] Moreover, given the underlying trend of a rise of 35,000 a month, most forecasters predicted that at least a further 500,000 would be added to the unemployment register during 1982, despite the steady improvement in the availability of job vacancies, and that unemployment would remain above the three million mark for a further three years or more.

The final problem area of the economy illustrated in Table 8.3 is the plight of the industrial and commercial sector. During the first three quarters of 1980 gross trading profits, in nominal terms, plummeted by 22 per cent (and by considerably more if North Sea activities are excluded), while the financial deficit rose to £1.7b. The combination of relatively high domestic cost inflation, deteriorating competitiveness and tight fiscal and monetary policies was responsible for both the slump in profits (the real rate of return, net of stock appreciation and depreciation, on non-North Sea operations declined to 4¼ per cent in the first half of 1980 compared to 4¾ per cent in the second half of 1979 and roughly 5¼ per cent in the recession of the mid-1970s) and, despite the cut-back in investment and stock-building, the growth in the financial deficit.[17] By the fourth quarter of 1980 the real rate of return on non-North Sea operations had fallen to 2 per cent, the level at which it remained during the first half of 1981. The subsequent improvement in the financial position of industrial and commercial companies resulted from further destocking, cut-backs in investment and manpower, a reduction in the extension of trade credit, an improvement in competitiveness, lower domestic interest rates and the reduction in the 'claw-back' of stock relief.

Having analysed the 'costs' of the MTFS, it is now time to assess the 'gains' made on the inflation front, for which the 'real' sacrifices were made. The striking features of the RPI index are the acceleration in inflation (particularly in the third quarter of 1979 because of the June budget increase in VAT) that occurred between end-March 1979 and end-June 1980, and the subsequent deceleration in the period to end-June 1981 (particularly in the third quarter of 1980 when the effect of the previous year's VAT increase disappeared from the index). Towards the end of 1981 the year-on-year change in the RPI stabilised at the 12 per cent level. In view of the severity of the depression, induced in the name of anti-inflation policy, this appears a particularly inauspicious achievement in both absolute and

relative terms. After two and a half years in power, the Tory administration had failed to lower inflation below the 10.2 per cent level
they inherited (this was not achieved until April 1982) and at
December 1981 Britain's inflation rate was higher than both the
OECD (11.6 per cent) and EEC (9.9 per cent) averages. Part of the
problem lay in the risks the government assumed in raising excise
duties (which introduced a once-and-for-all jump) and sanctioning
increases in public-sector charges (including rents and rates) in order
to reduce the PSBR, decisions which allowed for an acceleration in
inflation in the short run in the hope of a realisation of longer-run
gains. (A similar trade-off resulted from the mortgage-rate repercussions of any interest-rate hike engineered in the name of monetary
control.) Although a tax and price index (TPI) was introduced to
take account of *direct* tax changes, by providing a measure of the
increase in gross income needed to compensate taxpayers for any
rise in prices, this was conveniently dropped from official speeches
once it had risen above the RPI. The restraining effect of policy on
average earnings is evident from the fourth quarter of 1980, the
effect being greater in the manufacturing sector than for the economy
as a whole as a result of its greater exposure to foreign competition.
A comparison between the trend in TPI and average earnings figures
from the second quarter of 1981 indicates the extent of the squeeze
on real 'take-home' pay. The official inflation forecast for 1982,
given at the end of 1981, was 10 per cent, which represented yet
another departure from earlier MTFS projections.

In conclusion, in so far as the UK experienced a steeper recession
than most Western economies yet failed to reduce inflation in
relative terms, the Tory administration is open to the criticism of
mismanagement of the economy. A benign neglect of the exchange
rate, although containing inflationary pressures, led to a benign
neglect of domestic output and employment.[18] Obsession with
PSBR objectives, which were responsible for large cut-backs in public
investment (particularly in housing, which was asked to absorb three-
quarters of the planned expenditure cuts in the four-year period to
1983-4) aggravated the depression. While many argue that the
authorities cannot influence the (real) exchange rate, except in the
very short term, the latter obviously do not agree: witness the
official attempts to stem the fall in the effective rate of sterling in
the autumn of 1981. Likewise, apostles of the 'vertical long-run
Phillips curve' school (e.g. Brittan, 1981, ch.III) warn against demand
intervention to reduce unemployment because of their view of the
final outcome, i.e. higher inflation and higher unemployment, as
eventually steps have to be taken to reduce inflationary expectations.
Governments, therefore, are advised to remove 'labour-market

distortions' (often used as a euphemism for 'union bashing') if they are unhappy with the prevailing **natural rate of unemployment**.[19]

Unfortunately for the government, the significance of some of the distortions often alluded to in ministerial speeches looked distinctly suspect under close examination, as was the case with the official claims that many workers had 'priced themselves out of jobs' because prevailing real wages (maintained by union pressure) were too high, while others refused to work because the real value of benefit levels was too 'high'.[20] This is not to deny that improvements in mobility and reductions in overmanning in some industries, for example, are not desirable, but rather that each should be considered on its own merits. Sweeping generalisations, however, do little good and only serve to harden attitudes. Given the real 'costs' experienced in the UK's 'gradualist experiment', which will not be 'willed away' by 'rational expectations' exponents, and even accepting the natural-rate diagnosis, surely a further attempt to secure tripartite agreement on incomes and a possible reform of wage bargaining is necessary, if for no other reason than that the government can ill afford to do without it given the parlous state of the economy. Although welcome, the much heralded improvement in productivity[21] (though not necessarily in productive *potential*) that has resulted from a slimmer labour force, general commercial reaction to domestic and world depression, and persistent exposure to fierce international competition[22] provides little ground for optimism, for it has been achieved at the expense of undermining the productive capacity of the economy and an increase in long-term unemployment. In any case, it fails to tackle the basic problem of reducing the insupportable costs of anti-inflation policy.

With regard to nominal PSBR objectives, which stood in a void (in both a political and statistical sense) in relation to $£M_3$ targets at the end of 1981, one should be aware of their deficiencies as indicators of the pressure imposed on financial markets by public-sector activities. To the extent that it includes net lending to other sectors and net purchases of financial assets, the PSBR is likely to *overstate* the real pressures imposed on inflation and interest rates (although the exclusion of maturing public-sector debt works in the other direction). For example, in recent years the public-sector financial deficit (PSFD), which excludes loans, transactions in financial assets and similar transactions, has usually been lower than the PSBR because of the public sector's net lending to, and net purchases of financial assets from, the private sector. But public-sector borrowing from the private sector to finance these transactions is likely to have little net impact on financial markets.[23] In a similar vein, 'privatisation' plans that reduce the PSBR will cause the latter to *understate* the resultant pressures to the extent that the sale of public-sector assets to the private sector simply replaces sales of public-sector debt that would otherwise have been made. Changes in the composition of portfolios and concomitant shifts in yield patterns are unlikely to affect this result seriously.

Looking beyond purely monetary considerations of fiscal policy, there are strong grounds for arguing in favour of a 'cyclically adjusted' PSBR to reflect the fact that nominal PSBR figures will automatically rise and fall according to whether the economy is in a period of recession or boom. Adjustment for the recent recession indicates that Britain has become the most restrictive of all the major industrialised nations on the fiscal front and that *discretionary* cuts in the PSBR have been used to override automatic stabilisers in the economy. Finally, adjusting the nominal PSBR figures for the effects of inflation, which erodes the capital value of debt holdings and reduces the real burden to debt issuers, provides a remarkably different picture from that portrayed by ministers (Miller, 1982). Indeed, if one removes the gain to the government, as an issuer, by assuming that all its debt interest payments merely represent compensation for capital loss to debt holders (which implies an exclusion of debt charges from the PSBR), then since 1979 the UK has, in fact, run a budget *surplus*. Moreover, this makes no allowance for the effect of the recession! Clearly, then, there are a number of grounds on which the appropriateness of the nominal PSBR as an indicator may be seriously challenged.

# 9 The 'New' Monetary Arrangements

## CHANGES IN THE TECHNIQUES OF MONETARY CONTROL

The new arrangements for monetary control, which took effect from 20 August 1981, were set out in the Bank's paper entitled 'Monetary control - provisions' (*BEQB*, September 1981, p.347) and followed discussions on two of their earlier documents: 'Background note on methods of monetary control' (*BEQB*, December 1980, p.428) and 'Monetary control: next steps' (*BEQB*, March 1981, p.38). The main proposals were:

(1) The establishment of a new *monetary sector* (to replace the UK banking sector) to include all recognised banks and licensed deposit-taking institutions (LDTs), the National Girobank, banks in the Channel Islands and the Isle of Man which opt to accede to the new monetary provisions, the Trustee Savings Banks (TSBs) and the Banking Department of the Bank of England. The TSBs were expected to account for approximately three-quarters of the resultant increase (£8b. or 10 per cent) in £M$_3$.

(2) The imposition of a non-operational cash requirement of ½ per cent of eligible liabilities (ELs) on all those institutions falling within the monetary sector whose liabilities average £10m. or more in the latest period over which the requirement is calculated. (ELs were redefined to allow offsets for funds, other than cash ratio deposits or special deposits placed with the Bank, lent by one institution within the monetary sector to another and for appropriately secured money-at-call placed with money brokers and gilt-edged jobbers.)[1] This uniform ratio was designed to secure resources and income for the Bank, the volume of clearing bank balances voluntarily held at the Bank for the settlement of inter-bank indebtedness henceforth to serve as the fulcrum for money market management (previously represented by the London clearing banks' 1½ per cent bankers' deposits ratio). Concessions were granted to institutions whose principal place of business in the UK was Northern Ireland (the ratio was reduced to ¼ per cent for an initial trial period of two years) and to institutions not on the previous statistical list of banks which

122

experienced transitional problems. To discourage institutions from artificially depressing their ELs on reporting dates, the Bank reserved the right to make spot checks on non-reporting days.

(3) An extension in the range of banks, to include foreign banks for the first time, whose acceptances are eligible for discount at the Bank. This proposal was necessary to ensure that a sufficient supply of bills was available to the Bank to facilitate its open market operations in bills.[2] To achieve 'eligibility' status for its acceptances an institution had to agree to maintain secured money with members of the LDMA and/or secured call money with money brokers and gilt-edged jobbers sufficient to ensure that: (a) such funds normally averaged 6 per cent of its ELs; (b) the level of secured money lent to the LDMA did not normally fall below 4 per cent of its ELs on any day. Arrangements were put in hand to allow the Bank to monitor each institution's performance on this front. The requirements were necessary to ensure, first, that an adequate supply of funds continued to be made available to the discount market, the maker of the market in bills (through which most of the open market transactions would pass),[3] and second, that the Stock Exchange money brokers and gilt-edged jobbers received sufficient funds to allow for the continued efficient functioning of the gilt-edged market.

(4) The retention of the special deposits scheme (though it remained in abeyance) which applied, in the form of a uniform call for deposits as a percentage of ELs, to all institutions with ELs of £10m. or more at the latest make-up day for which figures were available.

(5) The abolition of the minimum reserve assets ratio, although those institutions previously subject to it had to discuss with the Bank, in advance, any intended changes in the composition of their liquidity or in their liquidity management policies. This latter measure was designed as a stop-gap to ensure adequate prudential regulation until agreement was reached with the institutions on a form of prudential control that would prove both practicable and effective.[4]

(6) The suspension of the minimum lending rate (MLR). Although MLR was no longer to be 'posted' on a continuous basis, the Bank reserved the right 'in some circumstances [to] announce in advance the minimum rate which, for a short period ahead, it would apply in any lending to the market'.

The moves were designed to allow the market a more important role (though how much more is open to debate) in the determination of short-term interest rates and to be consistent with further evolution in the direction of monetary base control. They also reflected an acknowledgement of the deficiencies of direct quantitative controls (i.e. they were distortive, ineffective, resources were misallocated, etc.), as interest-rate policy remained the sole weapon in the authorities' armoury for the fight against monetary expansion (assuming a political acceptance of the limits to which the size of the PSBR could be pared without damaging the social and economic fabric of a democratic society).

Whether or not the new framework of monetary control would prove to be 'superior' to the previous system would depend on its capacity for improving the authorities' ability to meet prescribed $£M_3$ targets and the extent to which the Bank (presumably under the direction of government ministers) allowed interest rates to perform their market-clearing function. Gains on the first front might accrue as a result of: (a) a reduction in 'hard arbitrage' induced by bank attempts either to link overdraft rates to money market rates[5] or run down overdraft facilities in favour of fixed-rate term loans;[6] (b) the stimulus given to the commercial bill market (an alternative to bank finance for commercial borrowers) when market shortages are relieved through open-market bill purchases (thereby causing bill yields to fall) and not **discount window** lending; (c) discount houses raising the effective marginal cost of money to the banks by extracting, perhaps at the instigation of the authorities, more favourable rates on the secured bank loans required under the new arrangements. The scale of benefits deriving from these sources, however, hinges on the second factor, namely the extent to which, *in practice,* the Bank will be guided solely by $£M_3$ considerations in formulating its money-market intervention plans. The new arrangements *per se* would appear to have little to offer in the way of improving the efficacy of control over autonomous bank credit creation and hence monetary growth.

The basis of the new system was laid in November 1980 with the switch in the authorities' official money-market operations away from discount window lending and towards open-market transactions in bills. The interest-rate decisions taken then, however, did not augur well for the future – at least from a monetarist standpoint.[7] On 24 November, in spite of the recent surge in $£M_3$ growth, MLR was cut from 16 per cent to 14 per cent. The decision was justified on the grounds that sterling bank lending to the private sector was moderating (it amounted to £2.5b. in the three-month period to mid-October, compared with £3.2b. in the previous three months), that the PSBR was expected to be substantially lower, at £3½b., in the second half of the financial year, and that policy was in danger of becoming unduly restrictive – witness the rise in *real* interest rates. The MLR cut followed two months of action by the authorities to prevent interest rates from rising: the **purchase-resale agreements** due to expire on 8 and 15 September were extended first to 6 and 13 October respectively, then to 7 and 17 November and finally to 24 November and 3 December; and general assistance was provided through the purchase of Treasury, local authority and commercial bills, mainly on a purchase-resale basis. By early December, however, all the special schemes for assistance had been unwound.

The transition to the present-day system of official money-market operations was a gradual, evolutionary process. The first attempt to facilitate the change in emphasis towards open-market operations in bills was made in August 1980 when the authorities announced that bids of over £50m. from outside the discount market at the Treasury bill tender were likely to be overlooked. This was a deliberate move to concentrate the ownership of bills in the hands of the discount market rather than the banks to accommodate the switch in intervention tactics away from discount window lending. The Bank also made it clear that any assistance provided at the discount window would only be available on less advantageous terms than hitherto. Further to this, the Bank modified its conventional structure of dealing rates in Treasury bills, to encourage discount houses to relieve their cash shortages by selling bills to the Bank, and abandoned the practice of quoting prices at which it would buy bills with over one month to maturity.[8] The latter policy was designed to allow the market a greater say in the determination of the structure of short-term interest rates. To encourage the issue of commercial bills[9] and to avoid worsening an already severe reserve asset squeeze, the Bank increased the proportion of open-market purchases in the form of eligible bank bills rather than Treasury or local authority bills. Moreover, purchases of eligible bank bills were usually made on an outright rather than a purchase-and-resale basis to avoid imposing an indirect constraint on the creation of reserve assets for the banking system. This proved necessary because the discount houses' undefined assets multiple limited their holdings of private-sector assets, including eligible bills, which made them reluctant to replace bills sold to the Bank on a resale basis by buying more bills in the market, since they were uncertain as to whether or not the Bank would roll forward the agreements when they matured.

From the end of February the Bank renewed its practice of providing assistance through bill purchase-resale agreements whenever cash shortages proved too large to be relieved through outright purchases. In so doing the Bank extended its range of options for the provision of cash to the market since some holders were not willing to sell outright in anticipation of interest-rate falls and hence of making capital gains on their eligible bill holdings. At the end of March the Bank terminated its practice of quoting prices at which it would buy or sell bills of under one month to maturity and asked those offering bills of under one month to maturity to quote separate prices for bills of up to fourteen days. As a result the Bank became free, over the whole range of maturities, to choose what offers to accept, if any, and the market was allowed more influence in the determination of very short interest rates. Finally, in May, the Bank increased the undefined assets multiple imposed on discount houses from twenty to twenty-five times their capital and reserves in order to raise their potential holdings of eligible bank bills which the Bank could buy if necessary. The decision was taken in the light of an expected severe cash shortage in the market following the end of the Civil Service pay dispute.

With the aid of these modifications to money-market operations, the authorities sought to influence very short-term interest rates (say up to two weeks) while allowing the market a greater say in the determination of longer-term rates. It soon became clear, although it had been the case for most of 1980, that $£M_3$ considerations would not be the sole (or often the main) factor determining official interest-rate policy. The year started with an attempt to forestall interest-rate rises as a result of the start of the tax-paying season through a reduction, on 5 January, in the reserve assets ratio from 12½ per cent to 10 per cent. This was followed four days later by a reduction in the amount of Treasury bills offered each week at the tender from £200m. (the level to which it had fallen following a similar £100m. reduction the previous August) to £100m. The rationale for this was to obviate the need for official open-market purchases whenever Treasury bills were sold in conditions of serious cash shortage. At the same time the Bank suspended the requirement whereby at least 15 per cent of the security lodged against a loan from the Bank had to be in the form of Treasury bills. Renewed pressure on very short rates in March, following heavy payments of Petroleum Revenue Tax (PRT), led to a further cut in the reserve assets ratio to 8 per cent. Initially intended to remain at this level between 2 and 10 March, it in fact went unaltered until 30 April.

The first adjustment to MLR occurred on 10 March when it was cut from 14 per cent to 12 per cent. On this occasion it was possible to argue that the change was consistent with $£M_3$ developments, since although annualised growth remained well outside the target range, it had decelerated sharply since the summer of 1980: in the four months to mid-February $£M_3$ grew by 4¼ per cent compared with 10¾ per cent in the previous four months. Other factors taken into account were the improving profile of the PSBR, the slow-down in bank lending to the private sector, and the rise in real interest rates as a consequence of the fall in the inflation rate. In the week prior to and on the days immediately following the MLR cut, assistance was provided, including discount window lending (at MLR on 2 and 10 March and at rates above MLR on 12 March and three further occasions) to prevent short money-market rates diverging from base rates to a degree sufficient to induce round-tripping. These instances of discount window lending were the first to occur since the previous Christmas and were justified on the grounds that the scale of assistance required could not have been provided through open-market purchases.

During the third quarter of 1981 the Bank became increasingly concerned with the fall in the exchange rate (both against the US dollar and in effective terms) and its money-market intervention tactics reflected this. A substantial fall in the 'underlying' level of official foreign exchange reserves in the second quarter provided evidence of earlier attempts to support the pound, and in July interest-rate policy was asked to make a contribution: 'In the face of the weakening of sterling in early July, the necessity for some increase in rates was accepted: thereafter market pressures, mostly making for higher rates, were resisted' (*BEQB*, September 1981, p.312). Such action reflected the authorities' overriding concern with the short-run inflationary dangers of a falling exchange rate (i.e. higher import prices) rather than with the need for urgent restraint of $£M_3$ growth in search of greater price stability in the medium to long term. Thus on 6 July, following a rejection of the bids made by the discount houses for a three-day purchase-and-resale agreement (they were deemed too low), the Bank lent for one week at 12¼ per cent, ¼ per cent above MLR. Towards the end of the month the stance of policy was reversed when in order to alleviate expected cash shortages the size of the Treasury bill tender for ninety-one-day bills was reduced to £100m.[10] and that for 1 September bills from £250m. to £100m.

During the two-month period to mid-September the Bank's intervention tactics in the money markets demonstrated a curious desire to satisfy money-supply, interest-rate and exchange-rate objectives simultaneously. Inter-bank rates for one month's money and longer were held two percentage points or more above MLR in an attempt to boost demand for sterling (which had sagged due to declining world oil prices, high US interest rates and waning international confidence in Britain's economic policies) without worsening the financial plight of industry. It was hoped that by holding down the rates on seven-day deposits relative to those for three months, round-tripping would be averted, as few would run the risk of a rise in base rates by holding anything other than a very short-term deposit. In the event, $£M_3$ accelerated (partly as a result of companies' drawing on overdrafts to pay the backlog of taxes rather than running down their money-market investments) and sterling came under further selling pressure, with the result that the authorities finally intervened (on 14 September) to engineer a rise of just over one percentage point in short-term rates by lending £77m. overnight to the discount market at 13¾ per cent. The action was designed to reduce the inflationary pressures associated with a falling exchange rate (particularly against 'hard' EMS currencies) and rising bank lending to the private sector, and as such was not incompatible with the pursuance of monetary targets, although the precedent of intervention in open support of sterling caused unease amongst some of the government's monetarist supporters. Within two days, clearing bank base rates had risen by 2 per cent, demolishing in the process the government's budget hopes of a regeneration of demand through interest-rate channels. The response of sterling to the government's initiative was initially encouraging but within a week the rising strength of the Deutschmark created renewed anxieties.

A rough indication of the extent of official support for sterling may be gauged from the size of the 'underlying' fall in foreign exchange reserves, which was $677m. in September. This followed successive falls of $388m., $438m. and $29m. in June, July and August respectively, and was in stark contrast to the $200m. average increases registered in the last three months of 1980 and the $3b. increase recorded for the thirteen-month period to mid-November 1980. The figures, betokening intervention, clearly demonstrated that the government had to some extent abandoned its earlier agnosticism, embodied within its 'smoothing' operations, towards the determination of the exchange rate, but no formal external objectives were announced. Instead, a pragmatic approach was instigated which involved (at different times and to differing degrees) concerns about the pound/dollar, pound/Deutschmark and trade-weighted-average exchange rates. In September 1981 increasing emphasis was given to the role of the effective exchange rate as a short-term indicator, given the obscurity surrounding monetary developments in the economy and in $£M_3$ in particular. But still the market was left guessing as to what the standard was, thereby denying businessmen stability of expectations. The question of Britain's entry to the EMS was again raised but rejected on the grounds[11] that: (a) sterling, as a petrocurrency, was unsuited to membership because of its vulnerability to movements in world oil prices; (b) instability in the EMS itself might be imminent because of the weakness of the French franc and other members' currencies and the divergence of member countries' inflation rates; (c) it might involve greater intervention than before on the part of the Bank and would run the risk that defence against upward movements would jeopardise the achievement of monetary targets; (d) despite the downward adjustment in sterling from its peak, 'overvalued' level and a lower domestic inflation rate, there is no way of ascertaining the 'correct' level to peg at. These disadvantages were deemed to outweigh the political benefits and economic gains that would have derived from linking sterling to the Deutschmark bloc countries (which, in November 1981, accounted for 54 per cent of Britain's foreign trade) in the form of greater stability for trade and industry and the establishment of a comprehensible, external, anti-inflation discipline in support of the government's internal policies.

The strengthening of sterling after the rise in market rates on 14 September was short-lived, as interest rates in the USA continued to climb. As a result UK market interest rates rose in the face of little resistance from the authorities, followed by a further two percentage points jump in base rates on 1 October. Market sentiment subsequently improved, following a decline in interest rates in the USA and, later, West Germany, allowing for a ½ per cent cut in base rates, but in the latter half of October sterling again came under attack. The upward movement in domestic rates was resisted by the authorities, however. The fall in US rates at the end of October once again eased the pressure on sterling, and the decline in UK market rates was initially accommodated by the authorities (a further ½ per cent cut in base rates was made on 9 November). However, owing to the uncertainty surrounding domestic monetary developments, the Bank subsequently acted to slow the rate of decline, lending overnight through the discount window on 16 November at $15\frac{1}{8}$ per cent, one-eighth of a percentage point above the clearing banks' base rates. Nevertheless, a further fall (½ per cent) in base rates was registered on 3 December. The underlying fall of $225m. in official foreign exchange reserves during October indicated that intervention on the foreign exchanges had been used to complement (and perhaps, latterly, as a substitute for) interest-rate policy, while the $147m. increase in November reflected the marked turnaround in sterling's fortunes.

The conduct of policy in the last quarter of 1981 served to illustrate how vulnerable the UK and other European countries were to policies implemented by a US administration determined to cure inflation through control of the money supply. Unlike in the UK, the brand of monetarism administered by the Federal Reserve was of a purer form, which entailed a free float of the dollar and a level and structure of interest rates consistent with the meeting of pre-specified targets for monetary aggregate growth. As a result, fluctuations in US interest rates conditioned policy-making in Europe, with insulation of domestic financial markets from international influences proving impossible except in the very short run. Nevertheless the UK attempt to 'de-politicise' the determination of short-term interest rates left much to be desired.

# Reflections

The history of UK monetary policy over the last decade or so strongly suggests that a fundamental revision of attitudes to its alleged potency is now in order. It has become clear, if it wasn't already so, that *effective* monetary control is extremely difficult, if not impossible, to achieve in a competitive financial system within a 'democratic', open economy. The conduct of policy through the systematic control of arbitrarily chosen monetary aggregates is palpably insufficient for the control of inflation. Technical control problems abound. For example, 'direct' controls, as well as being distortive and responsible for a misallocation of resources, can be readily avoided (*any* effective direct control provides 'disintermediation' incentives), particularly in an economy free of exchange control. Interest-rate control is deficient in the sense that it is likely to affect broad monetary aggregates perversely in the short run, has only a small and unpredictable effect on private-sector bank borrowing, and fails to secure control over interest-rate differentials, a necessity for ensuring adequate non-bank demand for public-sector debt and dealing with the problems posed by arbitrage and bank liability management. Beyond design deficiencies, the chosen method of operation of control systems has militated against tight monetary control. This, however, reflects a fundamental responsibility of governments and central banks to have due concern for interest rates and the exchange rate once they threaten to move beyond 'tolerance' levels, and would therefore seem to rule out the much-vaunted monetary base control mechanism, since tight control of the money supply could not be guaranteed under all conditions.

As indicators of the stance of policy, monetary aggregates may perform as poorly as the nominal interest-rate indicators they replaced – witness the distortions created for the £M$_3$ statistic by the 'corset' and the recession, variations on which would appear should any other single aggregate be targeted. Moreover, should tight control of monetary aggregates ever be effected (which implies the use of direct controls), history suggests that credit flows would bypass regulated channels and institutions, thereby offsetting the degree of restriction imposed on money stock growth. This would call into question the significance of the money stock as either an indicator or policy objective.

In conclusion, it would seem appropriate to downgrade monetary

131

policy's contribution to economic management, just as Friedman had previously done for fiscal policy, and instead allow monetary policy to play a more humble role, such as the maximisation of sales of public-sector debt to non-bank investors, to which it has proved to be better suited.

# Appendices

## A. RESERVE AVAILABILITY

Apart from the 'generation' and 'creation' of reserve assets by the banks and discount houses (discussed in Chapter 2), the activities of the public sector and the Bank of England play a fundamental role in determining the supply of reserves available to the banks. The public sector is involved because one option available for the funding of its **total financing requirement** (see below) is the issue of Treasury bills to the banks and discount houses, sometimes termed **residual financing** (see Table A1, row 10, for its significance during the 1973–80 period). This 'residual' financing represents that part of the public sector borrowing requirement (PSBR) (including any sterling resources required for intervening in the foreign exchange market or by the Issue Department of the Bank of England to purchase commercial bills) that is not financed by: (a) the overseas sector; (b) sales of public-sector debt to the non-bank private sector; (c) further issues of notes and coin; (d) sales of non-reserve asset public-sector debt to the banks and discount houses; and (e) the government increasing its indebtedness to the Bank of England. It is important to note that the residual finance is provided automatically by the banks and discount houses because of the agreement by the latter to 'cover' the Treasury bill tender.

The supply of reserve assets that emanates from the operations of the Bank of England[1] (ignoring open-market operations which are subsumed within the 'residual' supply) results from the release of special deposits and some types of 'assistance' given to the discount market. A net increase in reserve assets in the form of bankers' deposits will arise whenever the Bank: (a) purchases assets from non-banks; (b) purchases non-reserve assets from banks (including sale-and-repurchase agreements); (c) lends to local authorities via a securities management trust (if the money is used by the local authorities to repay bank loans then reserve assets expand by the size of the loan while the banks' deposit base remains unchanged, thereby creating the opportunity for further expansion of advances). Bank of England loans to, and purchase of non-reserve assets from, discount houses only cause a net increase in reserve assets (held by discount houses, not by the banks whose positions remain unchanged) to the extent that such finance is not used by the houses to repay call-money loans, i.e. it is used to purchase Treasury bills at the tender. Finally, assistance given in the form of Bank purchases of reserve assets, whether from the banks or the discount houses, will fail to generate a net increase in reserve assets for either the banks or discount houses. In the case of the banks passing on the assistance to the discount houses as call money and the latter using the call-money to reduce indebtedness at the Bank, neither the banks nor the discount houses will experience any change in their reserve asset holdings. However, in the situation where the Bank purchases reserve assets from the discount houses who use the funds to repay bank call-money loans, reserve assets held by the houses will actually fall, while the banks' position remains unaltered.

133

**TABLE A1**  **'Residual' supply of Treasury bills to banks and finance houses (i.e. public-sector 'contribution' to reserve availability)**

| | Transactions (on a net basis) | 1973 | 1974 | 1975 | 1976 | 1977 | 1978 | 1979 | 1980 | 1973–80 |
|---|---|---|---|---|---|---|---|---|---|---|
| | (1) Public sector borrowing requirement | 4186 | 6432 | 10480 | 9128 | 5995 | 8331 | 12587 | 12305 | 69444 |
| plus | (2) Acquisition of commercial bills by Issue Department of Bank of England | 301 | −299 | 2 | 326 | −304 | −12 | 12 | 403 | 429 |
| plus | (3) Increase in foreign exchange reserves | 228 | 105 | −655 | −853 | 9588 | −2329 | 1059 | 291 | 7434 |
| minus | (4) Official foreign currency borrowing from UK banks and overseas[1] | 2621 | 3817 | 1294 | 2753 | 3917 | −2082 | −1953 | −2512 | 7855 |
| minus | (5) Official sales of public-sector debt overseas[2] | 48 | 1023 | −349 | −587 | 1589 | −110 | 1198 | 1334 | 4146 |
| minus | (6) Increase in notes and coin in circulation with the banking sector and the non-bank private sector | 544 | 788 | 673 | 837 | 1044 | 1286 | 1199 | 392 | 6763 |
| minus | (7) Official sales of public-sector debt to non-bank private sector[3] | 2292 | 3230 | 5545 | 5765 | 8456 | 6026 | 10905 | 9586 | 51805 |
| minus | (8) Sales of non-reserve-asset, public-sector debt[4] to banks and discount houses | −137 | −597 | 1825 | −3 | 1346 | 603 | 1712 | 3125 | 7874 |
| minus | (9) Increase in net indebtedness of government to Bank of England Banking Department | 1027 | −241 | −103 | 412 | −264 | 150 | −251 | −864 | −134 |
| equals | (10) Residual supply of Treasury bills to banks and discount houses | 42 | 360 | 1506 | −576 | 555 | −711 | −322 | 430 | 1284 |

Notes  [1] Official foreign currency borrowing from overseas includes: 'direct borrowing' of central government, allocation of SDRs, 'other direct overseas official financing' of central government and the 'overseas official financing' of local authorities and public corporations. Official foreign currency borrowing from banks includes: 'indirect', local authority and public corporation 'overseas official financing' from banking sector.

[2] Equals central government net sales of Treasury bills and British government securities overseas plus 'other' overseas financing of local authorities and public corporations.

[3] Equals sales of National Savings, tax instruments, Treasury bills, British government securities, Northern Ireland central government debt, 'other non-marketable debt' and debt sales of the local authorities and public corporations.

[4] Includes: tax instruments, British government securities, Northern Ireland central government debt and debt issues of local authorities (including revenue bills, some of which are reserve assets) and public corporations.

\*Details for 1973 data may be slightly different.

Source: *Financial Statistics*, Table 2.6, July 1981 for 1975–80 data; Table 2.6, February 1979 for 1973 data.

To ascertain the *potential* monetary expansion associated with any given change in the supply of reserve assets available to the financial system it is necessary to look at the banks' acquisition of reserve assets. Quantification of this by source, however, is made virtually impossible by the following factors: (a) the acquisition of Treasury bills, as a result of the residual financing of the public sector's financing requirement, by discount houses and banks cannot be separately distinguished; (b) the supply of reserve assets to the banks resulting from the Bank of England's money-market operations will depend on the type of net assistance given to the market and the use to which such assistance is put – identification problems abound; (c) it is impossible to tell what proportion of reserve assets held by 'outside' holders are likely to be acquired by the banks. Despite these reservations, some items are capable of quantification and thus can provide an insight into how in practice one might obtain approximations to changes in bank holdings of reserve assets by source. Thus below we list those factors which influence the supply of reserve assets available to the banks.

(i) *The 'residual' financing of the public sector's total financing requirement*[1]

|          | (1)  | Public sector borrowing requirement |
|----------|------|--------------------------------------|
| plus     | (2)  | Acquisition of commercial bills by Issue Department of Bank of England |
| plus     | (3)  | Increase in foreign exchange reserves[2] |
| minus    | (4)  | Official foreign currency borrowing from UK banks and overseas |
| minus    | (5)  | Sales of (sterling) public-sector debt to non-residents |
| minus    | (6)  | Increase in notes and coin in circulation with banks and the public |
| minus    | (7)  | Sales of public-sector debt to non-bank private sector |
| minus    | (8)  | Sales of non-reserve-asset, public-sector debt to banks and discount houses |
| minus    | (9)  | Increase in net indebtedness of government to Bank of England Banking Department |
| equals   | (10) | 'Residual' supply of Treasury bills to banks and discount houses[3] |

Notes:  [1] Items (1)–(3). The public sector's domestic sterling borrowing requirement equals items (1)–(5).

[2] This represents the creation of reserve assets due to official foreign exchange market intervention (including currency 'swaps').

[3] This ignores the possibility that the government might run down its deposits at the Banking Department of the Bank of England (or alternatively sell Treasury bills to the Bank) in order to finance its domestic sterling borrowing requirement, which would augment the banks' holdings of reserve assets in the form of bankers' deposits, not Treasury bills.

## (ii) *Official[1] transactions (net) in the money markets*

|         | (1) Loans to the discount market[2] |
| --- | --- |
| plus    | (2) Purchases of assets from the discount market[2] |
| plus    | (3) Purchases of assets from non-banks |
| plus    | (4) Purchases of non-reserve assets from banks |
| plus    | (5) Loans to local authorities |
| equals  | (6) Resultant increases in reserve assets[3] held by banks |

Notes  [1] That is, undertaken by the Banking Department of the Bank of England.

[2] Assuming the funds are not used to repay bank call-money loans or to acquire reserve assets from the banks.

[3] The increase in reserves manifests itself as an increase in bankers' deposits.

## (iii) *The discount market's net creation of reserve assets for the banks*

|         | (1) Net increase in bank call-money loans to discount market[1] |
| --- | --- |
| minus   | (2) Net use of funds to make payments to the authorities[2] or to acquire reserve assets from the banks |
| equals  | (3) Net creation of bank reserves by discount market |

Notes  [1] This includes the reclassification of market loans to the discount market as call-money

[2] Payments may take the form of purchases of debt from, or repayments of loans to, the Bank of England.

## (iv) *Miscellaneous*

|         | (1) Net release of special deposits to banks |
| --- | --- |
| plus    | (2) Net increase in banks' 'eligible' commercial bills[1] |
| plus    | (3) Net increase in banks' holdings of 'eligible' government bonds due to the passage of time |
| plus    | (4) Net acquisition of reserve assets (e.g. local authority bills, Treasury bills and gilts of less than one year to maturity) from 'outside' holders |
| equals  | (5) Miscellaneous addition to banks' holdings of reserve assets |

Note  [1] Up to a maximum of 2 per cent of eligible liabilities.

## B. OFFICIAL TRANSACTIONS IN THE MONEY MARKETS[2]

*Example 1*: The 'special buyer', the Bank's operative in the money market, purchases £*x*m. of Treasury bills from the discount houses, who use the finance to
reduce indebtedness at the clearing banks, i.e. their reliance on 'call money' is
reduced:

*Balance-sheet adjustments*

| Liabilities (£m.) | | Assets (£m.) | |
|---|---|---|---|
| | Bank of England | | |
| Bankers' deposits | $+x$ | Treasury bills | $+x$ |
| | Clearing banks | | |
| | | Bankers' deposits | $+x$ |
| | | Call money | $-x$ |
| | Discount houses | | |
| Call money | $-x$ | Treasury bills | $-x$ |

*Analysis*: The extra finance obtained from the sale of Treasury bills is used by
the houses to reduce indebtedness at the clearing banks, for which an increase in
bankers' deposits is matched by a reduction in callable loans to the discount
market. The net result for the banks is zero change in total assets, total liabilities
and reserve assets, although the growth in non-interest-bearing bankers' deposits
is likely to evoke subsequent reaction. If the houses had sought to reduce bank
indebtedness by reducing their reliance on market loans, the results for the
clearers would have been the same as regards the growth in the balance sheet,
but reserve assets would have increased, thereby creating opportunities for credit
creation on the basis of a higher reserve assets ratio. (Under the cash ratio regime,
the reserve ratio rises in *both* cases.) Once again, however, although such transactions would have eased reserve-asset pressure for the banks, they would have
only served to aggravate IBELs pressure in the face of the corset.

In conclusion, it has been shown that bill purchases by the special buyer from
discount houses have no *direct* effect on £$M_3$, although secondary expansionary
effects may be experienced under the reserve asset ratio regime according to the
disposition of the houses' newly acquired finance.[3]

*Example 2*: The special buyer buys £*x*m. of Treasury bills from a secondary
bank:

*Balance-sheet adjustments*

| Liabilities (£m.) | | Assets (£m.) | |
|---|---|---|---|
| | Bank of England | | |
| Bankers' deposits | $+x$ | Treasury bills | $+x$ |
| | Clearing banks | | |
| Deposits | $+x$ | Bankers' deposits | $+x$ |
| (belonging to secondary banks) | | | |
| | Secondary banks | | |
| | | Treasury bills | $-x$ |
| | | Reserves (clearing bank deposits) | $+x$ |

*Analysis*: In this example the *direct* result of the official purchases is a rearrangement of secondary bank assets. Reserves, in the form of clearing bank deposits, of the secondary banks are augmented by the proceeds of the sale, the counterpart to the rise in reserves being a rise in bankers' deposits for the clearers when the Bank of England credits their accounts.

Once again it can be seen that, at the initial stage, the overall reserve asset position for the banks remains unchanged (the increase in bankers' deposits matches the decline in Treasury bill holdings of the secondary banks) although, on this occasion, while $£M_3$ is unaltered, bank deposits do rise. Subsequent adjustment under the reserve asset ratio regime might take place through the secondary banks restoring their reserve assets to the previous level by extending more call money to the discount houses, the latter using the finance to reduce their indebtedness (in the form of call money) to the clearing banks. The net result would be zero change in the banking system's level of deposits and reserve assets and in $£M_3$.[4] Identical results would be obtained if the Bank of England provided 'indirect' assistance to the discount market by buying Treasury bills from the clearing banks instead of the secondary banks. Indirect assistance provided through the purchase of non-reserve assets rather than Treasury bills, however, would cause bank reserve assets to rise and hence would allow the banks, under the reserve asset ratio control system, the opportunity to expand their deposit base.

## C. OFFICIAL TRANSACTIONS IN THE GILT-EDGED MARKET

*Example*: The Government Broker sells bonds ($£x$m. worth) to a non-bank private sector (NBPS) representative who has an account at a secondary bank:

*Balance-sheet adjustments (secondary effects shown in brackets)*

| Liabilities (£m.) | | Assets (£m.) | |
|---|---|---|---|
| | **Bank of England** | | |
| Bankers' deposits | $-x$ $(+x)$ | Bonds | $-x$ |
| | | Loans to discount houses | $(+x)$ |
| | **Clearing banks** | | |
| Deposits | $-x$ | Bankers' deposits | $-x$ $(+x)$ |
| (belonging to secondary banks) | | Call money | $(-x)$ |
| | **Secondary banks** | | |
| Deposits | $-x$ | Bank deposits | $-x$ |
| (belonging to NBPS) | | (at clearers) | |
| | **Discount houses** | | |
| Call money | $(-x)$ | | |
| Borrowing from Bank of England | $(+x)$ | | |

*Analysis*: The immediate effect of the sale of bonds to the NBPS is a reduction in the liabilities of the secondary banks, which forces a reduction in secondary bank deposits at the clearing banks, the counterpart to which is a reduction in the clearers' bankers' deposits at the Bank of England when the cheque drawn on the secondary banks is cleared. Thus, at this initial stage, both clearing and secondary banks have suffered losses on both sides of the balance sheet, the banking system as a whole having also lost reserve assets, i.e. the clearers' bankers' deposits. Consequently, the clearers attempt to replenish bankers' deposits (even under the reserve asset ratio regime they were non-interest-bearing and hence always held at a level close to the prescribed 1½ per cent of eligible liabilities minimum) by, for example, calling in call money from the discount houses who are forced to balance their books with further assistance from the Bank of England.

The net result is that the secondary banks have lost an equal amount of reserves (in the form of clearing bank deposits) and deposits, while the clearers likewise suffer an equal decline in deposits and reserve assets (although under the cash ratio regime, cash reserves are not affected). As far as the banking system as a whole is concerned, reserve assets fall by the same amount as sterling $M_3$,[5] i.e. by £$x$m. (the fall in £$M_3$ is equal to £$x$m. rather than £$2x$m. because £$M_3$ is defined to include only UK *non-bank* resident-owned sterling deposits). This implies a reduction in the reserve assets ratio. Attempts by the clearers to restore bankers' deposits without losing other reserve assets would crucially depend on the banks' IBELs positions relative to the penalty zone of the corset, for a reduction in 'market loans' to the discount market rather than a reduction in 'call' loans would indeed restore the level of reserve assets to their former position, but at the same time would increase IBELs pressure, since market loans are classified as negative IBELs.

The example clearly illustrates how open-market gilt operations can be used to control money stock growth: sales reduce £$M_3$ and purchases increase £$M_3$. The final balance-sheet adjustments (not shown) will depend on the methods chosen by the banks to relieve the induced reserve asset pressure under the reserve ratio control system (the presumption in 1971 was that bank loans to the non-bank private sector would be curtailed to some extent as non-reserve assets were disposed of) and cash (bankers' deposits) pressure under the cash ratio control regime.

## D. THE 'DIRECT' MONETARY EFFECTS OF THE BALANCE OF PAYMENTS

*Accounting identities*

Broadly speaking $\Delta M_3$[6] $\equiv$ DCE + reserve flows,
where DCE $\equiv$ PSBR plus increase in sterling bank lending to the non-bank private sector and overseas[7] minus increase in NBPS holdings of UK public-sector debt (PSD).

More importantly:

Increase in £$M_3$ $\equiv$    (1) DCE

     plus    (2) increase in official holdings of commercial bills[8]

     plus    (3) increase in foreign exchange reserves

    minus   (4) increase in non-resident holdings of UK PSD

minus (5) increase in public-sector foreign currency borrowing

minus (6) increase in non-resident-owned sterling deposits

minus (7) increase in banks' net foreign currency liability position

minus (8) increase in banks' non-deposit liabilities[9]

Items (3), (4) and (5) on the right hand of the identity sum (but with the opposite sign) to 'external and foreign currency finance of the public sector' ('ECF: public sector'), are presented in Table 11.3 in *BEQB* statistics. This is wider than the concept of 'official financing', as presented in the balance-of-payments statistics, since an amount equal to the net increase in official reserves held by the Exchange Equalisation Account is netted out from total overseas purchases of marketable UK public-sector debt plus all public-sector foreign currency borrowing (e.g. drawing on IMF facilities, foreign currency borrowing by nationalised industries and local authorities, etc.).[10] Despite the difficulties of identifying such external and foreign currency items in the balance-of-payments accounts, one may regard the sum of items (3), (4), (5), (6) and (7) – ECF, but with opposite sign – as broadly representing the counterpart in the payments accounts of the current account surplus (deficit) plus capital inflows (outflows) to the UK private sector.

Item (6), the increase in overseas sterling deposits, is netted out from the total on the right-hand side of the identity because non-resident-owned sterling bank deposits are formally excluded from $£M_3$. Hence, under a fixed exchange-rate regime and within a reserve assets control mechanism, sales of foreign currency for sterling (bank deposits) by non-residents will increase official reserves and the RAs of the banks, but will do nothing to change $£M_3$, the balancing entry being item (6), although, of course, the banks' eased RA position may lead to subsequent deposit expansion. Under 'floating' rates the acquisition of sterling finance from residents' bank deposits will cause $£M_3$ to fall, again requiring the balancing entry of item (6).

Finally, the banks' net foreign currency liability position is included as this represents the banks' 'switched-in' position or the extent to which they have acquired sterling finance by switching out of foreign currency and into sterling.[11] Under 'fixed' rates, the supply of RAs to the banks increases as the EEA purchases the foreign currency, and (IB)ELs are increased by virtue of the switch;[12] $£M_3$ remains the same, however. In order that this neutral situation be reflected in the identity, the increase in banks' net spot foreign currency liabilities must be subtracted from the increase in official reserves. Under 'floating' rates, the negative sign attached to item (6) can be justified by noting that, although official reserves necessarily remain constant, $£M_3$ will fall when residents purchase the foreign currency and finance the purchase by running down their sterling bank balances. If non-residents purchase the foreign currency then $£M_3$ remains unaltered, this being reflected by an increase in banks' net spot foreign currency liabilities matched by a *fall* in non-resident-owned sterling deposits.

Before moving on to make use of the basic accounting identity in analysing the effects of external and foreign currency transactions on the domestic money stock, it is worthwhile reviewing the role of the Exchange Equalisation Account (EEA). The EEA is a government agency required to hold the official foreign exchange reserves of the government. When the EEA absorbs (purchases) foreign currency, it provides sterling to the seller by borrowing from the main **Paymaster General Account** (prior to 1971, the EEA acquired the sterling by encashing short-term sterling claims – mainly Treasury bills). (Similarly, a reduction in reserves will be associated with payments to the Paymaster General Account, thereby providing the government with sterling finance.) The government therefore suffers an enlarged domestic borrowing requirement which may have to be partially met by borrowing from the banking system through increased supplies of Treasury bills. Although this in itself will not cause $£M_3$ to rise, an increase in the banks' consolidated reserve asset ratio position[13] may allow for subsequent deposit growth through, for example, an expansion in bank lending to the NBPS.

In the following section different types of external transaction are analysed from the standpoint of their effect on DCE, $£M_3$ and banks' RAs. A separate analysis is presented for both fixed and floating exchange-rate regimes, although strictly speaking the point at issue is whether or not the authorities are intervening. The difficulty, of course, in interpreting the results for policy purposes lies in the fact that the present regime of **dirty floating** conforms to neither paradigm. The analysis is conducted in terms of inflows (outflows would have the reverse effects) and only the 'impact effects' are considered. Subsequent reactions of the banking, public and private sectors to changes in reserve assets, interest rates, the exchange rate (with long-term effects on prices and incomes and hence on the demand for money) and liquidity are ignored.[14] The results are summarised at the end of this section (pp. 147–9).

## 'Fixed' exchange rates

Under a 'fixed' exchange-rate regime the authorities intervene in the foreign exchange market to maintain a particular parity or range of parities. Thus they satisfy any 'excess' demand for/supply of sterling that arises from domestic or foreign sources, which, in the case of a capital inflow, means they meet the 'excess' demand. The impact effect, therefore, of a capital inflow is to increase the public sector's need for sterling in order to finance the addition to official reserves. This enlarged domestic borrowing requirement may or may not lead to an increase in $£M_3$, depending on the nature of the transaction forming the counterpart to the increase in official reserves.

### (1) Current account flows

(a) *A net increase in UK exports paid for in sterling acquired from the EEA.* In this example, the foreign importer acquires the sterling required to pay for its imports from the EEA, which absorbs foreign currency into the reserves. The increase in official reserves is financed by selling more Treasury bills to the banking system, which in itself does not change $£M_3$ but does increase the banks' RAs. However, when payment for the imports is completed, UK resident-owned sterling bank deposits will rise, in line with the increase in banks' RAs, causing both $£M_3$ and the banks' reserve asset ratio to rise, the latter creating the potential for subsequent deposit creation. DCE, however, remains unchanged.

(b) *A net increase in UK exports paid for by a reduction in non-resident-owned sterling bank deposits.* In this example, official reserves do not change: non-residents' sterling bank deposits are simply transformed into resident-owned sterling bank deposits, thereby causing $£M_3$ to rise as only the latter are formally included in $£M_3$. RAs and DCE are unchanged.

(c) *A net increase in UK exports paid for in foreign currency which is held on deposit with UK banks.* In this case there is no change in official reserves, ECF, RAs, DCE or $£M_3$ (zero change in resident-owned sterling bank deposits). In the balance-of-payments accounts the increase in exports is matched by a reduction in UK banks' net overseas foreign currency borrowing.

(d) *A net increase in UK exports financed by a buyer credit provided by a UK bank.* The provision by UK banks of buyer credits to overseas residents is represented by an increase in sterling lending to the overseas sector, which causes DCE to rise. This rise in DCE is responsible for the increase in £M₃, residents' sterling deposits rising on completion of the foreigners' payments for imports. Neither official reserves nor bank-held RAs change.

(e) *A net increase in UK exports sold on deferred payments terms.* If the exporter agrees that overseas residents can defer payment for their imports and, in the interim, borrows from the banks, then £M₃ will increase by virtue of the increase in DCE resulting from an increase in sterling bank lending to the NBPS. No change will occur in official reserves or RAs available to the banking system.

(2) *Capital inflows to the private sector*

Examples of this form of transaction are resident sales of equities to non-residents (whose foreign currency asset realisations are assumed not to involve UK agents) and a transfer of funds by a multinational corporation to a UK subsidiary. The direct effects are precisely those specified under example 1(a) above: the expansion in reserves resulting from the sale of foreign currency by non-residents is financed by an increase in Treasury bills issued to the banking sector which expands its RAs; transfer of the sterling to those residents selling the equities will then expand (IB)ELs and £M₃ but leave DCE unchanged.¹⁵ The RA ratio will rise as a result of the transaction, which may give rise to further expansionary/inflationary pressures.

(3) *Capital inflows to the banks*

(a) *An increase in non-resident-owned sterling bank deposits.* The increase in official reserves is financed by extra sales of Treasury bills to the banks, causing their RAs to rise. However, £M₃ and DCE remain unaltered because non-resident-owned sterling bank deposits are excluded from £M₃. Nevertheless, (IB)ELs do rise, together with the RA ratio.

(b) *A reduction in non-resident sterling liabilities to UK banks.* Bank lending in sterling overseas falls causing DCE to fall. £M₃, however, is unaffected, as are (IB)ELs. The increase in official reserves is financed by borrowing from the banking system, thereby causing RAs and the RA ratio to rise.

(4) *Capital inflows to the public sector*

(a) *Increased non-resident purchases of public-sector debt from the authorities.* In this example the increase in official reserves is financed by the sales of public-sector debt to non-residents, so that RAs available to the banking system are unchanged. Likewise, DCE, (IB)ELs, £M₃ and the RA ratio all remain the same.

(b) *Foreign currency borrowing under the exchange cover scheme* by either the nationalised industries or local authorities, and borrowing from the IMF also leave £M₃ and DCE unaffected. Government receipts from the EEC reduce the PSBR but increase official reserves, leaving both RAs supplied to the banking system and £M₃ at their original levels although, of course, DCE falls.

(5) *Banks' foreign currency transactions*

It is important to distinguish between the banks' 'switched' position and their 'net external foreign currency' position. The former represents the banks' net spot foreign currency liability position *vis-à-vis all* their customers and is not classified as a balance-of-payments item because it can change without any transaction taking place with a non-UK resident. The latter *is* a balance-of-payments item and represents the banks' net external position *vis-à-vis* overseas customers only. The domestic money stock will only be affected when residents' sterling bank deposits increase as a result of the banks' foreign currency transactions.

(a) *'Switched' position unchanged.* Changes in the banks' 'net external foreign currency position' can only affect the money supply if the counterpart is a UK non-bank resident switch from foreign currency into sterling and the sterling is used domestically.

(i)    UK bank on-lends a foreign currency deposit to the public sector. The banks' 'switched' position is unchanged, but their net external liabilities have risen. Official reserves increase but this is financed by the foreign currency loan (i.e. ECF constant); there is no need for extra reserve assets to be supplied to the banking system. Hence RAs, DCE, (IB)ELs, the RA ratio and £M$_3$ remain unaltered.

(ii)    UK bank on-lends foreign currency borrowed abroad to a private sector UK customer who uses it to finance an investment abroad. Again, the banks' 'switched' position is unchanged, as are official reserves, (IB)ELs, RAs, the RA ratio, £M$_3$ and DCE.

(iii)    UK bank borrows foreign currency abroad and lends to UK NBPS which switches the foreign currency into sterling and uses it domestically. In this case, official reserves go up (when the EEA provides sterling to the NBPS) as do (IB)ELs, RAs, the RA ratio and £M$_3$. DCE, however, stays the same.

(b) *A changed 'switched' position*

(i)    UK banks switch foreign currency into sterling to acquire RAs. The banks sell the foreign currency to the EEA, which finances the addition to reserves by issuing more Treasury bills. Hence RAs and the RA ratio rise but £M$_3$ is unaffected. (IB)ELs, however, rise because of the switch itself – assuming net spot foreign currency liabilities were initially positive. Thus although £M$_3$ is initially unaffected by the switch, the improved RA position may induce banks to expand deposits by, for example, increasing their sterling lending to the NBPS.

(ii)    UK company transfers funds from a foreign currency account with a UK bank to a sterling account, on a book-keeping basis. In this case the banks' net foreign currency liabilities *vis-à-vis* all their customers (i.e. their switched position) has fallen with no effect on the balance of payments (since no non-resident is involved) or on official reserves. £M$_3$ rises, however, as UK resident-owned sterling bank deposits rise at the expense of resident-owned foreign currency deposits which are excluded from £M$_3$. DCE remains unaltered as do (IB)ELs (the increase arising from larger corporate-sector sterling deposits offsetting the decrease resulting from the switch) and the RA ratio.

(iii)    A UK bank and a UK-resident customer agree on a book-keeping transaction which replaces a foreign currency loan with a sterling loan. In this case, the bank's 'switched' position increases by virtue of a decline in foreign currency assets without the balance of payments or the official reserves being affected. (IB)ELs increase by virtue of the switch (with the same assumption as before about initial positive net spot foreign currency liabilities) causing the RA ratio to fall (no change in RAs) but leaving £M$_3$ unchanged. DCE rises, however, as bank lending in sterling to the UK NBPS is included in DCE, whereas foreign currency lending is not.

(iv)    Non-residents increase their foreign currency deposits with UK banks by running down their sterling deposits: transaction conducted on a book-keeping basis. Again, the banks' 'switched' position increases by virtue of their increased foreign currency liabilities, causing (IB)ELs to increase. However, this increase in (IB)ELs is offset by the contractionary effect resulting from the decrease in non-residents' sterling deposits, leaving (IB)ELs unaffected. Bank reserve assets are unchanged, as are DCE and $£M_3$ – the increased switched position cancelling out the (expansionary) effect of a reduction in non-residents' sterling deposits (see the $\Delta£M_3$ identity on pp. 139–40).

## 'Floating' exchange rates

Under floating exchange rates the *direct* effects of capital inflows on the domestic money stock are likely to be small, inflows leading to an appreciation of the exchange rate until equality between the supply of and demand for sterling is restored. Thus the counterpart to a capital inflow is initially a matching capital outflow leaving both the level of official reserves and the central government's domestic sterling borrowing requirement unchanged. However, the domestic money stock may be affected, depending on the composition of the payments' inflows and outflows: an inflow to one sector matched by an outflow from the same sector will leave $£M_3$ unaffected, a result which need not occur when the outflow is from a different sector to that which experiences the inflow. Various examples of possible combinations are illustrated below.

(1) *Capital inflows to the private sector*

(a) *An improvement in the private-sector component of the balance of payments current account financed by non-residents running down their sterling balances held at UK banks.*   This transaction is an example of an inflow to the private sector matched by an outflow from non-resident sterling bank deposits, and is identical to example (2) in the summary of results for fixed exchange rates. The run-down of non-resident-owned sterling bank deposits and the build-up of resident-owned sterling deposits leaves (IB)ELs unaffected but causes $£M_3$ to rise as only the latter are included in $£M_3$. The authorities do not intervene on the foreign exchanges, so that no extra reserve assets are supplied to the banking system and official reserves are unchanged. Likewise, the banks' RA ratio and DCE remain unaltered.

(b) *An improvement in the private-sector component of the balance of payments current account paid for in foreign currency held on deposit with UK banks.*   The change in the banks' balance sheet – increased resident holdings of foreign currency deposits and reduced non-resident holdings – does nothing to alter either DCE or $£M_3$ as all foreign currency assets and liabilities are excluded from both aggregates. (IB)ELs, RAs, the RA ratio and official reserves also remain unaltered (identical to example 3 under fixed exchange rates).

(c) *An improvement in the private-sector component of the current account paid for in sterling and financed by non-residents selling foreign currency held abroad.*

(i)    Residents purchase the foreign currency (financed by reducing their sterling bank deposits). The net result of residents purchasing the foreign currency will be to leave $£M_3$ at its original level. RAs and DCE will likewise remain unchanged, but (IB)ELs will rise as a result of the banks' enlarged switched position (residents' foreign currency deposits at UK banks have increased) causing the reserve asset ratio to fall.

(ii)   Non-residents purchase the foreign currency (financed by running down their UK sterling bank deposits). In this case both (IB)ELs (due to the banks' enlarged switched position) and $£M_3$ rise, the latter due to the rise in resident-owned sterling deposits. Official reserves, bank reserve assets and DCE all stay at their original levels, but the RA ratio falls.

(iii)  UK banks purchase the foreign currency (i.e. they acquire a foreign currency claim). The reduction in the banks' switched position will offset the rise in (IB)ELs associated with the increase in residents' sterling deposits, leaving (IB)ELs at their original level. $£M_3$ will nevertheless rise, while DCE, banks' RAs and the RA ratio are unaffected.

(d) *Similar current account improvement paid for in sterling and financed by non-residents selling foreign currency held at UK banks.*

(i)    Residents purchase the foreign currency (by depleting sterling bank deposits). On this occasion the banks' switched position does not change. Thus the net results will be: no change in $£M_3$, (IB)ELs, RAs, RA ratio or DCE.

(ii)   Non-residents purchase the foreign currency. As above, there is no change in the banks' switched position but $£M_3$ rises as a result of the increase in residents' sterling bank deposits. (IB)ELs, RAs, the RA ratio and DCE remain unchanged.

(iii)  UK banks purchase the foreign currency (i.e. foreign currency liabilities are reduced). On this occasion the banks' switched position falls, causing a reduction in (IB)ELs that offsets that arising from increased resident sterling deposits, leaving (IB)ELs unaffected. However, $£M_3$ rises, with DCE, banks' RAs and the RA ratio unaffected.

(e) *Similar current account improvement paid for in foreign currency held abroad.*
The banks' switched position increases by virtue of the increase in residents' foreign currency deposits causing (IB)ELs to rise. However, official reserves, $£M_3$, DCE and banks' RAs are unaffected, although the RA ratio does fall.

(f) *Overseas purchases of equities from UK NBPS (using foreign currency held abroad).*

(i)    Residents provide the sterling to overseas investors. The net results would be: an increase in the banks' switched position; (IB)ELs rise due to the changed switched position; $£M_3$, DCE and RAs remain unchanged; and the RA ratio is reduced.

(ii)   Non-residents provide the sterling to overseas investors. Net results: an increase in the banks' switched position; DCE and RAs are unchanged; $£M_3$ rises by virtue of the increase in residents' sterling deposits; (IB)ELs rise by virtue of the switch and the RA ratio falls.

(iii)  UK banks provide the sterling. Net results: a reduction in the banks' switched position; no change in (IB)ELs, RAs, the RA ratio or DCE; and an increase in $£M_3$ by virtue of the rise in resident-owned sterling bank deposits.

(g) *Overseas purchases of gilts from the UK NBPS (using foreign currency held abroad).*

(i)    Residents provide the sterling to the overseas sector. Net results: an increase in the banks' switched position; no change in RAs or $£M_3$; an increase in

DCE, resulting from reduced NBPS holdings of public-sector debt, and (IB)ELs, resulting from the banks' enlarged switched position; the RA ratio is reduced.

(ii) Non-residents provide the sterling. Net results: an increase in the banks' switched position by virtue of increased non-resident holdings of foreign currency deposits at UK banks; (IB)ELs increase by virtue of the switch; DCE and £M$_3$ rise; RAs remain constant and the RA ratio falls.

(iii) UK banks provide the sterling. Net results: a reduction in the banks' switched position; no change in (IB)ELs, RAs or the RA ratio; DCE and £M$_3$ rise.

(2) *Capital inflows to the banks*

(a) *An increase in non-resident-owned sterling deposits, financed by sales of foreign currency held abroad.*

(i) Residents provide the sterling to the overseas sector. Net results: an increase in the banks' switched position; (IB)ELs rise by virtue of the switch; RAs and DCE remain unchanged; the RA ratio is reduced; £M$_3$ is reduced in line with the fall in residents' sterling bank deposits.

(ii) Non-residents provide the sterling. Net results: an enlarged switched position; (IB)ELs rise by virtue of the switch; RAs, DCE and £M$_3$ remain unchanged; the RA ratio is reduced.

(iii) UK banks provide the sterling. Net results: a reduction in the banks' switched position; no change in (IB)ELs; DCE and £M$_3$ remain unchanged, as do banks' RAs and the RA ratio.

(b) *A reduction in non-resident sterling liabilities to UK banks financed by sales of foreign currency held abroad.*

(i) Residents provide the sterling used by the overseas sector to repay UK sterling bank loans. Net results: an enlarged switched position; (IB)ELs remain unchanged; DCE falls because of the decline in sterling bank lending overseas; £M$_3$ falls because residents' sterling deposits fall as a result of the foreign currency purchases; RAs remain the same, as does the RA ratio.

(ii) Non-residents provide the sterling. Net results: an enlarged switched position; (IB)ELs remain unchanged; DCE falls; £M$_3$, RAs and the RA ratio remain unchanged.

(iii) UK banks provide the sterling. Net results: a reduced switched position; (IB)ELs are reduced by virtue of the switch; £M$_3$ remains unchanged; DCE falls but RAs and the RA ratio are unaltered.

(3) *Capital inflows to the public sector*

(a) *Increased non-resident purchases of public-sector debt from the authorities financed by a reduction in non-resident-owned sterling bank deposits.* As public sector flows have no direct impact on the domestic money stock this type of transaction simply reflects an outflow from non-residents' sterling bank deposits. £M$_3$, DCE, and official reserves will all remain at their original level but (IB)ELs will fall (as will RAs because of the government's reduced need for bank borrowing). As a result, the RA ratio will also fall.

# TABLE A2  Fixed exchange rates: summary of results

| Transaction (*results hold for both fixed and floating exchange rates) | Direct effect upon | | | | | |
|---|---|---|---|---|---|---|
| | Official reserves | (IB)ELs | RAs | RA ratio | DCE | £M$_3$ |
| 1 Net increase in UK exports paid for in sterling acquired from the EEA | ↑ | ↑ | ↑ | ↑ | c | ↑ |
| 2* Net increase in UK exports paid for by a reduction in non-resident-owned sterling bank deposits | c | c | c | c | c | ↑ |
| 3* Net increase in UK exports paid for in foreign currency which is held on deposit with UK banks | c | c | c | c | c | c |
| 4* Net increase in UK exports financed by a buyer credit provided by a UK bank | c | ↑ | c | ↓ | ↑ | ↑ |
| 5* Net increase in UK exports sold on deferred payment terms | c | ↑ | c | ↓ | ↑ | ↑ |
| 6 Capital inflow to the private sector | ↑ | ↑ | ↑ | ↑ | c | ↑ |
| 7 Increase in non-resident-owned sterling bank deposits | ↑ | ↑ | ↑ | ↑ | c | ↑ |
| 8 Reduction in non-resident sterling liabilities to UK banks | ↑ | c | ↑ | ↑ | ↓ | c |
| 9 Increased non-resident purchases of UK PSD from the authorities (purchases from banks – results in brackets) | ↑ (↑) | c (c) | c (↑) | c (↑) | c (c) | c (c) |
| 10 Increased overseas purchases of gilts from UK NBPS | ↑ | ↑ | ↑ | ↑ | ↑ | ↑ |
| 11* Foreign currency borrowing by the public sector under the exchange cover scheme or borrowing from the IMF | ↑ | c | c | c | c | c |
| 12* Government receipts from the EEC | ↑ | c | c | c | ↓ | c |
| 13* UK bank on-lends a foreign currency deposit to the public sector (switched position unchanged). | ↑ | c | c | c | c | c |
| 14* UK bank on-lends foreign currency borrowed abroad to a private-sector, UK customer who uses it to finance an investment abroad (switched position unchanged) | c | c | c | c | c | c |
| 15 UK bank lends foreign currency borrowed abroad to UK NBPS which switches it into sterling for domestic use (switched position unchanged) | ↑ | ↑ | ↑ | ↑ | c | ↑ |
| 16 UK banks switch foreign currency into sterling (switched position increased) | ↑ | ↑ | ↑ | ↑ | c | c |
| 17* UK company transfers funds from a foreign currency account to a sterling account (switched position reduced) | c | c | c | c | c | ↑ |
| 18* Book-keeping transaction between UK bank and UK resident customer to replace a foreign currency loan with a sterling loan (switched position increased) | c | ↑ | c | ↓ | ↑ | c |
| 19* Non-residents increase foreign currency deposits at UK banks by running down sterling deposits (book-keeping transaction) (switched position increased) | c | c | c | c | c | c |

c = Constant
↑ = rise
↓ = fall

**TABLE A3  Floating exchange rates: summary of results**

| Transaction | Direct effect upon | | | | | | |
|---|---|---|---|---|---|---|---|
| | Official reserves | 'Switched' position | (IB)ELs | 'RAs' | RA ratio | DCE | £M₃ |
| 1. Improvement in private-sector component of current account financed by a reduction in non-resident-owned sterling deposits at UK banks | c | c | c | c | c | c | ↑ |
| 2. Improvement in private-sector component of current account and paid for in foreign currency held on deposit with UK banks | c | c | c | c | c | c | c |
| 3. Improvement in private-sector component of current account paid for in sterling raised by non-residents selling foreign currency held abroad to: (i) residents | c | ↑ | ↑ | c | → | c | c |
| 4. Ditto (ii) non-residents | c | ↑ | ↑ | c | → | c | ↑ |
| 5. Ditto (iii) UK banks | c | → | c | c | c | c | ↑ |
| 6. Improvement in private-sector component of current account and paid for in sterling raised by non-residents selling foreign currency held at UK banks to: (i) residents | c | c | c | c | c | c | c |
| 7. Ditto (ii) non-residents | c | c | c | c | c | c | ↑ |
| 8. Ditto (iii) UK banks | c | → | c | c | c | c | ↑ |
| 9. Improvement in private-sector component of current account and paid for in foreign currency held abroad | c | ↑ | ↑ | c | → | c | c |
| 10. Overseas purchases of equities from UK NBPS financed by sales of foreign currency held abroad to: (i) residents | c | ↑ | ↑ | c | → | c | c |
| 11. Ditto (ii) non-residents | c | ↑ | ↑ | c | → | c | ↑ |
| 12. Ditto (iii) UK banks | c | → | c | c | c | c | ↑ |

c = Constant
↑ = rise
↓ = fall

**TABLE A3 continued**

| Transaction | Direct effect upon | | | | | | |
|---|---|---|---|---|---|---|---|
| | Official reserves | 'Switched' position | (IB)ELs | 'RAs' | RA ratio | DCE | £M$_3$ |
| 13. Overseas purchases of gilts from UK NBPS, financed by sales of foreign currency held abroad to: (i) residents | c | ↑ | ↑ | c | ↓ | ↑ | c |
| 14. Ditto (ii) non-residents | c | ↑ | ↑ | c | ↓ | ↑ | ↑ |
| 15. Ditto (iii) UK banks | c | ↓ | c | c | c | ↑ | ↑ |
| 16. Increased non-resident-owned sterling bank deposits financed by sales of foreign currency held abroad to: (i) residents | c | ↑ | ↑ | c | ↓ | c | ↓ |
| 17. Ditto (ii) non-residents | c | ↑ | ↑ | c | ↓ | c | c |
| 18. Ditto (iii) UK banks | c | ↓ | c | c | c | c | c |
| 19. Reduction in non-resident sterling liabilities to UK banks financed by sales of foreign currency held abroad to: (i) residents | c | ↑ | c | c | c | ↓ | ↓ |
| 20. Ditto (ii) non-residents | c | ↑ | c | c | c | ↓ | c |
| 21. Ditto (iii) UK banks | c | ↓ | ↓ | c | c | ↓ | c |
| 22. Increased non-resident purchases of PSD from the authorities financed by a reduction in non-resident-owned sterling bank deposits | c | c | ↓ | ↓ | ↓ | c | c |
| 23. Increased non-resident purchases of PSD from the authorities financed by sales of UK equities to: (i) residents | c | c | ↓ | ↓ | ↓ | c | ↓ |
| 24. Ditto (ii) non-residents | c | c | ↓ | ↓ | ↓ | c | c |

c = Constant
↑ = rise
↓ = fall

(b) *Increased non-resident purchases of public-sector debt from the authorities financed by sales of non-resident-owned UK equities.* This example illustrates the direct monetary effects of a capital inflow to the public sector matched by a capital outflow from the private sector.

(i)   Residents purchase the equities. Net results: $\pounds M_3$ falls by virtue of the fall in resident-owned sterling bank deposits; (IB)ELs fall for similar reasons; bank-held RAs fall by virtue of the government's reduced need for sterling bank borrowing, thereby reducing the RA ratio; DCE remains unaltered.

(ii)  Non-residents purchase the equities. Net result: in this case resident-owned sterling bank deposits are not affected by the equity sales, so $\pounds M_3$ is unchanged, although (IB)ELs do fall (as they include all sterling bank deposits, resident and non-resident-owned); as in (i) above, RAs and the RA ratio fall but DCE remains unchanged.

The above samples are sufficient to indicate the wide range of results resulting from different combinations of capital inflows and outflows under a floating exchange-rate regime. They demonstrate that there can be no presumption that $\pounds M_3$ is unaffected just because official reserves do not change.

## E. THE ABOLITION OF EXCHANGE CONTROLS

*Implications for monetary control through observance of $\pounds M_3$ targets (only impact effects shown)*

(1) *Transactions responsible for tightening control (i.e. which induce a rise in $\pounds M_3$)*

(a)   Floating exchange rates (ER): NBPS switch from gilts (sold to the Government Broker) to foreign currency securities with UK residents providing the foreign currency.[7]

(b)   Fixed or floating ER: outflow from NBPS-held public-sector debt (PSD) (sold to the Government Broker) to Eurosterling market.[6,1]

(c)   Floating ER: UK banks switch from non-reserve-asset (RA) gilts to foreign currency with either: (i) non-residents purchasing the gilts while residents provide the foreign currency; or (ii) the Government Broker purchasing the gilts while residents or non-residents provide the foreign currency.

(d)   Fixed ER: Eurosterling banks switch from foreign currency to sterling in order to extend credit to UK residents.[6]

(e)   Floating ER: Eurosterling banks switch from foreign currency to sterling in order to extend credit to UK residents, and non-residents supply the sterling finance.[6,7]

(f)   Fixed ER: Uk banks borrow foreign currency in the Eurocurrency markets to lend to UK residents, who subsequently switch into sterling.

(g)   Floating ER: UK banks borrow foreign currency in the Eurocurrency markets to lend to UK residents, who subsequently switch into sterling (assuming non-residents purchase the foreign currency).[7]

(h)   Fixed or floating exchange rate: outflow from domestic equities to the Eurosterling market.[1,4,6]

(i)   Floating ER: NBPS switches from domestic equities to foreign currency securities, with UK residents supplying the foreign currency.[4,7]

(2) *Transactions responsible for easing control (i.e. which induce a fall in £M₃)*

(a) Fixed ER: NBPS switches from IBELs to foreign currency securities.
(b) Floating ER: NBPS switches from IBELs to foreign currency securities, with non-residents providing the foreign currency.[7]
(c) Fixed or floating ER: outflow from IBELs to Eurosterling market and funds on-lent to UK residents.[2,5]
(d) Fixed ER: UK banks switch from non-RA gilts to foreign currency, with UK residents purchasing the gilts.
(e) Floating ER: UK banks switch from non-RA gilts to foreign currency, with UK residents purchasing the gilts but non-residents providing the foreign currency.
(f) Floating ER: Eurosterling banks switch from foreign currency to sterling in order to extend credit to UK residents, with UK residents providing the sterling finance.[2,7,5]

(3) *Transactions not affecting control (i.e. £M₃ remains constant)*

(a) Fixed ER: NBPS switches from gilts (sold to the Government Broker) to foreign currency securities.
(b) Floating ER: NBPS switches from gilts (sold to the Government Broker) to foreign currency claims, with non-residents providing the foreign currency.
(c) Floating ER: NBPS switches from IBELs to foreign currency securities, with UK residents providing the foreign currency.
(d) Fixed ER: UK banks switch from (excess) reserves to foreign currency.
(e) Fixed ER: UK banks switch from non-RA gilts to foreign currency, with either non-residents or the Government Broker purchasing the gilts.
(f) Floating ER: UK banks switch from non-RA gilts to foreign currency, with (i) UK residents purchasing the gilts and providing the foreign currency, or (ii) non-residents purchasing the gilts and providing the foreign currency.
(g) Floating ER: UK banks borrow foreign currency in the Eurocurrency markets to lend to UK residents, who subsequently switch into sterling – assuming UK residents purchase the foreign currency.
(h) Fixed ER: NBPS switches from domestic equities to foreign currency securities.[3]
(i) Floating ER: NBPS switches from domestic equities to foreign currency securities, with non-residents providing the foreign currency.[3]

*Notes*

[1] Assuming UK residents are the ultimate recipients of Eurosterling loans – see note 2 below.
[2] The size of the fall in £M₃ will be equal to the change in the size of the Eurosterling bank's liquidity reserve held at a London bank. If the Eurosterling bank on-lends the newly acquired funds to non-residents, £M₃ will initially fall by the full amount of the deposits originally acquired, but eventually the size of the fall will return to more or less the position stated above as UK residents become the ultimate recipients of the loan.
[3] This represents the impact effect: if allowance is made for the subsequent fall in the equity market and the consequential rise in bank borrowing by the corporate sector, then £M₃ is likely to rise.
[4] If allowance is made for the secondary effects discussed in note 3 above, then a further rise in £M₃ would be recorded.
[5] Transactions that add to the total volume of sterling credit without raising the domestic money stock.

[6] Transactions that add to the total volume of sterling credit and also induce a rise in the domestic money stock.

[7] Balance-of-payments transactions that cause the domestic money stock to change even though a pure floating exchange-rate policy is being pursued.

## Implications for monetary control through the 'corset'

(1) *Transactions responsible for tightening control (i.e. which induce a rise in IBELs)*

(a)  Floating ER: switch by NBPS from gilts (sold to the Government Broker) to foreign currency securities, with either a resident or non-resident providing the foreign currency.[1,11]

(b)  Fixed or floating ER: outflow from NBPS-held PSD (sold to the Government Broker) to Eurosterling market.[1,2,9,10]

(c)  Fixed ER: Eurosterling bank switches from foreign currency to sterling in order to extend credit to UK residents.[1,9,10]

(d)  Fixed ER: UK banks borrow foreign currency in Eurocurrency markets to lend to UK residents, who subsequently switch into sterling.[1,10]

(2) *Transactions responsible for easing control (i.e. which induce a fall in IBELs)*

(a)  Fixed ER: NBPS switches from IBELs to foreign currency securities.[3]

(b)  Fixed ER: NBPS switches from domestic equities to foreign currency securities.[4]

(c)  Fixed ER: UK banks switch from (excess) reserves to foreign currency – assuming the initial net spot foreign currency liability position was positive.[5,12]

(d)  Floating ER: UK banks switch from non-RA gilts to foreign currency – assuming initial net spot foreign currency liability position of UK banks was positive.[6,13]

(3) *Transactions not affecting control (i.e. IBELs are unaffected)*

(a)  Fixed ER: NBPS switches from gilts (sold to the Government Broker) to foreign currency securities.

(b)  Floating ER: NBPS switches from IBELs to foreign currency securities with either a UK resident or non-resident providing the foreign currency.

(c)  Fixed or floating ER: outflow from IBELs to Eurosterling market.[2,8]

(d)  Floating ER: switch by NBPS from domestic equities to foreign currency securities with either a UK resident or non-resident supplying the foreign currency.[7]

(e)  Fixed or floating ER: outflow from NBPS-owned equities to Eurosterling market.[7,8]

(f)  Floating ER: Eurosterling banks switch from foreign currency to sterling in order to extend credit to UK residents; immaterial whether a UK resident or non-resident provides the sterling finance to the Eurosterling banks.[8,15]

(g)  Floating ER: UK banks borrow foreign currency in the Eurocurrency markets to lend to UK residents, who subsequently switch into sterling; immaterial whether UK resident or non-resident purchases the foreign currency.[15]

*Notes*

General assumption: a change in ownership of sterling bank deposits is assumed *not* to lead to a change in the proportion held in interest-earning form.

[1] This is only the initial impact on IBELs – the eased RA pressure may allow banks to reduce IBELs by shedding RAs through operations in the discount market, e.g. by reclassifying call-money loans as market loans.

[2] Assuming the Eurosterling bank (or ultimate borrower) is happy to retain the sterling as an interest-bearing deposit in the UK.

[3] This, again, is only the impact effect: increased RA pressure may lead banks to raise IBELs by switching from market loans to the discount market to call money.

[4] This is the impact effect: if allowance is made for the subsequent drop in the equity market and the consequential increase in corporate borrowing from the banks, IBELs are likely to remain the same.

[5] IBELs fall by even more if the switch from sterling involves banks selling other (non-RA) securities to the NBPS rather than running down excess reserves.

[6] If the Government Broker buys the gilts there will be a rise in IBELs, provided that, after the switch, the banks' net spot foreign currency liability position is still positive.

[7] Inclusion of secondary (equity market) effects discussed in note 4 would cause IBELs to rise.

[8] Transactions which raise the volume of sterling credit relative to IBELs.

[9] Transactions which depend on discount-market manoeuvres to raise the volume of sterling credit relative to IBELs.

[10] Transactions which depend on discount-market manoeuvres to raise $£M_3$ relative to IBELs.

[11] As note 10, with residents providing the foreign currency.

[12] Transactions which raise $£M_3$ relative to IBELs.

[13] As note 12, when (i) the gilts are sold to UK residents and the foreign currency is provided by UK residents, or (ii) the gilts are sold to non-residents and the foreign currency is provided either by a UK resident or non-resident.

[14] As note 12, with UK residents providing the foreign currency.

[15] As note 12, with foreign currency purchased by non-residents.

# Postcript: the March 1982 Budget

## MAJOR BUDGET MEASURES

(1) A cut in national insurance surcharge (NIS) by 1 percentage point to 2½ per cent. Net 'cost': £640m. in 1982–3.
(2) Personal allowances and tax thresholds raised by 2 percentage points more than required under the statutory indexation provision.
(3) Excise duties uprated in line with inflation.
(4) Package of assistance for the construction industry. 'Cost': £270m. in 1982–3.
(5) 'Enterprise' package. 'Cost': £80m. in a full year.
(6) Plan to cut unemployment and other benefits by 2 per cent in real terms abandoned.
(7) A further £250m. public expenditure cuts.
(8) 'Privatisation' plans: 1982–3 target sales figure set at £700m. (to come from sale of assets of: 51% stake in BNOC: British Telecom; British Gas offshore oil interests; British Transport Docks Board; British Airways; British Rail and the National Bus Company).
(9) £130m. aid for firms working in high technology areas (space and production engineering and information technology).

## IMPLICATIONS FOR THE PSBR AND PUBLIC-SECTOR EXPENDITURE PLANS

(1) As a result of the Budget measures, the PSBR was forecast to decline from £10.5b. (the actual out-turn figure was £8.6b.) in 1981–2 (4¼ per cent of GDP) to £9½b. (3½ per cent of GDP) in 1982–3. This represented a slight increase on the 1981 Budget forecast for a PSBR in 1982–3 of £9b. (3¼ per cent of GDP) and, as a proportion of GDP, a major increase on the initial MTFS projection of 2¼ per cent. Nevertheless, the PSBR was still forecast to fall, both absolutely and as a proportion of GDP, during 1982–3, in keeping with the principles of the MTFS.
(2) The revised public expenditure plans for 1982–3 onwards are higher than the cash equivalent of those in the March 1981 White Paper (shown in brackets): 1982–3, £115b. (£110b.); 1983–4, £121b. (£114b.); 1984–5, £128b. These revised plans were consistent with a progressive decline in total public expenditure as a proportion of GDP from 45 per cent in 1981–2 to 44½ per cent in 1982–3, to 42½ per cent in 1983–4, to 41 per cent in 1984–5.

## MONETARY MEASURES

(1) The target range for 1982-3 was revised upwards to 8-12 per cent (under the original MTFS proposals it was supposed to have been 5-9 per cent), and applied to $M_1$ and $PSL_2$ as well as $£M_3$. 'Illustrative' ranges for 1983-4 and 1984-5 were given as 7-11 per cent and 6-10 per cent respectively. The target range for 1982-3 was held to be consistent with money GDP growth of 10 per cent per annum.

(2) The National Savings sales target for 1982-3 was set at £3b., £0.5b. less than in 1981-2.

(3) Indexed gilts were made available to all investors, including non-residents.

# End-Notes

## CHAPTER 1

1. Cmnd 3292, May 1967.

2. House of Commons Paper 319, July 1968.

3. Ibid, para. 205.

4. Ibid, para. 206.

5. Ibid, para. 220.

6. Ibid, para. 222; Cmnd 3292, para. 19.

7. Cmnd 3292, para. 183.

8. Ibid, para. 59.

9. Ibid. paras 69 and 187.

10. Ibid, para. 59.

11. The likely outcome according to the PIB (para. 59).

12. A third factor commonly cited is the difficulty experienced by the government in funding the **public sector borrowing requirement** outside the banking system, but this, in fact, had not been a serious problem – e.g. see J. H. B. Tew, 'The implementation of monetary policy in post-war Britain', *Midland Bank Review*, Spring 1981.

13. *BEQB*, December 1969, pp. 455‒6.

14. Radcliffe Report, Memoranda of Evidence, Vol. 1, p. 36, para. 11 and p. 31, para. 114.

15. Ibid, p. 17, para. 7, Bank of England's oral evidence, Qs 12061 and 12062.

16. The concept of DCE was introduced to allow for the effect that when the balance of payments is in deficit the government obtains sterling finance through the operations of the **exchange equalisation account**, thus reducing its need to borrow at home. Broadly speaking DCE is the change in the money supply adjusted to take account of the balance of payments situation by adding on the deficit or deducting a surplus.

## CHAPTER 2

1. Apart from the (previously noted) deficiencies inherent in these forms of control their effectiveness was also called into question; see, for example, Allard (1974) and also the Crowther Report and Brechling and Lipsey (1972) with respect to hire-purchase terms control and ceilings respectively.

2. For details of the ramifications of the tender see Dennis, Hall, Llewellyn and Nellis (1982; ch. 6, pp. 169–70).

3. Borrowed funds were defined as all sterling loans taken *less* sterling lending to the discount market *plus* net foreign currency liabilities. The PSD comprised: British government and Northern Ireland Treasury bills; 'eligible' local authority bills and local authority negotiable bonds; British government, government-guaranteed and local authority stocks of not more than five years to maturity; and company tax reserve certificates.

4. The **public sector lending ratio** was replaced by the **undefined assets multiple** in 1973 (*BEQB*, September 1973) because of the practical disadvantages of the former control; under the new device, a house's holdings of 'undefined assets' could not exceed a sum equal to twenty times its equity capital and reserves.

5. 'Key issues in monetary and credit policy', *BEQB*, June 1971, p. 196.

6. The activities of the discount houses are important in this process, as the first response of the (clearing) banks to a loss of bankers' deposits will be to call in call money lent to the discount market in order to meet, once again, their bankers' deposits obligation (although, of course, their reserve position at this stage will remain depleted); the terms on which the Bank of England subsequently provides assistance to the discount market will then help to determine how far interest rates will rise.

7. The reforms comprised: (a) the offering by the Broker in December 1968 of long-dated tap stocks on the basis of a specified yield rather than a specified price (*Midland Bank Review*, May 1969); (b) the freeing of the official buying price for stocks within three months to maturity from their tie with the Treasury bill rate; and (c) the abolition of the authorities' practice of announcing the price at which they were prepared to sell tap stocks; bids were invited instead.

8. This refers strictly to the 'creation' of reserve assets by the operations of the banks and the discount market; the 'contributions' made by the public sector and the Bank of England to reserve availability are analysed in Appendix A.

9. One could also add a further desirable element which was absent from the scheme, namely that the reserve ratio had as its denominator the concept of bank deposits over which influence is sought and not some, supposedly, closely related variable (such as 'eligible liabilities').

10. A single bank, operating in isolation, is unlikely to achieve any lasting improvement in its reserve position through this channel: see Zawadzki (1981, pp. 52–4).

11. 'Competition and credit control', *BEQB*, September 1973, p. 307. Zawadzki (1981, pp. 56–7) asserts that under normal conditions the room for manoeuvre within the constraint would allow for an expansion in call money of the order of ½–1 per cent of eligible liabilities.

12. This is particularly true when the 'corset' is in operation (see Chapter 4), for the ability of banks to reclassify 'market' loans as call money crucially depends on their scope for manoeuvre within their IBELs' constraint (as well as on the magnitude of their 'market' loans outstanding).

## CHAPTER 3

1. The first occasion on which the Bank exercised its discretion was on 13 November 1973, when MLR was raised from 11¼ per cent to 13 per cent.

2. Earlier special deposit calls of 1 per cent of ELs on 30 November 1972 – half to be paid by the end of November and half by mid-December – and 2 per cent of ELs on 21 December 1972 (to be effective from January 1973) failed to register any significant impression on the banks' reserve asset ratios.

3. Lending guidelines first reappeared under CCC in August 1972.

4. Price, L. D. D., 'The demand for money in the United Kingdom: a further investigation', *BEQB*, March 1972. Price's income elasticity of demand for money calculations were later repudiated (*BEQB*, September 1974, p. 284).

5. For opposing views on the 'excess supply of money hypothesis' that arose as a result of discussion of the monetary implications of structural change, see Artis and Lewis (1974) and Hacche (1974).

6. Individual banks may gain from liability management by attracting deposits (and bankers' deposits) away from other banks or inducing switches out of public sector debt, the proceeds of which can be used as a source of liquidity (possibly to replace a certain proportion of liquid asset holdings) or to alleviate incipient or imminent reserve pressure, or as a springboard for growth. As a group, banks may 'successfully' compete for deposits and reserve assets through one or more of the following channels, the reaction of the authorities (e.g. to rising interest rates) determining the ultimate outcome: (a) under a fixed exchange rate, by inducing capital inflows from the overseas sector by, for example, raising sterling inter-bank rates relative to the appropriate Eurodollar rates; (b) by inducing a reduced non-bank demand for new public-sector debt and thereby raising the Exchequer's 'residual' borrowing requirement; (c) by inducing non-bank redemptions of non-marketable public-sector debt; and (d) by inducing non-bank sales of marketable public-sector debt to either the Bank of England or, in the case of the debt comprising reserve assets, to the banks.

7. For the banking system as a whole, eligible liabilities (CDs or deposits) and assets (loans) rise, while the reserve asset base remains unchanged.

8. The CD tax loophole further distorted the $M_3$ figures: see Gowland (1978, pp. 58–60).

## CHAPTER 4

1. The first time that the sterling component of $M_3$ was singled out for special attention was in December 1976. This was because the revaluation of the non-sterling component of $M_3$ at a time of intense pressure on sterling caused the total $M_3$ figures to expand at a rate which exaggerated the 'laxity' of domestic monetary policy.

2. Bank of England, *Report for the year ended 28 February 1975*, p. 14.

3. That is, those whose interest-bearing eligible liabilities (IBELs) averaged at

least £3m. (later raised to £5m. on 12 November 1974 and to £10m. on 8 June 1978) during a specified base period.

4. This power was assumed in 1975: see 'Credit control' notice, *BEQB*, March 1975.

5. The existence of an unsatisfied fringe of borrowers (which presupposes a 'non-competitive' financial system where markets do not clear) would, however, influence the rate of decline.

6. The degree of IBELs relief enjoyed depends upon the source of the CDs: if the CDs are bought from other banks, then that amount of IBELs pressure is passed on to them; if the CDs are purchased from the discount houses and financed by a reduction in call-money loans, then again IBELs relief equal to the full extent of purchases will be experienced (ignoring subsequent attempts by the discount houses to restore their assets and liabilities to previous levels, which will normally take place as depositors switch away from bank deposits and towards discount house deposits following the adjustment to relative yields); but if the CDs are purchased from non-bank private sector holders (including overseas residents) then IBELs will fall to the extent that the proceeds of the sale are not held as interest-bearing deposits with that bank.

7. Operations that reduce IBELs but neither ELs nor $£M_3$ (e.g. as a result of the banks' inducing, by whatever means, their customers to switch from deposit to current accounts) are also possible.

8. The results stem from the definitions of ELs and $£M_3$, which differ in the following respects: (a) items exclusive to ELs − non-resident-owned sterling bank deposits with an original maturity of up to two years, the discount houses' sterling deposits with UK banks, discount house holdings of CDs, sterling resources acquired by 'switching in' operations, and the banks' net liability in sterling to their overseas offices; (b) items exclusive to $£M_3$ − non-bank, private-sector sterling bank deposits with an original maturity of over two years, notes and coin in circulation with the public, sterling deposits of the public and non-bank private sectors with the discount market, and public-sector sterling deposits at banks.

   The following set of transactions, not involving the discount houses, would have the same effect of destroying IBELs relative to $£M_3$: (a) a reduction in non-resident-owned sterling deposits (with an original maturity of up to two years) at UK banks; (b) a reduction in the banks' net sterling liability to overseas offices; (c) a reduction in the banks' 'switched in' position (subject to the banks' net spot foreign currency liability position remaining positive); and (d) a switch to longer maturities of funds with an original maturity of up to two years held by the non-bank private or overseas sector with the banks.

9. If reserve pressure prevented this manoeuvre, then assuming net sales of non-reserve-asset, public-sector debt to the Government Broker are ruled out, the banks' likely response would be to reduce market lending to local authorities, who might restore the discount houses' undefined assets to their previous level by borrowing corresponding amounts from the discount market.

10. To the extent that these transactions provide unnecessary IBELs relief, the

banks might subsequently reclassify some market loans to the discount market as call money loans in order to add to their reserve asset bases.

11. This was not the case, however, at mid-July 1980. Because of the previous severe reserve asset squeeze, forty-seven institutions had SSDs lodged at the Bank to the value of £456m., £366m. of which had been incurred by eleven institutions (including at least one clearing bank) under the third tranche of the corset's penalty structure.

12. See, for example, the studies by Hacche and Coghlan in *BEQB*, September 1974 and March 1978 respectively.

13. Poole (1970) demonstrated that within the Hicksian IS/LM paradigm a money stock policy is superior to an interest rate policy as a means of stabilising income if the demand for money (LM) function is relatively more stable than the expenditure (IS) function and is not too responsive to interest rate changes. This assumes, however, that the policy-maker perceives a linear model as characterising the workings of the economy and that he is certain of the parameters of the model, thereby confining stochastic variability to additive disturbances – a most unlikely occurrence in the real world. An interesting review of the criticisms attacking the 'sub-optimality' of this approach, with and without an allowance for multiplicative disturbances, is contained in Courakis (1981, pp. 273–82).

14. This assumes, of course, that the information provided does not cause the authorities to revise their preconceptions about what constitutes the 'appropriate' structure and lag pattern within their representative model of the economy. For a detailed discussion of how, in theory, a policy indicator might be constructed, with and without allowance being made for ignorance of structure and lags, see Saving (1967) and Brunner and Meltzer (1969).

15. One has to ask, however, how announcements of annual target ranges for monetary growth are to affect wage and price expectations in the period relevant to the contracts to be negotiated when monetary aggregate growth only affects both demand and inflation with lengthy and unpredictable lags. Moreover, one can question the negotiators' ability to quantify and isolate the likely impact of monetary growth from the cumulative effect of all other possible influences on the price level.

16. This can be demonstrated (admitting the limiting nature of the assumptions of the model, such as a closed economy) using the Cambridge version of the **quantity theory of money** $M = kPy$. With the demand for money ($k$) held constant, the increase in nominal income ($Py$) is constrained by the increase in the money stock ($M$). Hence if money stock growth is held at or below the current level of inflation, the best that trade union negotiators can do to hold down unemployment is to ensure that wage bargains are struck at a level which does not result in firms being forced to raise their prices – which was undoubtedly the problem facing many firms in the 1979–81 period due to their unsustainably low profit levels.

17. *BEQB*, December 1977, p. 461.

18. *BEQB*, March 1978, p. 34.

19. *BEQB*, June 1978, p. 169.

20. *BEQB*, March 1978, p. 34.

21. For example, see Kaldor's evidence to the Treasury and Civil Service Committee (1980, pp. 103–14).

22. For evidence relating to the base see pp. 58–66 below, Budd (1981, p. 20) and Bade and Parkin (1981, especially pp. 20–3).

23. *BEQB*, March 1977, p. 49.

24. *BEQB*, March 1978, p. 36.

25. Goodhart (1981, p. 132).

26. See, for example, Coghlan's (1978) study. Despite the hopes raised by Coghlan, the subsequent predictive performance of the model proved very poor, although the basic parametric framework was not invalidated (Artis and Lewis, 1981, p. 20). Hendry (1979) also provides some evidence on the stability of a demand-for-$M_1$ function.

27. The logic of this had been accepted by the Governor in 1978 (witness his Mais Lecture, *BEQB*, March 1978, p. 37 and his speech to the Building Societies' Association, *BEQB*, June 1978, p. 247). It was given greater emphasis by the Bank's publication of the $PSL_1$ and $PSL_2$ series in the *BEQB*, September 1979, p. 278, and was finally implemented following the Chancellor's budget speech of March 1982 (see the Postscript on p. 155 for details).

28. Under 'statistical association with goal variables', most analysts have attempted to resolve the issue of causality by reference to Granger-type tests (see Granger, 1969). Unfortunately no clear consensus has emerged as to which monetary aggregates in the UK, if any, unambiguously 'Granger-cause' prices in a uni-directional manner: see Bade and Parkin (1981, pp. 13–23) for a review of some of the available literature and 'new' evidence.

29. *BEQB*, March 1978, p. 34.

30. Bockelmann (1977).

31. Dennis, Hall, Llewellin and Nellis (1982, pp. 228–32).

# CHAPTER 5

1. Until the system of 'stock relief' was changed in March 1981, companies also faced a financial disincentive to run down stocks.

2. Although this would alleviate some of the 'real' costs of tight monetary control, it would also induce upward pressure on the demand for 'narrow' money, indicating the difficult policy dilemmas likely to be faced by the incumbent administration.

3. Duck and Sheppard (1978) point out that the lower the banks' prescribed reserve ratio, the greater the influence fluctuations in the public's cash holdings exert on the money stock. To overcome the problem of variable non-bank cash holdings, Duck and Sheppard suggest that the authorities issue a new reserve instrument (a 'reserve deposit') which would act as the sole reserve asset for the banking system, could only be held by those deposit-taking institutions over which central control was sought, and would bear a competitive yield. A prescribed ratio of 'reserve deposits' to deposits

would be set and banks with insufficient holdings would be penalised at a progressive penal rate by being required to deposit 'supplementary penal deposits' at the Bank, while excess holdings would not receive interest. In this manner, banks face a financial disincentive to bid for the public's cash, for any 'excess' deposits, on a given 'reserve deposits' base, resulting from an expansion in loans will invoke penalties which can be made as harsh as the authorities wish.

4. See Goodhart (1975, pp. 154–5).

5. Note that, on the debt sales front, it is immaterial whether banks or non-banks purchase the public-sector securities, MBC thereby allowing for the possible extension of the range of public-sector debt instruments on offer.

6. The need for a flexible interest-rate policy to deal with the problem of maturing public-sector debt is considered in the *Midland Bank Review*, Spring 1980 (pp. 3–6).

7. The attraction of *lead* accounting, where today's holdings of base assets limit deposits at some future date, is that it would provide the authorities with information about the immediate future development of the money stock. Unfortunately this would depend on the banks' ability to predict their future balance sheets and then control them, an action severely circum-scribed by the degree of uncertainty associated with the utilisation of pre-viously agreed overdraft limits. The problem would be further compounded by the variability in short-term 'residual' Exchequer borrowing from the banking system. Moreover, should these difficulties prove surmountable, any effective penalty system required to deal with miscalculation about the level of required reserves is likely to induce disintermediation, with the same distortive effects as were experienced under the corset. Under *lagged* account-ing (on which the American system is based) current base requirements would be determined by past levels of deposits and so would have to be sup-plied to the system regardless of whether or not they coincided with the authorities' wishes. Similar problems would arise under a *current* accounting basis, for by the time the banks had decided on their desired base level, it would be too late to change it should it diverge significantly from the authorities' desired level. Suggested remedies carry their own drawbacks: (a) under a *mandatory* reserve requirement, the Bank could provide base assets required by the system on a progressive penalty basis, but this might induce disintermediation or liability management; (b) a low mandatory base requirement on which (excluding 'free reserves') interest was paid (as suggested by Greenwell & Co., 1979) might avoid the risks in (a), but most likely at the expense of weakening the relationship between the growth in holdings of base assets and the money stock, as would be the case under a non-mandatory reserve requirement system.

8. The question of the Eurosterling disintermediation incentive likely to be introduced under MBC is considered in Llewellyn (1981).

9. The government's move to support the pound on the foreign exchanges in September 1981 and earlier attempts to stabilise interest rates (*Midland Bank Review*, Spring 1981, p. 13) are prime examples of how an adminis-tration, whatever its political and economic prejudices, may be forced to temper its preferred policies in the face of real-world developments.

10. Artis and Lewis (1981, ch. 6) argue for a combination of MBC and interest-rate control, the former to deal with the retail banking function (mainly conducted by the 'deposit' banks) and the latter to deal with wholesale banking, conducted by 'deposit' and 'non-deposit' banks alike.

11. Innovations adopted after publication of the Green Paper included: further 'minimum price tenders'; full indexation of certain bond issues (which were issued by auction) – for pension fund holders (and insurance companies conducting pension business) initially (March and July 1981 and January 1982) but later (March 1982) for all investors; a greater use of unofficial tap stocks in the pursuit of a more flexible pricing policy (Pepper, 1981); and 'convertible' issues (January 1981).

12. This typically reflects demands for the issue of instruments akin to the Treasury bill, with maturities ranging from a few days up to, perhaps, two years. Even outside an MBC framework, such an innovation might result in a reduction in the average cost of financing a given volume of national debt, although the implications for 'liquidity' might act as a deterrent to their issue.

13. Coghlan and Sykes (1980), for example, propose the issue of 'certificates of gilt deposit' as a home for institutional funds awaiting the 'propitious' moment to move into gilts.

## CHAPTER 6

1. This was later to backfire on the administration when, following the Chancellor's refusal to index personal tax allowances in line with the **Rooker-Wise amendment** to the 1977 Finance Act (incorporated within the 'caretaker' budget of 3 April 1979), the TPI eventually rose above the RPI, subsequent to which official references to the usefulness of the TPI were conspicuous by their absence.

2. *Midland Bank Review*, Summer 1980, pp. 17–18.

3. For the financial year 1979–80 as a whole, bank lending to the private sector actually *exceeded* £M$_3$ growth; this was made possible by a rapid growth in overseas-owned sterling bank deposits.

4. *BEQB*, September 1979, p. 266; *BEQB*, June 1980, pp. 124, 141–2.

5. *BEQB*, March 1980, pp. 15–16, 20.

6. Earlier additions to the range of options open to the Bank of England in execution of its gilt-marketing strategy were warmly embraced by the new administration (e.g. the issue of 'partly paid' stocks and sales by tender, but with a minimum price stipulated, proved popular throughout the June 1979–April 1980 period) but no further reforms or additions to the range of public-sector debt instruments available for sale to the NBPS were forthcoming.

7. *Midland Bank Review*, May 1972, pp. 22–3.

8. As demonstrated by the frequent occurrence of currency crises while the controls were in force. The major problem was that the bulk of speculation was undertaken by foreign currency holders and traders (in the form of

'leads and lags') over whom the authorities had little influence, despite the existence of exchange controls.

9. For a more detailed description of post-1960 exchange controls and their effectiveness, see Tew (1978).

10. Although, as the Wilson Committee concluded, any lack of industrial investment in the UK was not due to a lack of funds but to a dearth of suitably profitable investment opportunities.

11. The work of Lessard (1975) suggested that international diversification in equity markets, particularly Japan, could be used to reduce portfolio risk arising from general market price movements (which affect equities on a domestic capital market more or less to an equal extent) because of the apparently low correlation between national market movements. Peters (1981) claims that, even allowing for exchange-rate risks, international diversification in equities allows the investor to obtain a higher return at *lower* overall risk.

12. The change in the latter is open to some doubt owing to the uncertainty surrounding the *net* impact on the interest-bearing component of ELs as bank deposits change hands.

13. The legal framework constraining institutional portfolio investment overseas applies mainly to pension funds and insurance companies: the combined overseas and property holdings are limited to 25 per cent of assets for local authority funds; actuaries advise suitable upper limits (typically 15 per cent of total assets) for private pension funds; and the Department of Industry, through the 1974 Insurance Companies Act, has the power to ensure that UK companies match their liabilities and assets to a sufficient degree by maturity *and* by currency.

14. For the source of these figures and others quoted see *BEQB*, September 1981, pp. 369–73.

15. The Bank estimated (*BEQB*, March 1980, p.13) that the removal of exchange controls generated an outflow, mainly in the form of repayments of foreign currency borrowing by the private sector, of between $£\frac{3}{4}$b. and $£\frac{1}{4}$b. in the third and fourth quarters of 1979.

16. Alternatively, Eurosterling banks can borrow foreign currency, switch into sterling and on-lend the proceeds.

17. The rise in sterling bank lending overseas, which was virtually zero during 1979 but grew to nearly £1.2b. in the first quarter of 1981, was due in part to the abolition of the exchange controls which once more allowed sterling financing of third-party trade, and in part to the abolition of the corset in June 1980.

18. UK banks have always been able to acquire funds to support sterling lending (or alternatively just to reduce IBELs on make-up day), without increasing IBELs or £M$_3$, by switching foreign currency into sterling, as long as their net spot foreign currency asset position has remained positive; once the banks reach a positive net spot foreign currency *liability* position, further 'switching in' will cause IBELs to rise. In the examples given, it is assumed that the banks' net spot foreign currency liability position is initially positive.

19. Foreign currency borrowing by the private sector from UK banks rose by £2.9b. between end-September 1979 and end-June 1981. In the same period, UK resident (private-sector) foreign currency borrowing from foreign banks grew by £0.9b. on a transactions basis.

20. UK residents' foreign currency deposits with foreign banks rose by £0.7b. on a transactions basis (i.e. not taking into account valuation changes) between end-September 1979 and end-March 1981.

21. As Kaldor (1979) points out, such a development could allow for the creation of a state of hyper-inflation, despite a rigid adherence to targets for sterling monetary aggregates.

## CHAPTER 7

1. Some of those whose opinions were canvassed by the Treasury and Civil Service Committee (TCSC) during the latter's inquiry into the conduct of monetary policy (e.g. Kaldor, 1980, pp. 104-14 and the NIESR, 1980, pp. 156-7) disputed the monetarists' claim of a uni-directional, causal, lagged relationship between changes in the money stock and inflation. Counter-evidence was provided by Beenstock (1980, pp. 59-60), HM Treasury (1981a, pp. 73-82 and 85-90) - but note Hendry's (1981, pp. 94-6) criticism - and Friedman (1980, p. 60, para. 23).

2. Under a fixed exchange rate, official foreign currency reserves will rise as the Exchange Equalisation Account absorbs the foreign currency being sold by the banks, but $£M_3$ will, at least initially, be unaffected as UK resident-owned sterling bank deposits are unchanged. The increase in bankers' deposits, however, resulting from the switch would increase the banks' lending potential under both the old reserve asset ratio regime and a cash ratio control system. With a floating exchange rate, official reserves remain constant, but $£M_3$ will fall or remain constant, according to whether residents or non-residents purchase the foreign currency from the banks; in the former case the fall in $£M_3$ is attributable to the fall in UK resident-owned sterling bank deposits (assuming the foreign currency purchases are financed in this way) while, in the latter case, $£M_3$ is unaffected if non-residents finance their foreign currency acquisitions by running down their UK sterling bank deposits, since these are formally excluded from $£M_3$.

3. The 'contributions' of local authorities and nationalised industries to the PSBR represent their own borrowing requirements less direct borrowing from central government, which features in the CGBR.

4. If that part of the PSBR derived from either the local authorities' or the public corporations' contributions to the PSBR is financed by public-sector debt sales to the non-bank private sector (e.g. government-guaranteed nationalised industries' stock or local authority stock and bonds) then all that is involved is a redistribution of the bank and non-bank private sector ownership of bankers' deposits and bank deposits respectively, with no change in the aggregate totals.

5. If the PSBR derives from the local authorities' or public corporations' contributions then the 'excess' public-sector expenditure will simply result in a redistribution of the ownership of existing bank deposits - away from the

public bodies' holdings and towards the NBPS, leaving £M$_3$ unchanged. The issuing of public securities to banks will then restore these public bodies' initial bank deposit levels but leave the NBPS with more bank deposits matched, on the banks' balance sheet, by larger security holdings. Thus the net monetary effects are the same as for CGBR financing through the issue of non-reserve assets to banks.

6. The other items in 'external finance' mentioned on p. 90 are considered in Appendix D.

7. Minford (1980b, p. 141, Q. 1).

8. Though note Hendry's (1981, pp. 94–5) criticism of HM Treasury's submission on the subject.

9. Kaldor (1980, pp. 119–21); Hahn (1980, p. 83, para. 3.6).

10. The 'crowding out' claim is yet another government assertion open to dispute – see Kaldor (1980, pp. 121–2).

11. Budd and Burns (1979, p. 28).

12. HM Treasury (1981b).

13. Taylor and Threadgold (1979).

14. The two most widely discussed proposals were the tax-based scheme of Professor Layard (1981) and the decentralised pay-bargaining scheme of Professor Meade (1981).

15. *Monetary Policy*, Vol. I, para. 11.3.

16. Ibid, para. 11.24.

17. Ibid, para. 11.27.

18. Ibid, para. 2.11.

19. Ibid, para. 2.10.

20. HM Treasury (1981a, p. 68, para. 1); Richardson (1981, p. 281, Q. 940).

21. For example, Tobin (1981, p. 214, Q. 766).

22. HM Treasury (1981c, p. 91, paras 34, 35).

23. Taylor and Threadgold (1979).

24. HM Treasury (1981c, p. 91, para. 36).

25. Ibid, para. 37.

26. Howe (1981, p. 195, para. 682).

27. Treasury's oral evidence, para. 41.

28. Ibid, para. 42.

29. Hendry (1981, p. 17, C(i)).

30. Laidler (1981, p. 177, Qs 608, 609).

31. Hahn (1980, pp. 79–81).

32. Howe (1981, p. 188, Q 652); Flemming (1981, p. 64, Q. 126) (Bank of England).

33. Minford (1980b).

34. Laidler (1980).

35. Ibid, para. 16.

36. NIESR (1980, pp. 150–2).

37. *Monetary Policy*, Vol. I, paras 11.16–11.18.

38. Ibid, para. 11.19.

39. Howe (1981, p. 199, Q. 702).

40. Walker (1981, p. 61, Q. 112); Richardson (1981, pp. 130–1, para. 401).

41. Richardson (1981, pp. 132–3, Q. 411, and p. 135, Qs 428, 429).

42. Howe (1981, p. 240, Qs 859, 860).

43. Scott and Godley (1980).

44. The relative merits of the CEPG, NIESR and London Business School (monetarist) strategies are discussed in Allsop and Joshi (1980), and, for the first two mentioned, are analysed by reference to simulations run on the Treasury model in Ormerod (1981).

45. To be fair, the special (youth) employment measures introduced in 1981 (the £1b. a year training plan announced on 15 December to take effect from 1983), and official concern with interest rates (witness the provision of £2b. of cash reserves to the banking system in the autumn of 1980) and in September 1981 with the effective exchange rate, indicate a measure of pragmatic realism in the conduct of economic and monetary policy respectively.

## CHAPTER 8

1. The money supply figures quoted are in seasonally adjusted form unless stated otherwise.

2. The picture in the previous month had been clouded by the existence of outstanding (mainly gilt) sale and repurchase facilities totalling £1.6b. To the extent that the facilities were taken up by the banks, their published holdings of public-sector securities would have been artificially depressed: figures relating to the month to mid-July 1980 show a fall in holdings of £670m., which, in the absence of the sale and repurchase facilities, might otherwise have indicated a rise of perhaps £0.7b. 'Window-dressing' attempts by banks to camouflage the 'true' level of £M$_3$ by their selling of gilts overnight to the NBPS on make-up day further complicate the analysis. As a result of continued purchases in August, the banks were eventually asked (on 14 August) to refrain from increasing significantly their holdings of gilts of more than one year to maturity, particularly since a sale and repurchase facility (of £150m.) was extended to September 15.

3. An attempt to unravel the monetary effects of the Civil Service pay dispute is presented in the *Midland Bank Review*, Autumn/Winter 1981, pp. 2–5.

4. Their conclusion (*BEQB*, December 1981, pp. 463–4) was based on evidence of house price movements and housing starts which demonstrated relative inactivity in the housing market in spite of the extremely rapid growth in bank lending for house purchase. One implication of this is that fraudulent claims for tax relief on interest payments may have been made where the finance was used to boost general consumption expenditure.

5. The adjustment period will not be without its own attendant problems, however, for the severe strain that will be imposed on banks' cash (bankers' deposits) positions is likely to involve the Bank in acquiring more bills than ever before over a comparable period (Bank purchases of eligible bank bills and Treasury bills in the three months to mid-November to relieve cash shortages induced by large official gilt sales totalled £2¾b., net).

6. The authorities calculated that the PSBR would be roughly £1b. higher (because, for example, of higher disbursements in the form of social security payments and unemployment benefit, lower tax revenue and reduced surpluses – higher deficits – of public corporations: see 'The impact of recession on the PSBR', *Economic Progress Report*, February 1981) for each 1 per cent by which GDP fell below its projected level, assuming that neither government spending nor higher taxes were the cause of the lower GDP figure.

7. Forces pulling in the opposite direction resulted from decisions to increase the cash limit for defence spending by £220m. (agreed in the summer) and to increase the external financing limits of the British Steel Corporation, British Shipbuilders and British Steel by £400m., £65m. and £40m. respectively, although finance for the latter set of decisions was to be taken from the unallocated contingency reserve already planned for. At the same time as the external financing limits were extended, an £800m. squeeze on nationalised industries' costs for 1981–2 was imposed.

8. The 'windfall' tax followed an unsuccessful attempt by the Treasury to raise between £100m. and £200m. from the clearers by reducing the subsidy paid by the Treasury on bank loans made under the **Export Credits Guarantee Scheme**, whereby banks charge a fixed rate of about 7½ per cent and receive a Treasury subsidy to raise loan rates to market levels. The clearers' own scheme – for taking up to £1.5b. of ECG lending, which had been refinanced by the Treasury, back on to their own books – was similarly rejected by the Treasury. For the clearing banks' response to the new tax see Lomax (1981) and Johnson (1981).

9. Subsequently reduced to £375m. following concessions granted to small banks – the tax-free level of non-interest-bearing deposits was raised from £10m. to £15m. and the rate of tax on the first £200m. of taxable deposits was reduced from 2.5 per cent to 2 per cent.

10. This is outlined in Board of Inland Revenue, 'Stock relief – a consultative document', November 1980.

11. The objective would be further assisted, through a reduction in company bank borrowing, if the reduced availability of public-sector assets resulting from the lower PSBR led investors to expand the proportion of their port-

folios held in company securities, the issue of which would be encouraged by lower interest rates. The significance of this effect, however, would be reduced to the extent that investors responded by adding to their portfolios of overseas assets.

12. In the event, both real and nominal interest rates rose following intervention by the Bank of England in the money markets in mid-September to stem the decline in the effective exchange rate of sterling. For example, by 16 September the London clearing banks' base rates were back to the levels that obtained before the MLR cut at the time of the budget, while the rate of inflation only marginally increased during the six-month period.

13. Although the savings ratio did subsequently fall, it is difficult to assess the relative size of the 'contributions' deriving from a multitude of other factors, such as the attempt by the private sector to maintain consumption in the face of a sharp fall in real disposable income. For further details see *Midland Bank Review*, Summer 1981, pp. 3–4.

14. Employers' contributions in cash terms would also rise in line with any increase in wages and salaries and as a result of the increase in the upper earnings limit.

15. For further details and alternative measures of competitiveness see HM Treasury (1981, pp. 122–7) and Buiter (1981).

16. As admitted by the Manpower Services Commission in its draft corporate plan published on 3 February 1982.

17. A further contributory factor was an extension of trade credit by companies to other sectors.

18. Pratten's (1982) crude attempt to estimate the 'Thatcher effect' on unemployment by using the combined experience of Germany, the Netherlands and Belgium as a control, suggested that perhaps 46 per cent of the increase in UK unemployment between 1979 and July 1981 was attributable to Mrs Thatcher's policies (including the North Sea oil effect).

19. The 'natural' rate of unemployment is that which prevails when prices are stable. Although a Treasury paper sent to the Commons all-party Treasury and Civil Service Committee early in 1981 suggested that the 'natural' rate for the UK was about 5 per cent (which, when compared with a prevailing rate of over 9 per cent, itself suggested that policy was not 'gradualist' enough), the Prime Minister herself disavowed belief in the concept (House of Commons, 26 March 1981).

20. NIESR (1981); Kay, Morris and Warren (1980).

21. The Bank estimated that output per man-hour in manufacturing rose by 2½ per cent in the year to the end of the first quarter 1981, by 3–4 per cent in the second quarter of 1981 compared to the fourth quarter of 1980, and by a further 2 per cent in the third quarter. Treasury estimates (*Economic Progress Report*, January 1981) put the improvement between the fourth quarter of 1980 and the third quarter of 1981 at 10 per cent.

22. The improvement in the trade balance is sometimes cited as evidence of this, although proof depends on the ultimate size of the lagged fall in exports compared to the depression-induced fall in imports.

23. This suggests that the PSFD is a superior, 'unadjusted' indicator on this score, but there are defects inherent within the PSFD itself. For example, a PSBR figure that reflects public-sector borrowing to finance loans to the private sector that could not have otherwise been financed from private sources represents a true statement of the pressures imposed on financial markets; yet this net inflationary pressure would not register any impact on the PSFD. Finally, it can be argued that a 'domestic cash flow' PSFD is superior to the present PSFD indicator (Dorrance, 1982).

## CHAPTER 9

1. Special arrangements exist for the calculation of ELs for members of the London Discount Market Association (LDMA) and certain banks with money-trading departments: see 'Monetary control – provisions', *BEQB*, September 1981, p. 347, para. 6.

2. As foreshadowed in the 'Background Note' issued on 24 November 1980, the old technique of deliberately creating cash shortages in the money markets by an overissue of Treasury bills at the weekly tender – designed to force the discount houses 'into the Bank' and so provide the authorities with the means (through variation of the terms on which assistance is given) by which control over short-term rates can be secured – gave way to open market transactions in bills, designed to keep very short-term interest rates within an unpublished band determined by the authorities. Accordingly, the lender-of-last-resort facility available at the discount window was to be available less frequently (thereby satisfying some of the monetarist critics of government policy who had argued that the facility had developed into providing 'first resort' assistance) and the market was, at least in theory, to be allowed a greater say in the determination of the structure and level of short-term interest rates.

3. Despite these arrangements, subsequent events indicated that the discount houses would not escape the winds of change. On 30 September 1981, Cater Ryder and Allen Harvey and Ross merged to become the third force in the discount market in order to secure general economies of scale and, it was claimed, to enable them to gain a fairer share of Bank business. On 17 January 1982 Smith St Aubyn announced a £15m. loss (three-quarters of its net worth) on its gilt dealings, indicating the problems faced by houses in trying to supplement profits on bill business.

4. The first Bank publication (Bank of England, 1975) on the subject of prudential control followed the report of a joint working party, consisting of Bank of England and clearing bank personnel, on the principles that should underlie the assessment of the adequacy of bank capital and liquidity. The issue of capital adequacy was returned to in June 1979 with the publication of a Bank consultative document on *The Measurement of Capital*, and in March 1980 a further consultative paper on *The Measurement of Liquidity* was published. On the assumptions that liquidity requirements for prudential purposes should be expressed as norms and not as minimum levels and that the liquidity tests prevailing at that time (e.g. the **quick assets ratio**) were incomplete, overlapped in coverage and failed to ensure that an adequate amount of 'primary' liquidity (i.e. readily convertible into cash under *all* circumstances) was maintained by the banking system as a whole, the latter

paper proposed an 'integrated test' for determining the adequacy of bank liquidity. This test involved assessing a bank's need both for immediate liquidity (e.g. to cover withdrawals of sight deposits) and for liquidity to cover unforeseeable difficulties in the financing of known future commitments. Accordingly, the Bank suggested that institutions observe both a *primary* liquidity requirement (expressed as a minimum ratio, i.e. 40 per cent, of liquid assets classified as primary liquidity to the 'total sterling deposit base', which is derived from the application of arbitrarily chosen coefficients to both *gross* 'maturity-uncertain' liabilities and to *net* liabilities on 'maturity-certain' business) and an *overall* liquidity requirement. The latter applies to foreign currency business also and is calculated by applying the same set of coefficients to gross maturity-uncertain liabilities and net maturity-certain liabilities, but, in this case, both primary and secondary liquidity count towards meeting the requirement.

Following the expression of widespread dissent by the banks (particularly with regard to the application of a uniform norm on all banks, irrespective of differences in operations, and to the suggested scale of coefficients – notably the 100 per cent coefficient on gross liabilities in respect of market deposits up to one month from banks which would effectively discriminate against 'wholesale' deposit-taking institutions) and amid fears that Euro-currency business might be lost to less regulated centres, the Bank duly dropped its proposals ('The liquidity of banks', *BEQB*, March 1981, p. 40). Instead it decided to continue monitoring banks' liquidity management (according to specific guidelines) during the normal course of its supervision until it had reached agreement on alternative proposals that would prove to be both a practicable and effective means of ensuring the overall liquidity adequacy of the banks (agreement reached in July 1982 – see 'The measurement of liquidity', *BEQB*, September 1982).

5. *Individual* banks have been slow to move in this direction for fear of losing borrowing customers to banks not so disposed.

6. The incentive for banks to do this depends on the extent of variability in short-term rates of interest tolerated by the authorities: the greater the variability, the greater the incentive.

7. Nor did decisions taken earlier in the 1980–1 financial year. To prevent interest rates rising 'beyond the level necessary to contain monetary growth', the authorities intervened 'heavily and persistently' (*BEQB*, June 1980, p. 124). On 14 April the authorities purchased £500m. of non-reserve-asset gilt-edged stock from the clearing banks for resale on 12 May. This agreement was subsequently extended to 12 June (the first sale-repurchase agreement – for £500m. – of 15 March was also extended for the third time to 17 June). At the same time, a 1 per cent recall of special deposits (SDs) due in on 8 April was postponed (to 16 June) and a second 1 per cent recall, due on 14 May, was cancelled. Further substantial assistance was provided in the period to mid-September, partly to prevent higher interest rates from compounding industry's problems directly or indirectly by raising the exchange rate and occasionally to stop round-tripping. The assistance took the following forms: (a) on 5 June, the second 1 per cent recall of SDs, due on 16 June, was cancelled; (b) on 27 June a £700m. gilt purchase-resale agreement, to run from 4 July to 11 August, was offered to all listed banks and finance houses; (c) a similar facility, to run from 11 July to 18 August, was announced on 4 July which, together with a separate facility relating to government-guaranteed and export and shipbuilding paper of over two years

to maturity, provided a further injection of £900m.; (d) further purchase–resale agreements, for £700m. and £750m. respectively, were announced on 7 August (for the period 11 August to 8 September) and 14 August (for the period 18 August to 15 September); and (e) additional purchase–resale agreements with the discount market involving eligible bills.

At the banking make-up day in September, nearly £2.5b. of assistance was outstanding. Some had, undoubtedly, prevented round-tripping from expanding the recorded $£M_3$ figures, but the figures for July (up 5 per cent) and August (up 3 per cent) pointed nevertheless to a monetary explosion. While the Bank attempted to play down the significance of the $£M_3$ statistic at a time of depression, no move was made to replace the $£M_3$ target as the central plank of policy. Clearly, though, interest-rate decisions were no longer geared to restraining $£M_3$ growth. In so far as the problem stemmed from the authorities' 'overfunding' of the PSBR in an attempt to offset the monetary effects of a rapid expansion in private-sector bank borrowing, the funding initiatives taken on the National Savings front were seen as the solution (on 17 November index-linked National Savings Certificates were made available to all residents aged 60 and over; the maximum holding was raised to £3,000, and the SAYE monthly limit was raised from £20 to £50). Relief would result from the fall in corporate bank borrowing that would accompany any revival in the new issue market ensuing from a fall in long-term yields.

8. The announcement was made in October for eligible bank bills and in January 1981 for Treasury bills.

9. Open-market purchases would cause bill yields to fall, thereby stimulating new issues and so adding to the stock of bills available for purchase as well as reducing company bank borrowing. The stock of bills was further augmented by the cut in the reserve asset ratio from 12½ per cent to 10 per cent announced on 2 January 1981.

10. It had been raised to £200m. for the two-week period from mid-July in order to drain excessive cash, resulting from the Civil Service pay dispute, from the system. At the same time £100m. of special short-term Treasury bills were issued to mature on 1 September to coincide with a cash drain associated with the payment of oil-related taxes.

11. Unlike the previous year, when joining would have meant large-scale intervention to hold down the value of sterling which would have compounded $£M_3$ targeting problems.

## APPENDICES

1. For the time being, foreign exchange market intervention is ignored: the full monetary and reserve asset implications of balance-of-payments transactions are presented in Appendix D.

2. The implications for both the 'old' minimum reserve asset ratio control regime and the post-August 1981 cash ratio regime are discussed, as is the case for Appendices C, D and E.

3. Although the opportunity for secondary credit creation may be presented to the banks, whether or not such monetary expansion occurs will depend

on a number of critical factors, not least of which are the state of demand for bank credit and the profitability of such operations to the banks.

4. This, however, would still leave the clearing banks with a higher level of bankers' deposits, which would probably lead to further balance-sheet adjustment, particularly under the cash ratio control system.

5. This would hold true even if the secondary banks were not involved and the NBPS representative happened to bank with a clearing bank.

6. The authorities concentrate on £M$_3$ as their target variable: it comprises all UK resident-owned sterling deposits with the UK monetary sector, plus notes and coin in circulation. Residents' foreign currency deposits held in UK banks are ignored because of: (a) the ease of substitution of residents' foreign currency deposits between banks situated in the UK and abroad (for which little information is available); and (b) evidence that such holdings relate mainly to residents' investment activity abroad, which does little to affect the domestic economy (this view may be questioned in the light of developments since the abolition of exchange controls – see *BEQB*, September 1981, p. 325). Likewise, non-resident-owned sterling bank deposits are excluded because they are thought to consist largely of speculative investment balances, changes in which barely reflect domestic economic developments.

7. Before the abolition of exchange controls, banks' sterling lending to overseas residents was largely connected with the finance of UK exports and had more or less the same effect on domestic liquidity as direct bank lending to UK exporters. Now, however, the finance of third-party trade and other transactions has also to be considered.

8. These commercial bills are acquired by the Issue Department of the Bank of England as a result of open-market purchases from banks or discount houses. As such they represent the temporary provision of credit to the UK private sector by the authorities.

9. Non-deposit liabilities include the banks' capital and reserves.

10. Frequently, offsetting entries will occur within the ECF section. For example, public-sector overseas borrowing (which boosts official reserves) neither affects the total for ECF nor £M$_3$. Similarly, a rise in reserves accompanied by an increase in non-resident-held sterling PSD, whether purchased from the authorities or the banking system, will neither alter DCE or £M$_3$, although in the latter case the banks' improved reserve asset ratio position may allow for subsequent expansion in £M$_3$ through, for example, increased bank lending to the NBPS.

11. Sterling finance acquired in this way does not affect (IB)ELs or £M$_3$ when the banks' net spot foreign currency asset position is positive; once net spot foreign currency liabilities are positive, (IB)ELs are affected, although, once again, £M$_3$ remains unchanged as resident-owned sterling bank deposits are not affected.

12. Assuming net spot foreign currency liabilities were initially positive.

13. 'Residual' financing of the enlarged domestic borrowing requirement will, however, leave banks' cash (bankers' deposits) untouched, so that the expansion in lending capacity experienced under the reserve asset ratio system

will not materialise under the present cash ratio control mechanism. The *direct* effect of external transactions on £M$_3$ is nevertheless the same under both ratio control regimes. To this extent the institutional change in control technique has not fundamentally altered the analysis, which in the text (including Appendix E) relates primarily to the minimum reserve asset ratio control regime.

14. It is also assumed that: (a) public-sector sterling bank deposits remain unchanged; (b) inflows to the private sector augment bank deposits and are not used to repay bank borrowing; and (c) inflows received by the public sector result in its borrowing less domestically.

15. Overseas purchases of gilts from the UK NBPS cause residents' holdings of public-sector debt to fall (= > DCE ↑) and holdings of sterling bank deposits to increase (= > £M$_3$ ↑). The increases in DCE and £M$_3$, however, are normally attributed to the residents' decisions to hold less public-sector debt rather than to the inflow.

# References

Asterisks denote references recommended for further reading.

## CHAPTER 1

* 'Recent developments in London's money markets', *Midland Bank Review*, August 1969.
  *Barclays Bank Ltd., Lloyds Bank Ltd. and Martins Bank Ltd., A Report on the Proposed Merger*, Monopolies Commission, HC Paper 319, July 1968.
  *Bank Charges*, Report No. 34 of the National Board for Prices and Incomes, May 1967.
* Tew, J. H. B., 'Monetary policy – Part I', in *British Economic Policy 1960–74: Demand Management*, NIESR (Cambridge University Press, 1978).
  *The Report of the Committee on the Working of the Monetary System* (Radcliffe Report), Cmnd 827, August 1959.

## CHAPTER 2

Allard, R., 'An economic analysis of the effects of regulating hire purchase', Government Economic Service, Occasional Paper 9, 1974.
Brechling, F. P. R. and Lipsey, R. J., 'Trade credit and monetary policy', in H. G. Johnson (ed.), *Readings in British Monetary Economics* (Oxford University Press, 1972).
Butler Till Ltd, *Money Services for Local Authorities*, 3rd edn (1978).
'Competition and credit control: modified arrangements for the discount market', *BEQB*, September 1973.
*Consumer Credit, Report of the Committee* (Crowther Report) Cmnd 4596, 1971.
Dennis, G. E. J., Hall, M. J. B., Llwellyn, D. T. and Nellis, J. G., *The Framework of UK Monetary Policy 1971–1981* (Heinemann, 1982).
'New tactics in the bond market', *Midland Bank Review*, May 1969.
Zawadzki, K. K. F., *Competition and Credit Control* (Basil Blackwell, 1981).

## CHAPTER 3

Artis, M. J. and Lewis, M. K., 'The demand for money – stable or unstable?', *The Banker*, March 1974.
Goodhart, C. 'Problems of monetary management – The UK experience', in A. S. Courakis (ed.), *Inflation, Depression and Economic Policy in the West: Lessons from the 1970s* (Mansell, 1981).
Gowland, D., *Monetary Policy and Credit Control* (Croom Helm, 1978).
Hacche, G., 'The demand for money in the United Kingdom: experience since 1971', *BEQB*, September 1974.
Price, L. D. D., 'The demand for money in the United Kingdom: a further investigation', *BEQB*, March 1972.

## CHAPTER 4

Artis, M. J. and Currie, D. A., 'Monetary targets and the exchange rate – a case for conditional targets', in W. A. Eltis and P. J. N. Sinclair (eds), *The Money Supply and the Exchange Rate* (Clarendon Press, 1981).

Artis, M. J. and Lewis, M. K., 'The demand for money – stable or unstable?', *The Banker*, March 1974.

Artis, M. J. and Lewis, M. K., *Monetary Control in the United Kingdom* (Philip Allan, 1981).

Bade, R. and Parkin, M., 'UK monetary policy in the 1970s', paper presented at the City University Conference on 'Monetarism in the UK', September 1981.

Bockelmann, H., 'Quantitative targets for monetary policy in Germany', in *Cahiers Economiques et Monetaires*, No. 6 (Banque de France, 1977) pp. 11–24.

Brunner, K., and Meltzer, A. H., 'The nature of the policy problem', in K. Brunner (ed.), *Targets and Indicators of Monetary Policy* (San Francisco: Chandler, 1969).

Budd, A. *et al.*, 'Does monetarism fit the UK facts?', paper presented at the City University Conference on 'Monetarism in the UK', September 1981.

Coghlan, R. T., 'A transactions demand for money', *BEQB*, March 1978.

Courakis, A. S. 'Monetary targets: conceptual antecedents and recent policies in the US, UK and West Germany', in A. S. Courakis (ed.) *Inflation, Depression and Economic Policy in the West* (Mansell, 1981).

* Friedman, B., 'The inefficiency of short-run monetary targets for monetary policy', *Brookings Papers on Economic Activity*, 1977.

Granger, C. W. J., 'Investigating causal relations by econometric models and cross spectral methods', *Econometrica*, Vol. 37, 1969.

Hacche, G. 'The demand for money in the United Kingdom: experience since 1971', *BEQB*, September 1974.

Hendry, D. F., 'Predictive failure and econometric modelling in macroeconomics: the transactions demand for money', in P. Ormerod (ed.), *Economic Modelling* (Heinemann, 1979).

Poole, W., 'Optimal choice of monetary policy instruments in a simple stochastic macro model', *Quarterly Journal of Economics*, May 1970, pp. 197–216.

Saving, T. R., 'Monetary targets and indicators', *Journal of Political Economy*, Vol. 75, 1967.

Smith, D., 'The demand for alternative moneys in the UK 1924–1977', *National Westminster Bank Quarterly Review*, November 1978.

Treasury and Civil Service Committee, *Memoranda on Monetary Policy*, HC 720, July 1980.

Volcker, P. A., 'A broader role for monetary targets', *Federal Reserve Bank of New York Quarterly Review*, Spring 1977.

## CHAPTER 5

Artis, M. J. and Lewis, M. K., *Monetary Control in the United Kingdom* (Philip Allan, 1981).

'Monetary base control', *BEQB*, June 1979.

Coghlan, R. and Sykes, C., 'Managing the money supply', *Lloyds Bank Review*, January 1980.

Congdon, T., 'Should Britain adopt monetary base control?', *The Banker*, February 1980.

Congdon, T., 'First principles of central banking', *The Banker*, April 1981.

Duck, N. W. and Sheppard, D. K., 'A proposal for the control of the UK money supply', *Economic Journal*, March 1978.

Goodhart, C. A. E., *Money, Information and Uncertainty* (Macmillan, 1975).

Goodhart, C. A. E. and Crockett, A. D., 'The importance of money', Appendix II, *BEQB*, June 1970.

Greenwell, W. & Co., Supplement to *Special Bulletin* of 2 March 1979, 2 July 1979.

Griffiths, B. *et al.*, 'Reforming monetary control in the United Kingdom', *The Banker*, April/May 1980.

Hansen, B., 'On the effects of fiscal and monetary policy: a taxonomic discussion', *American Economic Review*, Vol. 63, No. 4, pp. 546–71, September 1973.

*Monetary Control*, a consultation paper by HM Treasury and the Bank of England, Cmnd 7858, March 1980.

Hotson, A. C., 'The forecasting and control of bank lending', paper presented at Money Study Group Conference on Monetarism, Oxford, September 1979.

Llewellyn, D. T. L., 'The monetary base and its control', paper issued by Carr Sebag & Co., March 1981.

'Economic outlook', *Midland Bank Review*, Spring 1980.

Moore, B. J. and Threadgold, A. R., *Bank Lending and the Money Supply*, Bank of England Discussion Paper, No. 10, 1980.

Pepper, G., 'The gilt edged market', talk given at a seminar on Monetary Policy and Financial Institutions, W. Greenwell & Co., May 1981.

Pierce, D. G. and Shaw, D. M., *Monetary Economics – Theories, Evidence and Policy* (Butterworth, 1979, 4th edition).

Tew, J. H. B., 'The implementation of monetary policy in post-war Britain', *Midland Bank Review*, Spring 1981.

Wood, G. E., 'Cash base control of money supply: its institutional implications', *The Banker*, July 1979.

## CHAPTER 6

'The effects of exchange control abolition on capital flows', *BEQB*, September 1981.

Committee to Review the Functioning of Financial Institutions (Wilson Committee) *Reports* (various, 1977–80), HMSO.

Kaldor, N., 'Sir Geoffrey's phoney freedom', *The Guardian*, 29 October 1979.

Lessard, D. R., 'World, country and industrial relationships in equity returns', in E. Elton and N. Gruber (eds), *International Capital Markets* (North Holland, 1975).

Peters, R., 'Overseas portfolio investment – developments since the abolition of exchange controls', *National Westminster Quarterly Bank Review*, May 1981.

Tew, J. H. B., 'Policies aimed at improving the balance of payments', ch. 7 in *British Economic Policy: 1960–74*, NIESR (Cambridge University Press, 1978).

## CHAPTER 7

Allsop, C., and Joshi, V., 'Alternative strategies for the UK', *NIESR*, No. 91, February 1980.

Beenstock, M. and Longbottom, A., 'The statistical relationship between the money supply and the public sector borrowing requirement', *Economic Outlook*, June 1980, London Business School Forecasting Centre, June 1980.

Beenstock, M., *Memoranda on Monetary Policy*, Vol. II, pp. 54-77, Treasury and Civil Service Committee, HC 720-11, 6 November 1980.

Budd, A. and Burns, T. 'The role of the PSBR in controlling the money supply', *Economic Outlook*, Vol. 4, No. 2, LBS Forecasting Centre, November 1979.

CLARE Group, 'Macroeconomic policy in the UK: is there an alternative?', *Midland Bank Review*, pp. 7-16, Autumn/Winter 1981.

Committee of London Clearing Banks, 'Implications of a high exchange rate and steps that might be taken', *Monetary Policy*, Vol. III, Appendices, HC 163-III, 24 February 1981.

Flemming, J. S., oral evidence to the Treasury and Civil Service Committee, HC 163-II, 24 February, 1981.

Friedman, M., *Memoranda on Monetary Policy*, pp. 55-61, Treasury and Civil Service Committee, HC 720-II, 17 July 1980.

Galbraith, J. K., 'Suffering Britain sits the monetarist's test', reprinted in 'Guardian Agenda', *The Guardian*, 20 October 1980.

Hahn, F. H. *Memoranda On Monetary Policy*, pp. 79-85, Treasury and Civil Service Committee, HC 720, 17 July 1980.

Hendry, D., *Monetary Policy*, Vol. III (Appendices), pp. 1-21 and 94-6. Treasury and Civil Service Committee, HC 163-III, 24 February 1981.

HM Treasury, 'Background to the government's economic policy', *Monetary Policy*, Vol. III (Appendices), pp. 68-93, Treasury and Civil Service Committee, HC 163-III, 24 February 1981a.

HM Treasury, 'The impact of recession on the PSBR', *Economic Progress Report*, February 1981b.

HM Treasury, oral evidence to the Treasury and Civil Service Committee, *Monetary Policy*, Vol. II, Minutes of Evidence, HC 163-II, 24 February 1981c.

Howe, G., oral evidence to the Treasury and Civil Service Committee, *Monetary Policy*, Vol. II, Minutes of Evidence, HC 163-II, 24 February 1981.

Kaldor, N., *Memoranda on Monetary Policy*, pp. 86-130, Treasury and Civil Service Committee, HC 720, 17 July 1980.

Laidler, D. E. W., *Memoranda on Monetary Policy*, pp. 48-54, Treasury and Civil Service Committee, HC 720, 17 July 1980.

Laidler, D. E. W., oral evidence to the Treasury and Civil Service Committee, HC 163-II, 24 February 1981.

Layard, R., 'Is incomes policy the answer to unemployment?', inaugural lecture, the Centre for Labour Economics, LSE, October 1981.

Lawson, N., Speech delivered to *The Financial Times* Euromarkets Conference, London, 21 January 1980.

Meade, J., 'The fixing of money rates of pay', in *The Socialist Agenda*, ed. D. Lipsey and D. Leonard (Cape, 1981).

Middleton, P. *et al.*, 'Monetary targets and the PSBR', paper presented at the City University Conference on Monetary Targets, London, May 1979.

Minford, A. P., 'A rational expectations model of the UK under fixed and floating exchange rates', in *The State of Macroeconomics*, Carnegie-Rochester Conference Series on Public Policy, 12, 1980a.

Minford, A. P., *Memoranda on Monetary Policy*, pp. 131-43, Treasury and Civil Service Committee, HC 720, 17 July 1980b.

NIESR, *Memoranda on Monetary Policy*, pp. 147-59, Treasury and Civil Service Committee, HC 720, 17 July 1980.

Ormerod, P., 'Where devaluation fits into the protectionist strategy', 'Financial Extra', *The Guardian*, 29 September 1981.

Richardson, G., oral evidence to Treasury and Civil Service Committee, *Monetary Policy*, Vol. II, Minutes of Evidence, HC 163-II, 24 February 1981.

Scott, M.Fg., and Godley, W. A. H., 'The arguments for and against protectionism', paper presented to the Panel of Academic Consultants No. 10, Bank of England, January 1980.

Taylor, C. T. and Threadgold, A. R., 'Real national saving and its sectoral composition', *Bank of England Discussion Paper*, No. 6, October 1979.

Tobin, J., oral evidence to the Treasury and Civil Service Committee, HC 163-II, 24 February 1981.

Walker, D. A. oral evidence to the Treasury and Civil Service Committee, HC 163-III, 24 February 1981.

## CHAPTER 8

Brittan, S., *How to End the 'Monetarist' Controversy*, Hobart Paper 90, Institute of Economic Affairs, July 1981.

Buiter, W., 'Competitiveness', Appendices to the Minutes of Evidence taken before the Treasury and Civil Service Committee, pp. 102-20, HC 163-III, February 1981.

Dorrance, G., 'The PSBR: is it an appropriate indicator?', *The Banker*, January 1982.

Fleming, M. and Nellis, J., 'A new housing crisis?', *Lloyds Bank Review*, April 1982.

Greenwell, W. & Co., *Monetary Bulletin*, No. 124, November 1981.

Hall, M. J. B., 'Thatcher's financial strategy', *Hong Kong Economic Papers*, forthcoming 1983.

HM Treasury, oral evidence to the Treasury and Civil Service Committee, *Monetary Policy*, Vol. II, Minutes of Evidence, HC 163-II, 24 February 1981.

Johnson, C., 'Budget hits the banks', *Lloyds Bank Economic Bulletin*, April 1981.

Kay, J. A., Morris, C. N. and Warren, N. A., 'Tax, benefits and the incentive to seek work', *Fiscal Studies*, Vol. 1, No. 4, November 1980.

Lomax, D., 'The current account levy', *National Westminster Quarterly Bank Review*, May 1981.

Miller, M., 'Inflation - adjusting the public sector financial deficit', in J. Kay (ed.), *The 1982 Budget* (Basil Blackwell, 1982).

NIESR, 'The British Economy in the medium term', pp. 9-13, *National Institute Economic Review*, November 1981.

Pratten, C. F., 'Mrs. Thatcher's economic experiment', *Lloyds Bank Review*, January 1982.

## CHAPTER 9

Bank of England, 'The capital and liquidity adequacy of banks', *BEQB*, September 1975.

## APPENDICES

* *BEQB*, 'The domestic financial implications of financing a balance of payments deficit on current account', March 1975.

* *BEQB*, 'DCE and the money supply - a statistical note', March 1977.

* *BEQB*, 'External and foreign currency flows and the money supply', December 1978.
* Goodhart, C. A. E., 'Money in an open economy' in P. Ormerod (ed.), *Economic Modelling* (Heinemann, 1979).
* HM Treasury, *Balance of Payments Flows and the Monetary Aggregates in the United Kingdom*, 1978.

# Index